# PAN AM PIONEER

# PAN AM PIONEER

*A Manager's Memoir,*
*from Seaplane Clippers to Jumbo Jets*

*S. B. Kauffman*

*Edited by George Hopkins*

Texas Tech University Press

Cover photo: November 22, 1935—Pan Am's Martin M-130 flying boat, *China Clipper,* leaves San Francisco for Manila via Honolulu, Midway, Wake, and Guam carrying the first United States transpacific airmail. Pan American World Airways, Inc. Records, Archives and Special Collections Department, Otto G. Richter Library, University of Miami, Coral Gables, Florida.

Printed in the United States of America

Cover design by Kerri Carter

**Library of Congress Cataloging-in-Publication Data**

Kaufman, S. B. (Sanford B.), 1907-1993.
    Pan Am pioneer : a manager's memoir from seaplane clippers to jumbo jets / S. B. Kauffman ; edited by George Hopkins.
      p.  cm.
    Includes bibliographical references and index.
    ISBN 0-89672-357-7 (cloth : alk. paper)
    1. Pan American World Airways, inc.—History. 2. Kauffman, S. B. (Sanford B.), 1907-1993. 3. Businessmen—United States—Biography. I. Hopkins, George E. II. Title.
HE9803.K38A3  1995
387.7'06'573—dc20                     95-37144
                                          CIP

95 96 97 98 99 00 01 02 03 04 / 9 8 7 6 5 4 3 2 1

Texas Tech University Press
P. O. Box 41037
Lubbock, Texas 79409-1037 USA
1-800-832-4042

# *Acknowledgments*

Sincere thanks to Edward McVey, Professor of English, University of Western Ontario, Canada, who taped San's memoirs.. Without his provocative and penetrating questions, without his willingness to allow San to recollect his exciting, history-making adventures in his own words, this account would not have come to print. Special thanks to Robert Blake (retired co-woker and a fellow Pan Am engineer), who carefully researched the histories of the airplanes and the factories that produced them. Pat and Mitch Wolenski (Words Plus; New Milford, CT), spent many years transcribing various drafts of this memoir, always with great care.

Thanks to our daughter, Pam Graham, who did most of the compiling of the book. Sincere thanks are due to the many who contributed pieces necessary to connect these stories. Each took great care to clarify and correct San's recollection without sacrificing the tone his narration achieved. These include our son Robert, Pam Graham, my brother Charles Symington and many friends, especially Katharine Oliver, Margery Erickson, Nancy Tier, and Joyce Lubold.

I am grateful also to George Hopkins. Once Texas Tech University Press became interested in the memoir, George agreed to edit the volume and recognized immediately San's invaluable role in not only Pan Am, but also the published histories thereof. Judy Sacks ministered to the manuscript's progress through copyediting with well-measured doses of precision and sensitivity.

This story is presented with thanks to so many; in memory of an exceptional man, a fascinating life, and with hope that the excitement and romance of that era shall be remembered.

*Betty Gay Symington Kauffman*
wife of Sanford Bogert Kauffman

# Contents

# Foreword

✈ *Memories of Sanford Kauffman*

*M*uch has been made of the role of the pioneer in our national heritage. Though there has always been the recognition that many have assumed such worthy proportions in their living, the popular view usually only admits to the few: the enduring symbols of adventure, courage, and heroism. In the field of aviation, there have certainly been such heroes. Charles A. Lindbergh, Wiley Post, and Amelia Earhart immediately spring to mind; their daring feats brought aviation to life in the public mind. Suddenly the odd contrivances that had brought new wonder and thrills to the County Fair were recognized as an up-and-coming factor in the modern way of life.

Yet one year after Lindbergh's solo trans-Atlantic flight, in 1928, a commercially viable air-transportation system seemed an unlikely proposition at best. That summer, Sanford Kauffman was just graduating from Yale, and a year abroad seemed just the thing. His German professor had introduced him to the managing director of Lufthansa shortly before the term ended; and over dinner, plans were set. San spent the following year working in practically every department of the fledgling German airline. It was highly subsidized by the state, of course, and he departed the country still somewhat unimpressed by the potential of the industry as a whole. But fate, and excellent connections made while at Lufthansa, soon brought him to Pan American Airways in New York. In spite of his misgivings, a career opened up for him step by step. San had the sense of vision (and perhaps, the sense of humor) to simply stick with it . . . one step at a time.

The ensuing story is at the same time a recapitulation of the factors that shaped Pan Am, aviation as a whole, and the world of the mid-twentieth century, for they were intimately entwined. Being a station manager in Havana in 1933 was hardly a job for the faint-hearted. In the midst of revolution, corporate concern to curry the good favor of the State Department would leave a young man to his own devices as a departing dictator is secreted aboard the Miami-bound flight. Later in Port-au-Prince, Kingston, and then Manila, Anchorage, and Lisbon, the young aeronautical engineer often had more in common with the pioneering settlers of the American west than his white-collar counterparts in other industries of the day. While opening up routes for a new worldwide service, he found humor and adventure in foreign lands and cultures. But also in the relative comfort of the home offices in New York, there were labor negotiations and the design of standards, both of operating procedures and the performance of the new aircraft. As San says, "I thought of skipping out of Pan Am, but . . . I couldn't imagine that any of those other companies could be as much fun." How else would one find oneself in the cockpit of a Martin 130 "Flying Boat" on the first trans-Pacific flight by a commercial aircraft? How else indeed!

As Pan Am emerged from the War Years, it had established itself as the United States' premier world airline. There were daily flights to all parts of the globe. There were also many lucrative mail, cargo, and training contracts; but other than military personnel, passengers had not yet become a highly significant factor in the business equation. That was all to change as sleek new planes began to roll into service. Because of the particular vision of Juan Trippe, Pan Am's founder, as well as San and others, the Pan Am engineering team soon found itself enmeshed in far-reaching new projects with the Boeing and Douglas aircraft manufacturers. Through the early 1950s, the greatest revolution in the field of aviation was unfolding: the development of the jets. The general public would finally view flying as the most natural and common occurence. The daring days of the Wright brothers or even "Lucky" Lindy quickly receded from memory as legions started scrambling to catch their intercity flights. Through the consistent efforts of the many, a new age of travel had been born.

"A Pan Am Pioneer" is one man's perspective of this unique episode of twentieth century development. It is a highly personal account that takes many surprising turns as Sanford Kauffman's penchant for common sense and directness takes him to the core of each circumstance. He lived as a hero in many respects, but all for the purpose of doing a job effectively. After all, there were some remarkable people involved, and it *was* fun.

*Robert Kauffman*
Son

# Introduction

✈ *A Manager's Memoir, from Seaplane Clippers to Jumbo Jets*

$S$anford Bogert Kauffman's life closely paralleled that of Pan American World Airways. In a sense, Pan Am *was* Kauffman's life. Born August 8, 1907, into an upstate New York farming family of modest means, Kauffman launched his career in airline management after graduating from Yale in 1928. Just a year earlier, on October 19, 1927, Pan Am had made its inaugural flight from Key West to Havana.

Kauffman probably owed his job to Yale. When it came to hiring, Juan Terry Trippe (class of 1921), Pan Am's founder, showed a marked affinity for graduates of his *alma mater*. After a year of post-graduate work in Europe, where he polished his language skills while "interning" with the German airline, Lufthansa, Kauffman returned home in 1929 and immediately found employment with Pan Am. For the next 43 years, Kauffman served at Juan Trippe's elbow, an eye-witness to his handling of history's most famous airline. Kauffman saw it all, the years of glory as well as the beginning of Pan Am's decline. He died February 23, 1993, barely outliving the airline to which he had given his life. Pan Am flew its last flight in December, 1991—a nice symmetry.

Neither a pilot nor an engineer, Sanford B. Kauffman made his way in an industry dominated by those callings—an old-fashioned "generalist" among technical specialists. Juan Trippe staffed Pan Am's corporate offices with others like Kauffman—educated, urbane young men who knew foreign languages and something of the wider world—but none were so successful as he. Kauffman would eventually become Technical Vice President for the company—a remarkable feat of self-education for a man who lacked formal training in the arcane field of aeronautics.

Who was "San" Kauffman, other than a man who knew how to "manage?" This memoir tells us much about what he did, people he knew, and things he saw during his career at Pan Am. Few people were in a better position, for Kauffman's experiences were varied and important. Beginning as an assistant to André Priester, the crusty Dutchman who was the technical genius behind Pan Am's early successes, Kauffman participated in every phase of the airline's development. His career spanned the great bulk of 20th century aviation history, and he played an important role in Pan Am's glamorous rise, from the romantic era of gracious flying boats with their elite passengers, to the no-nonsense time of jumbo jets and mass-market travel.

But because Kauffman lived a life utterly subsumed by his career as a Pan Am executive, this memoir tells us much more about the airline than it does about himself. He fathered five children, but they are invisible in his story. He was married for over fifty years to a devoted wife, Betty Gay (Symington) Kauffman, but she finds mention only once, typically in the story of their 1939 "honeymoon," which was in reality a business trip!

"For my husband, like most men of his generation, the job always took precedence over personal and family matters," his widow, Betty Gay, remembers.

Trim and athletic in appearance, of medium height and build, Kauffman looked exactly like the Ivy League-educated corporate executive he was. From his conservative clothes to his distinguished-looking prematurely gray hair, San Kauffman might have been ordered up from central casting for a movie about corporate executives. Nobody would ever have suspected him of being anything other than what he was—a devoted servant of the corporate ethos, a man who embodied, in his personal habits and appearance, the corporate entity which gave his life structure and meaning. San Kauffman was, in short, the classic "organization man," a workaholic cut from an old-fashioned mold.

"San was completely loyal to Pan Am," his widow Betty Gay Kauffman declares. "Even though he had offers from other companies, he never considered them seriously."

Like many another hard-driving executive, Kauffman paid a price for his career. He worked himself into at least one "nervous breakdown," and the pressures he faced in Pan Am's Byzantine corporate polity we can only guess at. Kauffman mentions these pressures only indirectly, but it seems clear that they caused him a variety of problems, both physical and emotional.

So complete was Kauffman's devotion to Pan Am, that when he retired in June 1972, upon reaching the mandatory retirement age of 65, he had no hobbies or other interests with which to fill his days.

This memoir is the result.

Always a gifted raconteur, San Kauffman would, after retirement, regale friends and family with tales of a lifetime spent at the heart of Pan Am's body corporate. At the urging of his wife, who worried that his unique perspective on Pan Am's history would otherwise be lost, Kauffman began tape recording his memories, but he worked at it only desultorily. During his career, Kauffman had sporadically saved material relating to it, primarily by tossing documents and photos into a desk drawer in his Sharon, Connecticut home. He had kept neither systematic notes nor a diary during his working career, so the things he collected (reports, memos, newspaper clippings and the like), were the only sparks to memory available. Adding to the problem, he simply dumped most of the material into the same large desk drawer where other items had been accumulating for years. Occasionally Kauffman rummaged through the material in response to questions from historians and journalists, but he never systematically organized his personal materials.

By the mid-1970s, Pan Am was much in the news. As the airline slid into the morass of debt which would eventually kill it, journalists and historians called Kauffman more frequently. These distractions kept Kauffman from serious work on his memoir. Writing is hard, lonely work, and Kauffman had little taste for it. The ease with which he *talked* about Pan Am, the effortless tales he spun about Juan Trippe, flying boats, and the origins of jet travel, were hard to get down on paper. And so the memoir languished.

In desperation, Kauffman's wife took charge, arranging formal tape recording sessions, hoping not only to preserve his view of Pan Am's history, but also to goad him into getting down to work. And in truth, she also hoped to give some structure to his rather empty post-retirement existence.

The result of these efforts, after professional transcription and considerable editing by family and friends, is this memoir. By the late 1980s, something approaching a publishable manuscript finally began to emerge. Then tragedy struck—Kauffman fell victim to Alzheimer's disease. It was a sad ending for this once dominant, self-assured man, and it seemed to doom his unpublished memoir.

Undeterred by her husband's illness, Betty Gay Kauffman submitted the manuscript for publication anyway. But because her husband was unable to assist an editor in elaborating and expanding upon it, most publishers were reluctant to accept the manuscript. And there were other problems which made Kauffman's memoir less desirable.

Early in the 1980s, two large histories of Pan Am appeared, Robert Daley's *An American Saga: Juan Trippe and his Pan Am Empire* (1980), and Marilyn Bender's and Selig Altschul's *The Chosen Instrument* (1982). Both are important works which might well merit the description "definitive," when taken together, although neither deals with Pan Am's final days. The problem was that both Daley's friendly history, and Bender and Altschul's more hostile treatment, relied for many important details on Kauffman, who corresponded with them, answering their questions on issues great and small.

As Pan Am's financial crisis worsened, journalists seeking comment or requesting "backgrounders" became a nuisance, both on the telephone and in person—at least to Betty Gay Kauffman, who did not want her husband to give away all his good stories to others.

"These newspaper reporters and such would take up hours and hours of San's time," she recalls with exasperation. "Then, when their writings came out, it was just bits and pieces, not the whole story as San told it."

One can easily sympathize. When Texas Tech University Press sent me the manuscript in the fall of 1993, my immediate reaction was favorable. As an aviation historian, I had previously written about Pan Am and other airlines in both scholarly and popular venues. I had also spent many hours conducting oral history interviews with pioneer airline people, so I recognized the ring of authenticity in Kauffman's transcribed reminiscences.

But the manuscript needed work, and Sanford Kauffman was dead. Still, there was much good in it. Kauffman's reminiscences had the kind of dramatic immediacy which gives the "worm's eye view" of history such appeal. Was there a way to salvage the manuscript, to fill in the gaps Sanford Kauffman had left? Didn't his generous contributions to the writings of others entitle him to tell his own story in its entirety, rather than have the best bits and pieces cannibalized? Why should Kauffman have to settle for mere mention in their indexes and footnotes?

At the urging of Judith Keeling of Texas Tech Press, I agreed to add the kind of elaborative comment to the manuscript which Sanford Kauffman himself would undoubtedly have been encouraged to make, had he been able. I spoke on several occasions with Betty Gay Kauffman about her late husband. Although naturally defensive, she was nevertheless refreshingly frank in her descriptions his driven, "Pan Am comes first" attitude.

She was also helpful in confirming the stress generated by working for Juan Trippe, that strange, brooding presence who dominated American commercial aviation in its infancy. Ever the distant, imperious taskmaster, presiding over Pan Am from the magnificent tower bearing its name in the heart of Manhattan, Trippe ruled the airline with an iron hand from its beginnings in 1927, until his retirement on May 7, 1968. He left a mixed legacy.

"Trippe was Louis XIV, more feared than loved," Betty Gay Kauffman declares. "He would call San whenever there was an emergency, and off he would go, anywhere in the world. It was ridiculous, but San was completely loyal to Trippe, and his life was one hundred percent Pan Am. But he saw that Trippe had left a sinking ship. San said that Pan Am was going down, and he advised against buying stock. He said in 1972, that Pan Am wouldn't last five years. However, it did last longer."

I have tried, where possible, to allow Kauffman to tell his story in his own words, which means that occasionally his patterns of speech might offend modern sensibilities. In particular, when Kauffman describes the "backward" people living in countries served by Pan Am, his views are typical of men of his time and class. But I think we must take history in strong doses, "warts and all," which is plainly impossible if we sanitize the language of the past. Kauffman's values and attitudes often emerge in the way he expresses himself, and to arbitrarily change that would rob his memoir of authenticity. My elaborative comments are separate from his work, yet presented in a way which, I believe, enhances his story without interrupting it.

So for San Kauffman, his family, friends, and all those interested in a first-hand account by a pioneer airline manager who saw commercial aviation's history unfold before him over nearly half a century, here is the memoir.

*George E. Hopkins*
Western Illinois University
Macomb, Illinois
May 21, 1995

# Germany 1928

*M*uch *went into* the building of the airline industry. Today, we take it all for granted, but it was a long, hard, and exciting process, and I happened to be a part of a great deal of it. I was lucky enough to be in on the earliest beginnings: I experienced most of the fears, heartaches, and frustrations of the founding of commercial aviation, and then I participated in the excitement and fun of the beginnings of a whole new industry.

Pan American World Airlines was started by Juan Trippe in 1927, with a borrowed single-engine plane and a contract from the United States government to fly mail to Cuba. Early in 1928, Trippe obtained the first airmail contracts for seven routes to the Caribbean islands and to Central and South America. By the end of that year, Pan Am had only eleven aircraft. But with exclusive rights to fly to Latin America, it was well on its way to pioneering international air travel.

It was in late 1929 that I joined the new company and helped to develop the original routes to Latin America, Europe, and Asia. But in 1928, the year before I went to work for Pan Am, I didn't know anything about air travel. Nobody did. I was twenty years old, and just graduating from Yale University. Before going to college, I had never been anywhere to speak of. I was brought up on a big farm about eight miles from Poughkeepsie, New York, on land that is now the Dutchess County Airport. My father, in addition to running the farm, was a teacher of science courses at a high school outside of New York City and commuted weekends. There were seven kids, and we did everything on the farm: cared for chickens, milked cows, and, in the spring, tilled the fields, walking barefoot behind a plow. To make pocket money, I kept honey bees and trapped animals in the woods. We went to a one-room schoolhouse with one teacher, about twenty students, and a potbelly stove. Later, I went on to Poughkeepsie

High School but continued farming, doing my chores, working with my honey bees, and trapping fur-bearing animals—as well as riding my bicycle sixteen miles to and from school each day.

Having been a farm kid all my life, I'd gotten the nickname "Farmer" in high school, but I had great expectations for myself. I can trace that fact back to our little one-room schoolhouse, where that earnest young teacher kept pushing me ahead. She'd be surprised, I suppose, to learn that she had such a strong formative influence on one of her students.

Father's background was Pennsylvania Dutch, and they had a reputation, from Revolutionary times, of being the most methodical farmers and always making the most of the land. But my father's interest in science had a particular influence in pointing me toward a technical career. I didn't think about it until long afterwards, but now I realize how much I admired and respected him. My father had always thought highly of Yale, and not knowing anything about colleges myself, that's where I went.

On entering Yale I was sixteen, a year or two younger than the average freshman. I had played football in high school, so I also went out for the sport at Yale, arriving a week early to present myself for football practice. I showed up in the locker room wearing knickers, a kind of knee-length short pants. They were the only pair of pants I owned, but the coach thought I was a local boy coming to help clean up. One of the team members came over and said, "Kid, I'll tip you off; you'd better get a pair of long pants or you're going to have a lot of trouble around here." So I went down to a secondhand store and got my first pair of long pants.

Being a country boy, I found the big city of New Haven strange, but I loved Yale. The quality of the education received there and the perspectives it gave me have affected my entire life. They certainly helped me, a young college graduate without an engineering degree, to get into the management of a high-technology industry like aviation at its beginning. In a few years it would not have been possible.

I entered college thinking of majoring in engineering, but on finding that the advanced engineering courses were so technical and time-consuming that they ruled out any chance of taking humanities courses, I decided against it. My feeling was that unless humanities courses were taken in college, they'd never be taken later on. It was my plan to go to graduate school before a career in engineering.

I took a few basic engineering classes, however, and this elementary training stood me in good stead when I later had to deal with aeronautical engineers and other experts. I also took a number of related courses such as drafting, advanced chemistry, and physics. In fact, my professor in physics, a Russian, wanted me to work in his lab after graduation. He was trying to discover how to develop living tissue chemically, fifty years ahead of his time. This was indeed a tempting option because I would have been paid enough to get through graduate school; however, as his work seemed rather too mystical to me, I turned it down.

Professor Benson, my German professor, initiated the next option for my future.[1] He urged me to go to Germany in order to study the language. Benson thought it mandatory, if one wished to speak the language properly, to learn German among native speakers, and he pointed out that German science and engineering at that time just about led the world. This was a tempting idea, but as the oldest boy in a family of seven children, I felt that I couldn't be a burden on my family any longer. After Yale I would have to get a job.

Toward the end of the fall semester in my senior year, Professor Benson invited me to his house to meet a German friend of his named Otto Merkel.[2] He and Professor Benson had been at Harvard Graduate School together, and every time Merkel came to America on business, he and his wife stayed with Benson. Merkel was managing director of Lufthansa, the German state-owned airline, and he offered me a job. His idea was to send me through all of Lufthansa's different departments while paying me enough to live on in Germany. Professor Benson's Germany option was now not only feasible but also very appealing.

I sailed on a German ship to Hamburg in September 1928. It was that country's biggest ship, and it certainly was my biggest thrill up to that time. Once we arrived, I drove to Berlin with a fellow passenger from the boat. He had connections in Berlin with an American woman who was married to a German, and we stayed with them for the first couple of days. This woman found a room for me to rent near the center of the city, by the Gedankness Memorial Church, in the Kurfurstendam area. I lived there.

During the months in Germany, from September 1928 to August 1929, I worked in practically every department of the airline: engineering, finance, traffic, and operations. The work was very intense and concentrated. In my free time, I socialized with my contemporaries at Lufthansa, as well as with several students at Berlin University. The manager of the airport, who was a graduate of Berlin University, put me in touch with a fraternity group there. They had use of a boathouse out on Lake Wansee where we did a lot of rowing, and I also went hiking with some German students. They loved to hike, but it amused me that they always hiked in formation as if they were on parade.

Generally, I experienced no anti-American feelings from the Germans with whom I associated, no "American, go home!" or things like that. My German friends all wanted me to speak English with them so they could improve their pronunciation. There was just one Prussian in the traffic department who was hostile, but the other people I worked with couldn't have been nicer.

Contrary to the image some might have of the wild, young American bachelor living abroad, I did not have much chance to see Berlin night life. Although the city offered a very active theater and cabaret life, I experienced little of it because I didn't have much money. My desire was to speak German all the time, and I associated almost entirely with Germans who didn't have much money either.

Often I used to walk in the park, and I started visiting the Berlin Zoo on my walks. There I made friends with a gorilla; when he saw me coming he would always stick his arm through the bars for my peanuts. When I went back to Berlin after the war, I wondered what had become of my gorilla friend during those years of bombings and burnings. Imagine my surprise when I walked up to his cage and there he was, with his hand held out, waiting for my peanuts.

Most historians I've read who look back at the early thirties point their fingers at the streets of Berlin as the place where the country's future history was formed. The city was a terrible place, a moral sinkhole. Coming from a Protestant New England background, I found it unbelievable. There were no limits at all to behavior. On one occasion, a male homosexual in a garish outfit and makeup interrupted my date with a German girl and asked me to dance. I thought the guy was out of his mind, but my date was quite blasé and said, "Oh, they do that all the time." The conservative German middle class seemed to feel that this sexual excessiveness was one more example of why Germany needed new, strong leadership. The younger people I knew, the university boys in particular, felt that a new leader had to come along to lead the country back to stability. Moral decay was just one of several areas about which they felt strongly. The major problems, of course, were economic distress and unemployment.

My impression was that most Germans were hard up as a result of this inflationary period. It was different for me; I had enough money to go out for dinner and get a fairly substantial meal, all for one mark, which was equal to about twenty-five cents. But for Germans it was pretty rough, which may be why they were so susceptible to all kinds of extremist activities. They felt that the economic problems resulted from the harsh terms of the Versailles peace treaty. Specifically, they put the blame on France, Britain, Italy, and the United States. If you asked a German of the middle or upper classes what he thought were the greatest problems in Germany, he would likely say "Unemployment, Communism, and the Versailles Treaty."

I had a few friends who were members of the aristocracy, and they often got together to discuss bringing back the monarchy. They were largely Prussians, former members of the German officer corps. They were looking for someone to take the lead, a new man with public recognition who was connected with the old monarchy system. The Prussians were disdainful of the workers' movement but also scared of it, and they wanted to restore prewar conditions. They were pretty annoyed with some of their contemporaries, big businessmen and industrialists who were looking around for a right-wing leader from any party who had leadership ability and who would be charismatic enough to sway the masses and keep out the Communists. Right after I left Germany, those same businessmen started financing Adolf Hitler.[3]

My only knowledge of Hitler came from a little vegetarian place where I used to eat, because it was much cheaper than the regular restaurants. Often on entering I would notice a man sitting alone in a corner booth. One day I asked the proprietor who the man was and if he might want company. I was told that his name was Adolf Hitler and he was the delegate from Munich in the Reichstag. I was also told that he liked to eat alone and would refuse company. Strange to think now that that unassuming little man was to involve the planet in another world war.[4]

At one point, I discovered that the German government was opening my mail. A policeman came around to the Lufthansa office and asked me to come with him to the police station. He was courteous but wouldn't tell me what the trouble was. He simply said I had broken the law. I called the United States embassy for assistance, and it was not long before one of the attachés came over. After he talked to the police, he explained the whole thing to me. It seems they had opened an envelope addressed to me from the War Department that my mother had forwarded to me. Inside was my ROTC commission, which had been sent after my twenty-first birthday. The attache said it was "just a tempest in a teapot; however, you will have to renounce your army commission. By German law, it's illegal to be inducted as an officer of a foreign government while you're a resident here." I immediately gave up my commission, but it was an upsetting experience.[5]

Another unpleasant incident occurred when an embassy fellow named Cook tried to appeal to my patriotism and asked me to be a spy for the U.S. He knew I was visiting the Junkers factory to look at their planes for Lufthansa, and he wanted me to see if bomb racks were being built into the passenger planes and report back to him. I gave him a flat "no" and told him that I would not spy on my friends in the company. When that didn't work, he tried to scare me by implying that he could get my brand-new commission canceled, the one I had already given up.[6]

In the middle to late twenties, young Germans interested in aeronautical matters joined one of the many glider clubs flourishing in Germany. Gliding was the only way they were allowed to learn to fly because of the Versailles Treaty. While these aircraft were, in fact, just gliders, their engineering was superior to anything else in the world at the time. It has often been said that the pilots who trained in them later formed the nucleus of the Luftwaffe, Hitler's air force. Whether or not they intentionally used the clubs that way, the kids who learned to glide then were certainly more easily trained to fly powered airplanes later. The press in the Allied countries speculated on this possibility, but since the Germans were obeying the strict letter of the peace accord, nothing could be done about it.

The Germans were also able to do a good deal of experimental work in their civil aviation program, which was allowed under the Versailles Treaty. A name I heard frequently was that of Wilhelm, "Willi," Messerschmidt. My employer took me to see his little factory outside of Berlin where he was building a prototype of a single-engine cargo plane that he was trying to sell to Lufthansa. Messerschmidt was an enterprising engineer and businessman, and he later designed the military Messerschmidt planes which turned out to be so important in the Second World War.[7]

During my year in Germany, the German Communists were very active and very visible. The problems of unemployment and inflation gave the Communist message a lot of appeal among the workers. They came to Berlin from all over Germany waving their red flags, and they marched through the streets constantly. The atmosphere of tension grew stronger, and when I left Germany in 1929, I felt that an outbreak of civil violence was likely. It seemed to me that there would be a violent revolution and that the Germans would either go Communist or turn to a fascist dictatorship.

On May Day the Communists marched all day long. In the afternoon one of the Lufthansa pilots who was a friend of mine said to me, "Let's go down to the working-class district, and see what's going on." We were walking down the street when suddenly guns started going off and bullets came flying all around us. They weren't shooting at us, they were shooting at each other, but unfortunately, we were right in the middle of the two groups, the right wing and the left wing. We quickly dove into the nearest store door! The next thing we knew, a miniature tank came down our street, and then a squad of soldiers and some mounted police with drawn sabres appeared. A truck came along with loudspeakers blaring a message that the soldiers and police were going to search every house in the area for the next half hour, and that if they found guns in any apartment, all the people in that apartment would be shot. "If you have guns in your apartment, and don't want to get shot, throw them out the window." Well, you should have seen the guns come flying out all over the street, including even a couple of machine guns! Those frightened workers knew they were not hearing empty threats. In my view, that little episode was a clear example of how much the Communist message concerned those in power, and why anybody who came along with a program to contain this leftist movement would receive a hearing in German political circles.[8]

In terms of my subsequent career, the key thing that happened during my time in Germany was the contact I made with Clarence Young, under secretary for the newly created office of U.S. Secretary of Commerce for Air.[9] The American government was planning to build a lighted airway, known as the beacon system, across the United States. The beacons were illuminated cones, consisting of clusters of fluorescent tubes about ten feet high. The Germans had set up the system already, and Young, as a guest of the German government and Lufthansa, came over to look at it. My boss at Lufthansa sent me along to translate for Young.

Clarence Young was the one who paved the way for my future in aviation. He asked me if I was planning on going into aviation, and I replied, "I'm not over here for that reason; I'm really just trying to perfect my ability to speak German. As a matter of fact, aviation doesn't look to me like a very viable business. From what I see, the various airlines are subsidized by their governments and can't make money on their own." This was not a very shrewd thing to say to the Assistant Secretary of Commerce for Air, but he simply said, "I happen to think you're wrong. It's going to take a while, but sooner or later aviation's going to be a big industry." This was far-sighted, since U.S. aviation consisted mainly of the zany barnstormers and the primitive post office airmail operation.

Young told me that a new outfit called Pan American was, in his opinion, going to become a great international carrier. He thought that was where I should apply for a job. "I can give you a letter to the chief engineer and tell him how fluent you are in German." The letter he wrote was my introduction to Pan American World Airways and to my future career.[10]

Before leaving Germany, I was invited to a dinner at the German Aeronautics Club with the chief military general presiding. There were pictures of all the flying aces around the walls, including a large picture of von Richthofen, who was the top aviation ace of World War I. His seat at the head of the table, under the picture, was always left empty. After dinner the general stood up and toasted von Richthofen; then he toasted me with an invitation to stay in Germany and take a commission as a colonel in the Luftwaffe, the newly formed German Air Force.[11] I was embarrassed; it was quite an honor to be asked, and they did not expect me to refuse. I explained that all my family was in America, so I had to think it over. I wasn't sure if the invitation was an order or a request, but thought I had better not wait to find out. I left Berlin that night.[12]

# The First Routes to Latin America

*In the fall of 1929,* I took the letter of introduction from Clarence Young to André Priester, the chief engineer at Pan Am. Pan Am had been in business as a corporation for two years, having started with just a couple of airplanes and a few flights to Key West. They were just beginning to look at international aviation, surveying routes into Central America and down to Brazil and Buenos Aires.

Juan Trippe ran Pan Am from day one, although he had started the corporation with C. V. Whitney and John Hambleton, who was later killed in an airplane accident.[1] Trippe's key to success was that he managed to secure for Pan Am the U.S. Post Office airmail contracts out of Miami and Brownsville, Texas. Planes went out of Brownsville to Panama, and out of Miami to Panama, Venezuela, Trinidad, Puerto Rico, and some other islands. The contract was worth three dollars for every air mile, whether you carried one pound or a hundred pounds. That contract provided Pan Am with some guaranteed income and was the basis for its future routes.

My meeting with André Priester took place in New York only about a week after I got back to America. We talked about European aviation, and he asked me many questions. Then he said, "You had better come to work tomorrow." I thought he was kidding, and since I hadn't expected anything to come of the meeting, I got ready to leave. But he said again, "Can you come to work tomorrow?" and I finally realized he was serious. I was very excited, but I told him I would need a couple of weeks because I'd been away from family and friends for a year. This was in the summer of 1929, just before the infamous Black Friday market crash.

It is my belief that you can't run any business by sitting in the home office. You have to get out in the field and find out what it's all about. Luckily, Priester felt the same way, and a few days after I went to work for him, he said, "I want you to go down to Miami as an assistant to the operations manager. Help him get that chop suey straightened out." Pan Am's base of operations was then in Miami, and "chop suey" was Priester's way of saying that everything down there was a confused mess. Scheduling was nonexistent, there were no rules, no procedures, nobody had uniforms, and the pilots were walking around in sport shirts.[2] I had already shown him the Lufthansa operations manual, which I had translated into English, and he said, "That's what we need."

I found out quickly from the operations manager in Miami that Priester was right about the whole thing down there being "chop suey." The operations manager was responsible for everything: pilot training and employment, scheduling all flights, ground operations, and airport staff. Everything on the technical side was under him, except the maintenance shop. A major cause of his problems was that he had no operations manual, no rule book, with which he could hold people's feet to the fire and get things done right.[3]

Pan Am was using amphibians, airplanes that could land on both land and water, for the runs to Central America. One day, a pilot got into an airplane to get ready for a flight, and when he tried to start the engines he began cursing a blue streak: "This is a hell of an operation," he shouted. "The damned throttle control just came off in my hand!" Even the planes were "chop suey." Departures weren't scheduled by the hour, but only by the day, because the manager never knew when an airplane would be able to fly!

In addition to maintenance problems, there were also pilot problems; the manager never knew if the scheduled pilot would show up. Priester had asked me to adapt that Lufthansa operations manual to something applicable to Pan Am's situation, so that's what I did. The manual had everything spelled out: a uniform code, regulations for the pilots (such as no drinking), maintenance procedures, ground operations, scheduling and flight procedures.[4]

In both Miami and Brownsville, I got the operations manager's comments and then went to the maintenance manager. In talking with them, I was grateful for the maintenance, operations, and engineering experience I had received while working at Lufthansa. I made up a detailed draft of the adapted Lufthansa manual, incorporating the comments in each area from the Miami and Brownsville people. I then sent the revised document out again for more comments from the field, and within six months we had a new operations manual in effect for everybody except traffic and sales. The new manual seemed to help morale in the company; people knew what was expected of them, even though there were some complaints about "going by the book." This was the true organizational beginning, you might say, of Pan American flight operations, based on the model provided by Lufthansa.[5]

In early 1930, I returned to the New York office, but I soon asked Priester for more experience in the field. He sent me back down to Brownsville. Pan Am had recently bought control of a Mexican airline that was started originally to carry gold out of the mines into Mexico City by air because robbers had been grabbing the bullion on the road. That small operation expanded into an airline of sorts that flew to destinations around Mexico and on south to Panama. Priester wanted me to look the operation over and make a report on how it was functioning.

I was rooming in New York City with a college classmate of mine named Duncan Cox. He had come to New York to work for the Aviation Corporation of America, a financial holding company that had a lot of money invested in Pan Am.[6] When Duncan told his boss about my Mexican assignment, he said, "Why don't you go along with him and see what they're doing with this money we're giving them?" So we happily agreed to make the trip together. Duncan was to meet me in San Salvador, which was fine with me because I planned to spend a couple of days in St. Louis at the home of my college roommate, Bill, William McChesney Martin, who became the youngest head of the New York Stock Exchange.[7]

I started out on the trip via the Pennsylvania Railroad and TWA, one of the domestic airlines. This trip took several days because you rode on a sleeper train at night and then in a plane when daylight returned. In those days, passenger planes could not fly safely through the night. I got aboard the train at New York's Pennsylvania Station and got off at daybreak in Columbus, Ohio.[8] A man in a ramshackle little automobile then took me out to the airport, where there was a Ford Trimotor plane all warmed up and ready to go. I got aboard the plane and we rattled off. I think there were only three passengers aboard, and the other two were going all the way to the West Coast. After a couple of days in St. Louis, I got on a plane owned by an outfit called Universal Airlines and headed south toward Dallas.[9]

When I reached Dallas it was almost dark. There was no way to get to town, and there were no hotels near the airport. I was booked on an early-morning flight to Brownsville on Braniff, an airline that had just started up with a few single-engine airplanes.[10] Luckily, the caretaker at the airport felt sorry for me, and he told me there was a meeting room upstairs that had a big sofa I could use. So I went up there to sleep. At about three or four in the morning I woke up and discovered a big conference going on around me. I thought, "This is embarrassing—I'd better announce myself." So I rose up and they were quite startled to see me. Tom Braniff was having a meeting with his regional representatives, so I met that group for the first time under quite unusual circumstances.[11] At daybreak I got aboard a Braniff two-seater for Brownsville and discovered that my "seat" would be atop a pile of mailbags.[12]

I had bought my ticket through to Brownsville from the Pennsylvania Railroad, including the air-trip portion. Today, one might think it odd that a railroad would cooperate with the airlines that would eventually put them out of the passenger business. But at that time, such an outcome was inconceivable. The railroad/airline combination was called the Lindbergh Line. This was three years after Lindbergh's fabulous flight, and he let the railroads use his name.[13]

I arrived in Brownsville after a very exhausting trip in the little single-engine plane and was met by George Kraigher, head of operations and chief pilot for the Mexican airline we had acquired. He was a Yugoslavian who had been a Serbian fighter pilot in the first world war. George loved horses; he'd had them all his life, and we went riding while I was there. Wonderful old George! In those days, because the outfits were so small, many of the fellows wore two hats like George. A man stationed there named Ed Snyder was engineer in charge of maintenance for all the Central American routes. Due to the clouds he had found ringing Mexico City, Ed was the one who developed instrument flying.[14]

I was in Brownsville for several days, talking to the employees and busily writing in my notebook. Then George and I flew down to Mexico City, again in a Ford Trimotor. We stayed at the YMCA in Mexico City, where all the pilots had cots in one big room.

That night George got into a discussion with a number of us about the changes that were happening, and I informed him that in the new organization we were going to have airport managers on the ground. George took great exception to that. He feared that the pilot's authority was going to be reduced, and he said that no pilot was going to take orders from a ground person who didn't know flying.[15]

I saw that we had a basic problem; in those days the pilot was the big hero, parachuting from planes at county fairs and doing stunts above the crowd. In his leather helmet with the goggles and his aviator jacket, he had captured the public's imagination and had become an heroic figure. But I told George that there had to be somebody with tight control over the airline's ground services. We were putting in an interconnecting radio telegraph system, with a radio operator at each station all the way down to Panama. We were sending messages and booking people, and we had a lot of administrative things to do, along with watching the weather. I tried to explain that this new man wouldn't be in charge of flight operations, and I emphasized that his main purpose, as far as the pilots were concerned, was to get them weather reports. But George thought that the managers would soon start telling the pilots what to do. The only ground personnel George was interested in were the maintenance people. The pilots should continue to be in charge of the whole operation, just as they had been since the beginning.

Though we argued back and forth, George and I parted on friendly terms in Mexico City without having resolved our different points of view. I told him that regardless of what he thought, we were going to put in a small organization at each airport to run our business, but that its purpose wouldn't be to tell pilots how to fly the airplanes. After it was established, George did get used to it.

The next stop was supposed to be Guatemala City, but it was fogged in, so we landed at a place on the coast called Tapachula, just a dirt strip cut among the palm trees that the Mexican airline had built a couple of years earlier for one of their mail routes. The next day we flew up to Guatemala and then on to San Salvador. We had just inaugurated a flight from Miami to San Salvador to connect with the southbound flight from Texas to Mexico, in order to link the East Coast with the West Coast.

Duncan Cox was scheduled to arrive in San Salvador to continue on with me for the rest of the trip. Pan Am and the Salvadorian government had just built a little terminal at the airport. It had airy rooms and an awning running out so the passengers would not have to walk in from the planes exposed to the scorching tropical sun. I was standing out there with a couple of other people when Duncan came in on a Sikorsky amphibian S-38. As the pilot came taxiing up to the terminal at a pretty good clip, one of his brakes failed and the plane came crashing right into the awning, with all of us running for our lives. When I turned around, there was the funniest sight: my roommate, in his fancy New York duds, pushing up on the plane's top hatch and finally coming up with the awning's torn canvas draped around his head. I could tell that Duncan was enjoying the burlesque nature of the scene, because he had a huge grin on his face. As he crawled out of the awning wreckage he said, "What kind of an airline do you have here anyway, San?"[16]

Fortunately, the incident didn't do much damage to the amphibian. Even though Duncan's company was heavily invested in Pan Am, I never worried about this incident damaging Pan Am's finances. Duncan was a practical fellow with a sense of humor, as well as being a friend.

We took off the next day in a Ford Trimotor that had come down from Texas, and we went south through Central America. Before reaching the Canal Zone, we stopped at a place called David, in the northern part of the state of Panama. There had been a lot of rain, and the plane promptly sank up to its hubs in the mud. While the crew tried to free it, Duncan and I found a place to stay that had mosquito nets over the beds, a necessity as the mosquitoes were as big as robins.

That first night we walked through the town and soon saw some Panamanian kids playing basketball on an outdoor court. Duncan, an avid sportsman, asked if we could play. A couple of them understood English, and we told them that Duncan had been on the Yale basketball team and was also a football star. The English-speaking boys consulted with the others, and then finally said that they would like to have us play. So the two of us got on one team, and, since Duncan and I were each about a foot taller than any of those little guys, we began shooting baskets like crazy. They quickly objected and said we would have to be on opposite teams. This height difference was something I ran into constantly wherever I went in South America; even as an American of moderate height, I always towered over almost everyone else.

Although most of the players couldn't speak our language, we all played by the same rules, and we didn't have any difficulty understanding one another. The basketball game soon turned into a battle between Duncan and me. The local guys were elated, and every time Duncan, the famous football star, bowled me over, cheers went up in the stands. An Americano was getting knocked down! We were such a hit that they insisted we come over and play more basketball with them the next two nights. One of our first exercises in public relations!

The mud was so deep that it took three days before our plane was dug out and we could fly out.[17]

We arrived in Cristobal, Canal Zone, on the fourth day. After having had the minor crash in San Salvador and the big delay in David, it wasn't a very successful schedule up until then. When we were ready to take off for Maracaibo in Venezuela, we switched to a Sikorsky twin-engined amphibian. This was a safety factor, because we would be flying over water for quite a while on that route.[18]

The plane didn't have enough range to fly nonstop to Maracaibo, so there was a fuel supply of five-gallon tins stationed on the beach at the lower San Blas Islands. A caretaker was assigned to guard the fuel supply, but the pilot told us he might not be there because three caretakers had vanished in three weeks. Sure enough, no one was there.

The pilot said that he believed the local Indians who were not very friendly in that area were killing the Panamanian caretakers. They were fishermen and hunters who didn't have much sympathy for Western concepts of working, with regular hours and responsibility. They were free spirits, and wouldn't act as caretakers for the fuel. But they didn't like the Panamanians being there either.

Luckily, the fuel was still there. With nobody to fuel us, the passengers got out to do it. Besides Duncan and myself, there was a Marine on his way to see a girl he'd met in Maracaibo, and an accountant who was going down to Colombia for some unstated purpose. We began passing the five-gallon tins of gasoline and filling the tanks on the wings when suddenly we noticed that the airplane had its nose down on the beach, pushed into the sand, and we realized that it was sinking. We checked inside and found that the water already was above the floorboards, so we swam under the plane, but we couldn't find a leak anywhere.

I talked to the pilot and told him we had better get the plane out of there before it sank for good. He agreed to try to take off while there was still light in the sky, so we emptied the plane. Even though it had all that water in it, he was able to stagger into the air, leaving all the cargo, the mail, and the four of us sitting on the gasoline drums at the edge of the jungle.

Every plane was supposed to carry a can marked "Emergency Rations," but when we opened ours, we discovered there had been a terrible mistake. It contained tools, not food. So we had nothing to eat but a huge layer cake the Marine was taking to his girl. Of course, I kept writing all this information in my notebook for the New York office.

The Marine was absolutely furious. He didn't want us to eat his cake, but we finally took it away from him and ate it anyway. Then we had to make some arrangements for the night, which was coming on rapidly. When we had landed, we had seen a village about a mile down the beach, and Duncan wanted to go down and visit. I replied, "Let's stay away from there. We'll stir up a hornets' nest." But Duncan insisted, so reluctantly, I went along with him down the beach. As we neared the village, some of the

Indians spotted us and came storming out of their huts. We took off as fast as we could. Fortunately, they turned around when they saw us disappearing along the beach.

Needless to say, the other two passengers were scared to death that the Indians would attack us that night. If they did, we would be dead ducks, since we didn't have any weapons with which to defend ourselves. And that gloomy fact also went into my notebook. In fact, we did almost die from attacks by huge mosquitoes and snarling bugs all through the night. It was horrible. We started a fire and sat coughing and choking in the smoke, but with little relief. The Marine and the accountant, a New York business type with starched collar and tie, were red-eyed from the smoke of the fire and lack of sleep, so at that point they didn't think too highly of the airline business.

All the same, the next morning we were still alive when the plane returned and landed out in the bay. The pilot explained that the runway at Cristobal, where we had taken off the previous morning, was covered with crushed rock, and a rock thrown up by our tires had punched right through the plane's aluminum hull. It hit high up in the joint, out of sight, which was why we could never find it. We took off without incident, flew to Maracaibo, and then went on to Barranquilla, Colombia.

Duncan and I spent the night in Barranquilla and the next day visited the Colombian airline, SCADTA, a national airline run entirely by German personnel. When I was in Berlin in 1929, I had met Peter Paul Von Bauer, the German who was head of the Colombian operation. It was an internal domestic service, but it was trying to get rights from the U.S. to begin scheduled flights up to Miami. However, certain American interests were doing everything they could to keep the airline from getting such rights because it wasn't truly a Colombian but rather, for all practical purposes, a German airline.[19] It was also one of the best-run airlines in the Western hemisphere.

By 1930, Von Bauer saw that it would never get into the United States as a German-run airline. Pan Am already had quite a bit of money invested in SCADTA, and Von Bauer decided that the only way to get into the United States was through Pan Am. So he gave up, and the airline was acquired by Pan Am, although the Germans continued to run it. Just before World War II, at the request of the U.S. government, Pan Am exercised its ownership rights to dismiss all the German employees and replace them with Colombians. The name was changed from SCADTA to Avianca, and today it is totally Colombian owned.

Getting into the Latin American countries was the single biggest challenge that Pan Am had to face in the early days. We had begun negotiating the landing rights for all those countries prior to my scouting trip down there. If Pan Am had operated by the book, such negotiations would have been carried out by a U.S. diplomatic mission. Pan Am would have had to go through the embassies to get each of the landing rights, and there is no telling how long that would have dragged on. But we had to do things fast. Pan Am had its own "ambassador," so to speak. David Grant Mason was our main negotiator, and he put together many of the agreements with Latin American countries. He was still in his twenties (Trippe was only thirty in 1929; Priester was an "old man" of thirty-five).[20]

As it turned out, we didn't always have landing rights when we made some of our survey flights. I'm not sure we had rights in all the countries when I went down there, but fortunately the countries enthusiastically welcomed us anyway. It was a very exciting event; people would come down to see the airplane, and there would be a lot of flag waving. We were often invited in for cocktails at the hotel by high government officials, as almost all of them were very interested in the whole enterprise. It was a matter of pride for their countries to have airline service.

We were still getting landing agreements signed as late as 1939, just before the war. But then the State Department finally got on to what we were doing, and they got mad because we were treading on their turf; it is against the law for any private citizen or corporation to negotiate with a foreign government. However, Trippe always claimed that we were negotiating as an agency of the government. In fact, he wanted to nationalize Pan Am after the second World War, and he tried unsuccessfully to get all the other U.S. airlines to come in and join us. His idea was to create a single, giant, government-owned airline that would operate all over the world. All other countries had only one airline, and so should we.[21]

Pan Am began building an international route system in Central and South America because it was the only place we could get to besides Canada. There were no planes with enough range to go any farther than Latin America. We were already in the Caribbean, so we just extended our routes to connect with all the Central and South American routes before someone else got there. We operated with a firm policy that we would not compete with other domestic U.S. airlines once they had routes established. Trippe thought that if the airlines got into competition, they would destroy one another. He was later proven to be right.[22]

# Stationed in Honduras

*After my trip through Central America* to Colombia, I flew back to Miami and finally to New York. I had completed my survey tour about ten days behind schedule, what with all the delays and adventures. New York wanted a report from me on how their Mexican airline was doing, and Duncan Cox was to give his company a sense of how wisely their money was invested.

Neither of us had a very high opinion of our Latin affiliates at that time. I completed my report and turned it in, but I don't think it was spread around very much; it wasn't a very encouraging report. It was exhaustive, covering the needs for passenger accommodations and reviewing deficiencies in maintenance, in airport runways, in scheduling, and in all sorts of other categories. It let management know that we would have to spend a lot more time and money in order to develop a first-class passenger service to Central and South America. If my document had been a report card for a scheduled airline, the grade would have been a C-minus.[1]

The primary result of that report was management's decision to install airport managers in all the Latin countries so that our people could handle local problems on the spot. The manager would be the man in charge in each country, not only of the airport but of everything connected with the airline. Furthermore, each manager would be Pan Am's ambassador, our diplomatic "front man." We recruited most of them from around the Miami division, rather than from New York. They were young fellows in their twenties, preferably with flying experience, but at least with business experience. After we hired them, they were trained in a four-week course in Miami.

Next I went through the station manager experience myself. After I finished my report and submitted it to New York, I had a talk with André Priester, my boss. I told him that if it was possible, I would again like to move out of headquarters into the field, because I didn't see that I could accomplish anything more at the moment in New York City. He agreed to send me down to Miami where I could become a station manager and start from the bottom up. There were no positions available then, so the Miami people said they would let me be a traveling vacation-relief manager. Each manager was given one month vacation a year, and there was about a six-week overlap when somebody from Miami would have to go down and take over.[2]

As far as reporting to my superiors went, I never reported directly to New York. I told the people in New York that if I went to work in Miami, I would report only to my boss in Miami. I didn't want to be a management spy from the main office, or even be seen by my coworkers as one; it wouldn't work. My condition was accepted, so I reported to Miami after each tour of duty as a station manager. Much of what I reported was very routine and boring, such as keeping tallies of number of gallons of fuel used per week.

To learn the ropes, they started me at the Miami airport for a month or so as assistant to the airport manager. Then I started doing vacation-relief work. My first assignment was Tela, which is on the north coast in Spanish Honduras. I had been in Honduras two or three weeks when a revolution broke out. The revolutionaries had hired some World War I airplanes, old Spads, Jennies and Sopwith Camels, and they were dropping bombs by hand over the side of the planes onto the airfield. I telegraphed Miami and told them that I was closing the airport, and that our planes should fly directly from Belize, British Honduras, over to San Salvador, skipping our airport. After I sent that telegram, the next flight passed us by.

Right away my phone rang. It was the manager of the nearby United Fruit banana plantation. The manager was an Englishman, as were most of the top managers of United Fruit. He asked me to come over right away because something serious had happened. As soon as I got there, he said, "We didn't get our mail today."

I replied, "Of course you didn't get it. Those guys were throwing bombs all over the airport the day before yesterday. And we're just not going to land our planes there. We have only a few airplanes, and we can't afford to lose any; we don't have the money to buy new ones."

"Why didn't you come and tell me that?" he said brightly. "We're controlling this revolution, and I'll simply tell them to stop bombing you."

I stared at him, shocked by what I had heard. He explained to me that the current president of Honduras was put in by United Fruit several years ago, with the firm understanding that he would not raise the price of bananas to the point where United Fruit could not sell them at a profit. But he had completely ignored that gentlemen's agreement and had begun charging such a high tax on the bananas that United Fruit lost its profits. They were losing money. "When that happens," he said, "and you can't reason with the man because he's become too greedy, you can always find someone else who would like to be president.

"There's a general," he continued, "who would love to be president, and he has quite a big following. So we're supplying him with funds to buy ammunition and equipment. He has gotten this revolution going, and he'll be the next president. Of course," he added in a lowered voice, "I don't want you to talk about this, although I think most people realize what's going on."

I was amazed, but I kept my mouth shut.

"So," he said quite cheerily, "the planes should come in tomorrow around two o'clock as normal, correct?"

I reminded him that the flights were canceled because of gunfire. But he replied, "If you'll let me know when the plane's due, I'll have the chaps on each side stop shooting. Right now the revolutionaries are entrenched on one side of the airport and the government troops are on the far side. They always do that, because they don't want to get hit. They like to shoot across the airport where it's all open. But some of the men want their mail, too."

I couldn't believe what I'd just heard. United Fruit was in total charge. They were financing both groups. They could cut off the funds to either side or to both of them. They were going to see that the revolutionaries got in and this other guy got out, because they had a new deal in place regarding taxes on the bananas with the new people.[3]

I sent a few messages back and forth by code to Miami. At first, they would not think of sending down the plane, so I said, "I'll stand out in the middle of the field waving the Pan Am flag; if the pilot doesn't see me there waving the flag, that means stay off. However, if I'm waving the flag, that means everything is okay and the plane can land." So they finally persuaded the pilot to make a pass over the field. He came in, saw me there with my flag, and landed. The shooting had stopped at least an hour before, and there were no shots fired at any time while we unloaded the mail. Everybody was happy.

The only trouble was that a Honduran guy in uniform wanted to get aboard the plane for San Salvador with his pistol on his belt. I said, "You can't carry that into the passenger cabin. It just isn't allowed." I was concerned that he might hijack the airplane, or God knows what. We had a big argument with him, and finally he let us put the gun in the cargo hold. I did not know whose side he was on. It was hard to tell in those days because they all wore similar uniforms.

The term *banana republic* must have come into being as a result of ridiculous situations such as this, with the plantation managers pulling the strings of both sides. One can question the moral position of the companies, of course, but actually the manipulation done in Honduras by United Fruit gave the people of the country more than their own government could. They got jobs, and the company provided hospital and medical services. They had the railroads operating throughout the country, hauling out bananas. Some people of the country were far better off with United Fruit there than they had ever been before. This was all rather startling to a youngster who was raised on a quiet farm in Poughkeepsie. My first revolution had been the May 1 uprising in Berlin. In Honduras, I experienced my second revolution, all by the age of twenty-three.

Our village was truly in a back-of-the-beyond location. There were no roads except right around the village and at the airport. But even if we had had roads, there was no place to go. There was no hotel or other accommodations for pilots and passengers who might have to stay overnight; there was nothing. United Fruit, as a courtesy, would put up people at the hospital if they had empty beds. It was the only place we could stay. I lived in a little hut on the beach, although most of the time I ate with the United Fruit people in their big restaurant.[4]

Being young and highly interested in what was going on down there, I spent all the time I could sightseeing. Planes came through my airport only three times a week, so I had lots of time for excursions. I visited San Pedro Sula, which is now a big city but was then just a little shanty town with dirt roads. The only way to get there was on the network of narrow-gauge banana railroads, riding on top of the piles of bananas. Then there was a ten-mile link through the jungle that one covered aboard a riverboat. That was a very exciting trip because there were all sorts of wonderful colored birds and other fascinating treetop creatures.

A little way up from where I lived there was a float off the beach. I was on the float one day with a native friend, and he pointed out a shark through a knothole in the middle of the float. The shark was right under the raft. I asked him if it was dangerous, and he said, "No, no, it won't bite." As a matter of fact, there was a native in a rowboat, about a hundred yards further out, where he was catching sharks on a baited hand-line. It turned out that the local people ate them.

One rainy day, I learned a lot more about the sharks. I started to swim out to the float, but my native friend said, "No, don't go out to the float; the water's muddy. If you swim out today, the sharks will bite. When it's clear, they see how big you are and they don't attack you. But if you go out in muddy water they can't see all of you; they see only a flash of white once in a while—like the belly of a fish, you know. Then bang, they bite, and once you bleed, you've had it." So nobody went in. I used that same technique later in Cuba when I was stationed there, and swam off a dock in the same way: clear water, fine; dirty water, never.

While I was in Tela, I lived in a hut on the beach with a Guatemalan assistant. His job title was field clerk; he made out all the papers and did all the running around. He was a Guatemalan Indian, and very well educated. He'd been to a prep school in the States, and I understood that his family was quite well off. He was a very nice guy who wanted to get into aviation, and he was in Honduras, like me, to advance his career.

He took over for me when I got my first case of malaria. It was with me for about six weeks. I was terribly sick, shivering all over; I'd be standing out at the airport with a plane coming in, and I'd just shake. I had alternate heat flashes and chills. Right there in the tropics I'd feel as cold as if I were at the North Pole. Finally, I went to the United Fruit hospital; they gave me some pills. I went back to the hut and was so exhausted that I went straight to bed. When my Guatemalan Indian friend came in, I showed him the pills. "Oh, no," he said. "Take the Indian cure." And he left to get it.

I thought he'd come back with some witch-doctor type of potion: spiders, fried frogs, and things like that. But no; he came back with two gallons of red wine. He said, "In Guatemala, this is the way we cure malaria. Now, don't drink it too fast, because you'll get sick. Just drink as much as you can, get into bed with lots of blankets, and really work up a terrific sweat. It's the only way you can cure it." And it worked!

Many years later I asked a friend who was a medical doctor experienced in tropical diseases about this, and he said, "Yes, the treatment would work, but it puts an awful strain on the body. Young people can take it, but older people might die from the shock of getting so hot." He explained that if you get hot enough, you kill the malaria organism.

After that experience, I never had any further difficulties with tropical diseases. I learned to be very careful of what I ate and drank. Boiled water and no raw vegetables was the rule. If you were in doubt about the local food, you could always eat bananas. You could peel your own bananas and be sure they were clean. Nature's own protection, that banana skin.

In addition to my clerk friend, we also had a radio telegrapher and one mechanic. Fortunately, he didn't have much to do, since he wasn't very good. He just supervised the fueling of planes and things like that. The aviation fuel came to us aboard United Fruit freighters. They loaded the fuel cans onto the dock, and we'd drive down to get them.

Everything came in via freighter, even our food. It was interesting to watch the bananas being loaded. United Fruit did not need a mechanical device for loading the bunches of bananas because labor was so cheap. When the freighter arrived it would blow its steam horn, and hordes of people would come out of the jungle to do the loading. The bananas came right out on the dock on the narrow-gauge railroad. The Indians would pick the bunches of bananas right off the trains and carry them up planks and ladders placed along the side of the freighter. One train would unload and go out as another train came in. It was very efficient and well run.

While I was there, I went hiking a short distance from town and came out on an opening in the jungle. I saw natives playing cricket under the palm trees! I went over to a substantial brick house and knocked on the door. An elderly Scotsman opened it and invited me in. He said he had taught the natives the game. His wife had died, and he continued to live out there in the jungle a couple of miles from the village. He had a beautiful house with a fine library. The fellow was a scientist and had been sent to Honduras to crossbreed the local Indian cattle with American cattle in an attempt to develop a tropics-resistant beef cow. He called his experimental animals Brahmas, and maybe they were the origin of the current Texas herds.

Being a station manager in these out-of-the-way places was truly a lonely job. There was little social life in the evening for the United Fruit executives, the Scottish research scientist, or me, because there was nothing to do. Besides, we all were working full days and the heat made you pretty sleepy. The one thing I remember is that we had card games at the United Fruit lounge in the hospital. It was sort of a club, a place where you could just sit and read as well as meet people.

The station manager I'd relieved went home for six weeks. For spending ten and one-half months in Honduras he got extra money, which we called station allowance. This was truly "found money," since it was far cheaper to live there than in Miami. Pan Am had to offer it, since nobody wanted to put up with living in that awful heat, with all the diseases and snakes and bugs, and of course the boredom if you were there for a long time.

# Jamaica and Haiti

*After leaving Honduras,* I went on to Jamaica, then part of the British West Indies. The British establishment lived in Kingston, the capital of the West Indies, in quite high style. I met the son of the governor general at the tennis club there, and through him I met his father, who invited me to the governor's mansion for tea and tennis on Sunday afternoons. Under British rule, the islands were very orderly and tightly run. Even the little children wore uniforms when they went to school. I have been back down there since independence and found it greatly changed for the worse.

An incident that occurred one day shortly after I arrived in Jamaica illustrates the effect of English leadership. We had moved to our new docking location a couple of miles from the city office. My clerk would bring the incoming airmail in a pickup truck from the docking area to our office in Kingston, where we would separate out the Jamaican mail for delivery to the post office. One day the clerk got back to town and discovered there was a bag of mail missing from the pickup. So I jumped into the company sedan and raced off back toward the landing dock. I got about halfway there when I saw a crowd standing alongside the road. I stopped the car and saw the missing mailbag. It had fallen out of the truck, and a policeman was guarding it, but obviously no one had thought of stealing it; the rule of law dominated.

In terms of activity at the airport, Jamaica was a big step up from my first station. We had flights through Jamaica every day: one that went from Miami to Cristobal, Panama, and a short shuttle flight that went from Jamaica to Port-au-Prince, Haiti. We had a Sikorsky 38 for the Haiti run, but we used the bigger planes for the trip to Panama.[1]

I saw passengers for the first time while I was a station manager in Jamaica. They were mostly tourists, but the increase in their numbers was slow. Airlines had not yet become sophisticated in matters of marketing for passengers. Special off-season fares, tourist packages, and other such ideas came later. Hotels were few, but the Myrtlebank, built and run by the United Fruit Company and the only hotel in Kingston, was one of the finest hotels I had ever been in: it was a beautiful place with a swimming pool, delicious food, and all the luxuries, and I lived there for the six weeks I was in Jamaica. What a change from the beach hut in Honduras![2]

As usual, the bay was our "airport" in Kingston. We used the dock of a swimming club near town, but when a storm came up we couldn't dock there, because the waves got so high that the passengers would get wet. I thought this was a terrible arrangement, and I had already discussed a change with the regular station manager. Finally I went to our local agent, a Jamaican lawyer, and told him that our present docking location was unsatisfactory. I said, "Up at the end of the harbor, on the British military installation, they have a nice dock. The inlet is very narrow there and the waves don't build up so badly. It's the ideal place for us."

He answered, "Oh, you can't use that. The military won't let you do that." And that was the end of the conversation.

However, I was having tea with the governor general the next Sunday afternoon, and he mentioned the dock subject. He said, "Why don't you chaps move your base? The water conditions where you are now are terrible. It's much calmer up at the other end of the bay." What a marvelous break, I thought to myself.

I answered, "I doubt if we can get permission."

"Oh, I'll give you permission," he replied easily.

I later found out that the governor general was in command of the West Indian armed forces, but at the time I still felt skeptical. "Well, you know, this agent of ours is a lawyer, and I asked him about it, and he said there was absolutely no chance of getting permission from the military."

The governor smiled. "Oh, that fellow—he's a crook, didn't you know? He wants to get paid off. He wanted to present himself to you as the in-between man between Pan Am and us, and he was waiting for you to offer a bribe." I was still a pretty naive kid from the farm and I didn't suspect people of things like that.

I asked the governor general what I had to do to arrange the move. He said, "Just move up. I give you permission."

"How about Monday?" I said. "I'll move a floating dock over there, anchor it, and we'll just move a ramp into the nose of the plane from the dock to swing with the wind. Are you sure I don't need any formal permission or anything?" I was still stunned at this turn of events.

"No, no," he said. "I'll send you a letter on Monday saying that we are pleased to know that you are going to move up to calmer water."

So I hired a small tug and towed the floating dock to the new location, at the other end of the harbor. The pilots all thought it was great even though I did this without checking with the main operations office in Miami.

I subsequently told our local agent about the move and that I had gotten the permission from the governor general. He didn't say any more to me about it, but he did raise a ruckus with Miami on the subject, and Miami wired to complain to me about stirring up trouble in Jamaica. They kept sending me messages to move back to the old location. But my response was that the safety of the planes, pilots, and passengers had priority, and this had dictated the move. Furthermore, our schedules, which had been delayed because of the rough water, were now being maintained. For a while the affair also got me in a bit of hot water with some of the local people, who had made money when we were in the old location by providing assorted services to our passengers, but that soon cleared up.[3]

Out in the field, I began learning in a practical way about these human conflicts. People at the home office couldn't understand how problems get solved out in the field. But if the man in the field is afraid to move in a reasonable way on a problem or an opportunity because he can't cover himself with the home office, everybody loses. Conditions in the Latin countries were so unpredictable that the station manager had to make snap decisions and not worry about being fired. To me, if some project made sense, it was the right thing to do. I didn't care whether I got fired or not.

After returning to Miami, I was assigned to Haiti as temporary manager. Haiti was a fascinating place, with incredible contrasts. There were native Indians living next door to the people the French brought in, of both black and French descent. Most of the people were very poor; the pay of a station hand when I was there in 1932 was about forty cents a day, the going wage in the country, but the rich had a very luxurious and exotic society. Being there was quite an experience.

We had a seaplane base in Port-au-Prince. The local people we hired to work there were completely unreliable, and we never knew who was coming to work. When they did come, they were likely to fall asleep on the job. For example, we sent a rowboat out to tow every plane that landed in to the dock. The day after I got there, a plane came in. I saw that the rowboat was out there, but I couldn't see anybody in it. I thought, "This fellow's fallen overboard," and I hurriedly rowed out. But there he was, asleep in the bottom of the boat, while the pilot circled around, waiting for him. To be fair to the people, I think that part of this sleepiness was due to tropical diseases, their diet, and their generally poor health.

These people had never followed any sort of a schedule. I would explain to them that they were supposed to show up every day at certain hours. They would say yes; but the habit was not there. As a result, we had to hire twice as many employees as we needed. I finally told the people that they had to show up or they would be laid off. When the next workday came along, one worker didn't show up. So when he came in on Monday, I told him he didn't have a job anymore. He got very upset and quickly left. When he came back, he had his wife and five children with him, and as they entered they all started to weep. He had it orchestrated perfectly to play on my sympathy. And it worked; I finally gave him a second chance.

Kite contests were the big sport in Port-au-Prince. A young guy from the U.S. embassy joined me in entering kite contests held on an airfield built and occupied by the U.S. Marines. Sunday was the big day for the contests, and several hundred people would cheer the kite fliers on. The contest consisted of trying to fly your kite the highest, and then diving it in such a way that it would crash another kite. Although some people had fancy box kites, we just had the old-fashioned V-type, but with a good tail and good twine, it did all right.

The Marines were all over the American part of the capital then. My impression was that they were a sad group. They were a self-contained unit, and they separated themselves from Haitian society. With not much to do, both the Marines and their wives drank too much. Some of them would show up at the club each morning and start ordering drinks. Alcoholism was, and is, a real problem with the people stationed in the tropics.

Stenio Vincent was the president in Haiti, and his people negotiated the operating rights with Pan Am. Here again, we did business directly with a foreign government. Contrary to what I had come to expect, the Haitians did not try to shake the company down and look for payoffs. We never had any trouble with the president. In fact we didn't see him; he stayed inside his palace in the center of town with heavily guarded concrete walls around it.

We had six landings a week at Port-au-Prince, every day except Sunday, carrying mostly mail and a few passengers. There weren't many tourists, but lots of salesmen came in and out, most of them bringing all kinds of trinkets that they could foist off on the poor locals. Aside from that stuff, and bananas, there wasn't any real business to be done in Haiti.

There was only one hotel in Port-au-Prince, owned and run by the Pauley family. They were quite a family; one of them went out West and made himself a fortune in the oil business. I often had dinner there. The dining room was open all around, and goats would wander in right off the street, come to the tables, and beg for something to eat, which amused everyone. On arriving in Haiti I stayed there, but later I moved to a boardinghouse up on the mountain, where it was cooler.

When I was leaving Haiti, I found out for the first time how bad things were for blacks in the United States. On a flight back to Miami, I met a black Haitian and his twelve-year-old son. They sat in the back of the plane, which was where I always sat in order to let the paying passengers have the better seats with the windows. I started chatting with the father, who was very well educated and was connected with the Haitian embassy in Washington. The young boy spoke English, too, and I asked him if he wanted to see the cockpit. I took him up and let him sit in the copilot's seat, while the pilot explained what he was doing.

When I took him back to his father, the man was in tears, and I said, "What's the matter, are you sick?"

He replied, "No, I'm just overwhelmed; for the first time in my life a white American has been nice to me and my son. Although I'm in the diplomatic corps, when I get to Miami I have to go to a Negro hotel in the working section, and although they provide facilities in Washington, we're still treated like we're nobodies. This is my son's first trip, and I'm so disturbed about what his reaction will be when he encounters the way most Americans treat us." His son had always been treated with dignity in Haiti; he had gone to private school and was a member of the elite. Suddenly he was going to find himself treated as an inferior. The Haitian said, "Taking him up to the cockpit will give him a good start—he'll always remember that he had friendly treatment from the first white American he had ever met."

I was shocked at how serious the breach was between blacks and whites. It made a deep impression on me. At the time, I couldn't believe racial prejudice was so strong, but I learned better later on. Prejudice was totally outside my personal experience when I was growing up. We had a black man working on our farm, who lived in our house, shared our meals, and was treated like a member of the family.

Of course, the trouble wasn't as obvious in the North as in the South. But in Miami, and the South in general, there were shabby, segregated hotels for blacks. There were different drinking fountains, different toilets, and the restaurants had those little side windows: if a black man wanted to buy food from a restaurant, he couldn't go inside and sit down. He would have to go to a window, and the people inside would open a screen and pass the food out to him.[4]

# A Revolution in Cuba

*In early 1933,* the operations manager in Miami called me in and said, "How about going over to Havana? They are expecting a revolution in Cuba very shortly, and someone needs to take the place of the manager there." This made sense: The manager had several children and was concerned about his family. But since I was single, and eager for a new experience, I was quite willing to go, provided that I would be relieved around the beginning of October, when I was planning to go back to graduate school.

I wanted to learn Cuban Spanish, so on my arrival I rented a room in the private residence of a widow living with her two daughters. Her husband had been master of the Port of Havana. After I moved in, I asked the family to speak only Spanish at mealtimes. They countered by putting a dish in the middle of the table and said I had to put money in the dish to pay for the language lessons. That seemed fair, so each night I paid up. Then, after the evening meal, we would frequently all go to the movies.

Since my Spanish wasn't great, I immediately hired a part-time translator and clerk, a bright young Army sergeant who did an excellent job. His name was Fulgencio Batista, a name that would later become very familiar, while he was dictator of Cuba. But at that time I found him to be a simple, unassuming man and a good employee.

The president of Cuba was Gerado Machado y Morales, a black Cuban who had started out as a political figure in the city of Puegas. He had held the office for eight years as a Wall Street-backed dictator. Machado was a man of the people, and wherever he went there was great cheering and yelling. But as time went by, he became progressively more greedy and unscrupulous. By the time I got there, he had made a lot of enemies. To offset this, Machado had built up a secret police force called Poirra. He'd say to them, "Get rid of this fellow; he double-crossed me." They would immediately shoot the person, and his body would just disappear.[1]

The killings became so frequent that an underground revolutionary movement called ABC got started in order to overthrow him. This was copied after a secret society formed before the French Revolution, comprised of cells. Its members were both civilian and military, anyone who was against the government. The way ABC worked was quite clever. "A" represented a section of the country, and the members within it would be numbered. Likewise "B" and "C." In this way, the actual names of the members would be unknown to one another, so that they would not expose other members under torture.

Through friends, I had received a guest membership at the Radato Tennis Club, an exclusive club in Havana where I played tennis nearly every afternoon. What I didn't realize was that my regular tennis partner, a young lawyer, was the top man in the ABC organization.

The whole country was involved in graft and bribery. The government customs clearance clerk came in to me one day complaining that he hadn't been paid. "Get paid for what?" I asked him.

"You people flew in a load of military stuff from Mexico, and I let it go through. You know that's illegal, since it's going to be used for warfare here. I do all these favors for you and I only get paid four hundred dollars per month. United Fruit pays much more than that. They pay me a thousand dollars a month."

"The former manager never told me about this," I said. "Anyway, you're working for the government, we pay the government for your services—and now we're supposed to pay *you*, too?"

"Oh yes, that's very common here," he said. "It's not a form of bribery, it's just to help me out. The government pay is poor, so the various companies help me out." I said I'd get back to him.

I contacted Miami about this, and they said I shouldn't have anything to do with it. I knew beforehand that would be the answer; Juan Trippe was very strict on this matter. Everybody knew that taking gifts and bribes was quite common in Latin America. But Trippe's philosophy was that the airline business was a new industry and didn't have the resources to deal in that kind of funny business. It was a very good policy; the problem with bribery is that once you start, they want more and more all the time.

I told the customs man that we had a policy against such payment, but he said he had previously gotten the money from the local manager.

Apparently the local manager had paid him off out of the petty cash fund. After that he'd drop by regularly, always expecting a tip for this or that alleged service relating to our cargo. But when the revolution finally broke out, the opposition group went after this guy, and he just disappeared.[2]

Two interesting places that tourists loved were Sloppy Joe's and Harry's Bar, where Ernest Hemingway hung out. They were gambling casinos out near the country club, and they both were classy places run on a very elegant scale. Gambling was a very popular activity in Havana.

I met a rich American named Harvey Firestone, a sad, elderly man. He had known Thomas Edison and Henry Ford Sr., among other famous people, but now he lived alone on a big estate outside the city with his servants. His hobby was gambling. I asked him one time, "Do you make money at this?"

And he said, "I don't know. If you have to keep track of what you make or lose, you shouldn't be doing it."[3]

Other gambling places around Havana were operated by really sinister types. There were some American professional gamblers in Havana who I would run into at a hotel in town; apparently that was where they had their offices. The story was that they were brought down to Havana by the American publicity people whom Machado had hired to improve his image in the United States. They bragged about their Cuban activities on their trips back to Chicago, but they were rather unsavory characters who may have had Mafia connections. They left pretty fast when the whole situation blew up into a revolution.[4]

After I got to Cuba, things were relatively quiet in the country for about six months. The revolution didn't occur until around July or August, but well before that time there was constant talk of an uprising and all kinds of minor trouble. Machado's days in office were numbered. His secret police were awful: they'd break into citizens' homes in the middle of the night and kill people, or take them away never to be seen again. Finally, the State Department sent Sumner Welles down in an effort to resolve the trouble.

Americans down there weren't told anything about what was going on; we had very little contact with our embassy, and they didn't know much anyway. I learned everything through my friends at the British embassy, who seemed to know everything that was happening. Apparently, Welles proposed to Machado that he leave the country with guaranteed safe conduct, which would have been the sensible thing for him to do.

The next thing I knew, an American destroyer steamed up to the Havana waterfront with a bunch of Marines and dropped anchor right off our seaplane dock. A launch came to our dock with a uniformed man who got off it and came into my office. He was the commanding officer. He announced, "We want to use your dock to come in and get water and food and supplies."

"Well, what are you doing here?" I asked.

"Damned if I know," said he. "We were just told to come down here and anchor in the harbor. I guess we're supposed to impress the Cubans for Sumner Welles's visit."

"You know, there's going to be a revolution down here. And when it happens, I hope you're going to help the rest of us get out of here on your destroyer."

He replied that they had orders not to intervene in any way. "Even if you're shot, we can't do anything about it."

So that was that, and any thoughts of "U.S. Navy to the rescue" were abandoned. I later learned that the Navy Special Service Squadron based in the Canal Zone had been moved to St. Petersburg, Florida, and increased from three ships to twenty-three. The Navy was prepared if Roosevelt said the word. However, nonintervention was the FDR policy.[5]

It was sometime in early August when I got a call at home early in the morning from one of my Cuban employees. "The revolution's going to break out sometime today," he said. "I thought I'd better tell you so you can redirect the planes or something."

Right away I had a problem. I had no basis for canceling the incoming plane except for this rumor, so I had to let the plane come in on schedule. Everything seemed normal, but since my informant was pretty dependable, I thought I'd better play it safe. Instead of leaving the plane at the dock as usual, I had it moved to a buoy anchored about a half-mile out in the bay, where I figured it would be safer. I could get it out of there in a hurry if necessary, and I could load passengers and cargo by means of a shore launch.

It was about noon when all hell broke loose. There was a lot of gunfire, and soon a whole bunch of Cubans waving rifles and sticks came marching down to the passenger terminal at the dock. They cornered me in the office and demanded that they be taken out to the plane; they said the plane belonged to Cuba and that the Americans were stealing everything.

I had already arranged to have the crew stay aboard the plane as a precaution, and I'd instructed them that if they saw a red flag being waved out of the radio-room window on the second floor, they were to take off immediately and fly back to Miami. The revolutionaries were running all over the place, and while they milled about, I slipped upstairs, got out our red signal flag, and waved it from the window. Almost immediately the crew on the plane dropped their mooring and prepared to take off. They had trouble getting one of the engines going, so they took off on just one engine and circled the dock while they worked on getting the other engine started. At one point the plane passed right over the pier, and the revolutionaries, both uniformed soldiers with military weapons and civilians with sporting guns, all let go at the plane with everything they had. I later learned that they hit it eleven times, including one round that passed right behind the pilot's head. But the crew finally got the second engine started, and they flew off toward Miami. It was a close call.

In the meantime, Sumner Welles and his aides had left Havana to hide out at somebody's country estate. The windows of the U.S. embassy were all broken, and you couldn't find anybody there. They had all run off to hide. I made an attempt to get half a dozen Marines assigned to our dock office, just to keep Cuban revolutionaries from raising hell there, but the American military brass wouldn't do anything. The Marines weren't allowed to leave the ship except to get food. So I just stayed in my office and tried to keep things going as normally as possible.

The revolutionaries' primary complaint against the United States, as best I could understand it, was that we were stealing from Cuba and the Cuban people. They thought that Machado was a puppet of the Yankees and that we were in league with him.

Later, I got a call from the Cuban manager at our landing field, which was twelve miles outside of Havana. Pan Am owned a local Cuban airline, Cubana, that operated out of the field using one Sikorsky amphibian plane that was kept there. The manager said, "Your taxi just arrived." Then he explained that Machado, the president of the country, was outside the office on the floor of a taxi, hiding under his wife's skirts. He was demanding that Pan Am fly him to Nassau. Apparently, Sumner Welles had promised him safe conduct by the Americans. I'm sure he had received such a promise, on the condition that he resign from the presidential office, but he had waited too long.

Right in the middle of all this confusion I got a call from our senior manager in Washington asking what was going on. I told him that Machado was requesting a flight out of our landing field and asked him what I should do. He replied, "Regarding Machado, Trippe says the State Department wants his escape carried out if possible, provided you don't endanger yourself or any of your employees." Then he hung up. I called the airport, and I told them to take Machado out. I heard later that he wouldn't even let his wife go with him. There were also two or three of his senators who wanted to go, but he wouldn't take anyone; he just wanted to save himself.[6]

I was leery of getting involved with this man, and with good reason. Even then, just a few hours after the start of the revolution, you could go past the university and see people's bodies hung up and burning on the metal telephone poles outside the school wall. They were members of the hated Machado secret police who the mobs had caught and executed. I saw one fellow who was alive but was being dragged around town behind a car at high speed with a rope tied around his waist. It was a gruesome sight. At that time I attributed these awful excesses to the Latin temperament, but when I later read a lot of history and learned some of the horrible things that have been done through the ages, especially under Hitler, I realized that such acts aren't peculiar to Latins. And these revolutionaries weren't any particular group of zealots. They were a cross-section of the ordinary public.

But I had plenty to deal with at the dock. When the Pan Am plane flew out, it infuriated the revolutionaries. They had sent their gunmen to the dock to seize the plane that had gotten away, and though they put some bullet holes in it, they were frustrated. So they then came back to the terminal and cornered me in my office. A Cuban employee had carried a revolver in to me. I tried to refuse it, but he said, "I'll put it here in your desk drawer. You may need it." I had no idea of using a revolver, but when a screaming mob came to my office door shouting that they were going to hang me from the statue of Jose Marti, the liberator of Cuba, I began to think I would need that gun after all. I figured if they were going to kill me, I was going to get a few of them at the same time. The picture that flashed across my mind, as I looked at all those nondescript characters running around out in the waiting room, was an illustration out of a childhood history book of a mob scene in the French Revolution.

While the gunmen were milling around on the dock, they got the word that I was the one who'd helped Machado escape. With that news, things got even worse; before that, they had just been yelling at me from the doorway, but now they raised their guns and pointed them at me. Since the U.S. embassy was abandoned, I called the British embassy and got hold of a friend of mine there. He told me to try to come right over. I hung up, and just then a man in a business suit pushed his way through the crowd in a no-nonsense, take-charge sort of way.

It was my Cuban tennis partner. "I heard you were in trouble down here," he said, speaking in English. The tension of the situation had left me speechless. Then he made a stunning revelation: he was the leader of the revolutionary underground movement!

He gestured his head toward the crowd of rebels surrounding us. "They're pretty touchy, these people. All the years of pent-up anger and frustration has suddenly broken loose, and there's no telling what they might do. I am not sure I can restrain them." Then he lowered his voice. "I hear that Machado got away." I just nodded. He winced and shook his head. "Well, that's going to make things real difficult. They know that even though you don't run things directly out at the airfield, you had to have something to do with the escape, since you're the man in overall charge of airline operations in Cuba."

My instincts told me that, with this man, honesty would be the best policy. "Yes," I said, "I gave the permission to take him out."

He looked at me silently for a very long moment, then tapped my arm as he stepped away. "I'll take care of it," he said. He gestured to the people around us and led them a distance away. A vigorous conversation then took place between him and the armed revolutionaries, and I could tell from their expressions that they did not like what he was telling them. But after several minutes of talk he came back to me. "Let's get out of here," he said, and, gripping my arm, he led me through the crowd, out the office door, and across the road to a bar. What a lucky break to have played tennis with him all those months.

"What will you have?" he asked.

"I'd like a triple shot, followed by another triple shot," I told him. I wasn't much of a drinker, but I sure drank a lot of whiskey that day, and it didn't affect me at all.

"Tell me what is going on," said he, and, happy to get it out, I told him the whole story: how I got both the amphibian and the landplane with Machado aboard out of the country, that both planes had arrived in Miami, and that Machado's trip out was requested by the United States government, not something I'd dreamed up.

"Yes," said my friend, "but as my deputies see it, you personally were the one who got the amphibian away from them, and they wanted it. Also, they wanted Machado, and your company owns the Cuban airline that got him away from them, thereby frustrating one of the main targets of the revolution. So there are pretty hard feelings against you, and selling your innocence is something that's going to be hard to do."

But sell it he did, by putting all the blame on the pilot of the plane, Captain Bill McCullough. He passed the word around that Machado's escape was engineered entirely out at the airfield, and that I had nothing to do with it. Later, the revolutionaries announced on radio that if they ever got their hands on the pilot, they'd murder him. But they were frustrated in their chief objective, which was to hang Machado.

Later my friend suggested, "You'd better not go home tonight. Come with me; our headquarters are in one of those high-rise apartment buildings downtown, and you can stay there tonight." Fortunately, I did as he suggested. I later learned that a bunch of revolutionaries came to my boardinghouse that night, nearly scaring my landlady to death. They went through my room, scattered my belongings all over the place, and opened all my luggage.

After work I went up to my friend's office, and from then on we were all identified by numbers. I was so scared and really traumatized by the flareup that I completely forgot my friend's name and have never been able to remember it since. The polished operation at my friend's office was quite a contrast to what I had seen earlier. A group of people were huddled over several long lists, which turned out to be the names and addresses of Machado's cronies and government officials. There were at least a hundred names on the lists. One list was of people who would just be hauled in and questioned, one was of people who were to be stripped of all their property, and one list was of people they intended to shoot.

In one room at the headquarters, ABC people were being assigned to murder squads. In the middle of the room was a large, opened wooden case filled with .45-caliber Colt revolvers they were handing out to the squads of gunmen. Each man was given a gun, assigned to a murder squad, and handed his list of what were called "confiscation cases." These were the names of the people he was to kill.

While I was waiting for my friend to arrive, I called Miami and told them that we should shut down Pan Am operations in Cuba for the present. When my tennis friend arrived, I took him aside and said, "Pan Am doesn't have any role in all this that's hostile to the purposes of the revolution. I mean, we're an American company with no role whatsoever in your internal politics. As to Machado's escape, we had orders from the U.S. State Department to do it; we had no choice. To help cool things down, I've canceled the flights."

My friend shook his head in a vigorous negative. "I think we'd be better off if you had one daily flight coming in with the mail. Ask Miami if they will authorize this. We want open communications with the world. Also, we have many exiled friends in Florida who want to know what's going on, and who want to come back if things are now safe."

I was worried about the safety of the airplanes. But my friend promised, "We will not touch your airplanes." He did suggest that, as a safety procedure, we should moor our planes offshore at the buoy and not come in to the dock. "I don't have total control over our people," he said.

I asked for a moment to think about his request, but I knew that I would comply with it. How could I refuse? I undoubtedly owed him my life! From the revolutionary headquarters I went over to the Pan Am office and got our Miami manager on the radio. I said I had talked with the revolutionaries and had their promise that we could keep our flights operating without interference. I told them about the lawyer's suggestion of mooring offshore, and I added that I would be at the dock when a plane was due in, and if I held aloft a red flag, that would be a signal to the pilot that something was wrong and to return to Miami. Well, Miami thought it over, then called back and told me they were resuming a daily flight.

The first flight arrived the next morning, and revolutionaries were swarming all over the dock. When the launch brought in a number of returning exiles, the crowd broke into a big roaring cheer. There was great rejoicing and embracing on the dock. The returnees were heroes to them. It was like a carnival. This happy scene made Pan Am people heroes that morning. But it became a different situation in the afternoon, when the plane was about to depart.

By the time the passengers were ashore and gone, it was midday, and I went downtown to one of my regular lunch places, a Chinese restaurant. The door was locked, but the owner once told me that if a revolution should break out, I should come to his back door and he'd feed me. So I knocked at his back door, and when he let me in I saw lots of his other patrons and friends already there. Just as I started on my food, the phone rang. It was my office. "You'd better get down here fast," the clerk said. "There's a fellow here who's trying to flee the country. He's gotten aboard the plane and won't get off—says we have to take him to safety in Miami."

When I got to the terminal and went out to the plane, there he was with his wife, sitting in front passenger seats. He was holding a pistol on his lap. I knew him by sight: Orestes Ferrara. He had been the equivalent of the Attorney General of Cuba, a top justice minister under Machado, and he had condemned lots of relatives and friends of the revolutionaries to death. He was also in charge of the secret police, and a really bad guy.

"You don't have a reservation, and you'll have to get off the plane," I told him.

He looked me back right in the eye and refused. He claimed that if anything happened to him, it would be my responsibility, and that he was under the protection of the American flag. He made it clear that he would not get off the plane and would use his gun if necessary.

"If you stay on here," I said, "they're going to come out and sink this plane or burn it with you in it. People at the station waiting area saw you go through. You'd better get off while the getting is good. I can drop you anywhere at another dock or somewhere; I'll have our launch put you off. So you'd better get off."

He said he wouldn't do it. He knew his last chance was to stay on that airplane, and he wouldn't budge. So I tried another tack. I said, "I have a couple of my workmen equipped with guns outside the plane. We'll bring them aboard, and if you don't get the hell out of here, they'll shoot you."

It was a bluff, and he knew it; he got back in the corner and said, "Anybody comes through that door with a gun, he'll get shot." I wasn't going to sacrifice any of our poor mechanics for that s.o.b., so I had no choice but to let the plane take off with him aboard.

Luckily, the engines kicked right over and started up, with Captain Leo Terletsky as pilot. That airplane got off without having to circle in front of those guys with their Army rifles. But, boy, the revolutionaries hated that pilot! They immediately got on the telephone to Miami, and when the plane got there, a bunch of exiles with guns were waiting for it. Fortunately, no one was killed.[7]

After the plane lifted off and was gone, I went back to the dock in the launch. There I discovered a bunch of American schoolteachers who had reserved tickets sometime in advance for that flight back to Miami. They were, to put it mildly, dismayed to see the plane take off. They started screaming and yelling at me, and a couple of them fainted. I said, "Sorry, but you'll have to go back to the hotel. It was too dangerous to put you on that airplane." Many of them lost their luggage to the mob that was outside the terminal.

However, things quickly settled down into a kind of normalcy. We kept the mail coming and going every day. Most of the time we didn't have passengers, but when we did, it was cheers and jeers; big cheers when a plane arrived in the morning with some of the returning exiles aboard, and jeers and violence in the afternoon when Machado supporters came to the dock to try to escape on the departing plane. Some were caught and murdered right there in the terminal if they were desperate enough to come down to the dock. The rest of them were smart enough to stay in hiding out in the countryside somewhere. This kind of violence tapered off, and by the end of four or five days we started tying the plane up to the dock again.

The revolution was only a few weeks old when the military aristocracy decided to pull off a coup against the ABC group and kick my young tennis friend out of power. Their replacement was to be General Garcia Menocal, who had been president of Cuba just before Machado. This is when my former translator and clerk, Batista, came into the picture.

The revolutionaries had selected Sergeant Fulgencio Batista to be the head of the Army. When the officers got wind of this, they knew that the sergeants and the corporals would soon gang up on them. Some two hundred of the officers gathered in the ballroom of the National Hotel, a big American luxury hotel near where I lived, to discuss what to do next. While they were talking, a gang of sergeants and corporals organized by Batista marched up to the front of the hotel and ordered them to come out. The officers refused.

The next day, as I was coming home from the airport, I noticed that the noncoms were still waiting outside the hotel. They were setting up a French 75-mm artillery piece in a park right beside the Mallacon road that runs along the ocean. I knew about French 75's from college ROTC field artillery training, and I was curious, so I went over and talked to the revolutionaries. They said that they intended to fire at the hotel because they couldn't get the officers to come out. Then they loaded the cannon and fired, and the first round went right over the hotel and landed near my dock terminal in the lower part of the bay. I quickly saw that if something weren't done, they might put me out of business.

"Wait, stop!" I shouted. "You can't do this. You're going to blow up a lot of homes and kill a lot of innocent people over there in the poor section." But it was clear that what I'd said hadn't impressed them. I said, "What you want to do is hit the hotel, right?" They agreed, and I told them, "I'm an expert in artillery—let me set up the cannon so you'll hit only your target."

At that moment, I was in a situation with no easy solution. If I helped them, there might be serious consequences for me, from both their government and my own. But I wasn't thinking of that; all I had on my mind was protecting Pan Am property and innocent lives. I knew that even if I didn't help them, they would keep banging away until eventually they hit the hotel.

So I showed them how to set up the gun, and they pumped a few high explosive shells into the hotel. Each round made a big hole in the walls. It wasn't long before the officers stuck out a white flag; a spokesman appeared and said they would all come out if their safety were guaranteed. The rebels gave them this promise, and the officers began filing out of the hotel and lined up in the parking lot. As the last of them got there, a rifle shot rang out from a second-story window of the hotel. Nobody knew who did it, or why. Immediately the revolutionaries opened up with their rifles and machine guns, firing at point-blank range into the crowd of unarmed young officers. It was horrible; they just mowed them down. Blood ran in a stream across the asphalt and down the parking lot rain grates. The bodies were just piled one on another. I don't know how many were murdered there, and the few survivors fled.

I got out of there fast. The next day Batista's people seized Radio Havana, the national radio station, and announced that he was taking over. Batista went on the air personally and tried to calm everybody. He declared a general curfew and said that if everybody just went home and did what they were told, nobody would be harmed. Very soon everything did simmer down, and he was made Colonel Batista, Chief of Staff. He ran Cuba but did not actually become president until 1940.

The time came for me to take off for Harvard Business School, so Pan Am sent some poor guy over to replace me. He was a trained airport manager, but under the new regime he had very few problems.

When Batista first took power, he started public works projects, roads and other things, in order to put people back to work. He was chased out for a while, and Dr. Ramon Grau San Martin became president for a couple of years. San Martin was a professor at the University of Havana, and he was a complete bust, so Batista was asked to come back. Living fairly well, even though in exile in California, he wasn't too anxious to go back, but they persuaded him to return and calm things down. He was in and out of power until Castro took over in 1959.

I had come to know Batista very well, as he had been my translator and secretary for a few months when I was first in Cuba; he did an excellent job. At the time, I wouldn't have picked him as a guy who was tough enough to head up that government. He was quiet and modest with me. I followed his career for years after I left Cuba, out of curiosity and interest. He tried to help the poor people, and he managed to do a lot of things that Machado didn't know or care about.

Batista had to deal with the powerful influence of the big American sugar corporations over there. Back then, any Cuban government had to have the blessings of U.S. interests before they dared move. But it was a two-way street; the big corporations tried to be friendly with the government so they could stay in business in Cuba. Batista tried to work with them, and he got a lot of taxes out of them, which he used for his various improvement programs.

One thing I learned during my stay in Cuba was that the British were a bigger help to me than the U.S. embassy. If I wanted to know anything at a time of crisis, I called the British; and this was true all over the world. The British had a really professional foreign service. They were trained people, they mixed well with the local people, they spoke the languages, and they had common sense and practical experience. They were quite different from our State Department people. I don't know if this is still true today, but at that time, the difference was striking.

When I returned to New York, I was worried that there might be some discussion about my actions in Cuba. But nothing much happened. I didn't get any medals, nor did I get any brickbats. The only comment from my superiors was, "You had a tough situation down there, and you were lucky to get by the way you did. It was pretty rough." Because Pan Am was so small in those days, we didn't have all the formalities that exist now. A station manager had to make decisions on his own, frequently without assistance from his senior manager miles away. Management didn't look too closely at how things were done as long as the planes kept flying.

# Planes and Pilots in the Thirties

$P$an Am operated with Sikorsky amphibians from 1929 through at least 1931. In my experience, they were fine on the water but not so good on land, because their wheels were too heavy and cumbersome. But in those days, most of our landing facilities were on water, and we used them to Miami, San Puetas, Cuba, Jamaica, and then Colombia and Panama. Newly assigned pilots required special training on judging wind conditions, making approaches and takeoffs, and handling all phases of sea landings. We trained the pilots in seamanship, although we had quite a few ex-Navy pilots who already had that experience.[1]

In addition to the Sikorskys, we had a fleet of twin-engine Commodore flying boats. We had acquired them from the New York-Rio-Buenos Aires (NYRBA) airline that had tried to compete with us but folded because they didn't have any mail contracts.[2] We took over all NYRBA planes that had not yet left the factory. I was in New York and went up to the Consolidated factory in Buffalo to inspect the airplanes. I checked them out thoroughly and discovered that there was no saltwater protection at all on the lower surfaces. That meant they'd corrode very quickly once in service, destroying the hull and the electrical system. We had had the Sikorskys for some time and had gained a lot of experience with corrosion. So I rejected the planes and said, "You'll have to spray the wings with a special corrosion-resistant paint we use, or its equivalent, before we'd accept them." Whitman, the general manager of the plant, got very upset. They were hard up for money, since this was the depths of the Depression, and he said he would get me fired.

I wouldn't back down for Whitman, and shortly thereafter I received a telephone call from Juan Trippe in New York. I thought I might get bawled out because the plant manager had raised hell with Trippe. But Trippe's first remark to me was, "How long do you think you can hold those planes up? We're a little short on cash; it would be real nice if you could hold them up for a week." It turned out that my rejection of the planes was just what was needed to help Pan Am's cash flow situation.

Trippe asked me how long I could hold them off. I said, "Well, it'll take them at least a week to do the job that has to be done—they have to open up all the ports and spray internally all through." That made Trippe very happy; he told the manager to do what I said or Pan Am would not accept the planes. Whitman was furious, but he did do the corrosion-protection job on all the planes. Once we got them into service, they were good little flying boats, but they were very slow and could only cruise at 90 to 100 mph. Because of the protection, the planes we got in that deal were still being used in 1939 for training navigators in Europe at the beginning of World War II.[3]

Before I left New York, I worked with André Priester on some procedures for air-crew promotions. He wanted to have promotions based on skill, experience, and written examinations, with graduated cockpit ranks of copilot, first officer, captain, and, finally, master pilot. To become a master pilot, a man had to pass all those other levels and was likely to be an older pilot who could not fly anymore. It was analogous to the mercantile marine ranks of second officer, first officer, and master mariner. Priester and I had an argument over this idea, and I asked him whether he had talked to the pilots about his notion of having a nonflying master pilot on our flying boats. I told him that I didn't think an older man could walk around on our flying boats giving orders to the guys doing the actual flying. Maybe it could be done on a real boat, but not on an aerial boat. We had pilots already who had the experience to be called master pilots.[4]

We had developed a very good crew-training school. The trainees went through the different levels, with many flying tests. Priester wanted me to add courses with written examinations to the training. I said, "We don't want to get into that on our own. We'd have too many people involved administering it, we don't have the expertise, and it would be too expensive." I had seen ads in *Collier's* and the *Saturday Evening Post* for the International Correspondence Schools (I.C.S.). So I had lunch with the instructors there and told them what I wanted: a series of courses and examinations that our pilots could take in the areas of seamanship, celestial navigation, world political problems, world history, and engineering.

I.C.S. did an excellent job, and they were able to find people with the specific skills necessary to develop the courses. Once the courses were put together, they handled the whole thing: they saw to the printing of the course material and the examinations; they mailed the materials out to the pilots; they corrected the returned exams; and they sent the grades out. In effect, they had set up a system of mail-order education. It worked out very well, especially since our pilots were jumping around to different places all the time: Miami, San Francisco, the Caribbean, Central America. This way, no matter where a pilot was, he could study for the next level of promotion.

Then we developed a promotion plan that required a pilot to have a certain number of flying hours in his logbook before he could sit for his first officer exam, then so many more hours before he could take the exam for chief officer, and so forth. There also had to be a vacancy in order to move up; for example, if someone passed the exam for chief officer but there didn't happen to be an opening, he would have to wait until he was next in line.[6]

We did have one problem with the training. In the mid-thirties, right in the heart of the Depression, we were hiring many young naval pilots who were also graduates of good colleges. They came to us with an attitude problem; they all thought of themselves as officers and gentlemen to whom we civilians couldn't teach anything. They put up a stink when we put them in the maintenance shops in Miami for a month and reduced them right down to grease monkeys; they had to scrape paint at the lowest level to qualify for a pilot's position. It was similar to boot camp. However, they admitted afterwards that it was a valuable experience. And I'll say this: we had the cream of the crop. They were generally highly educated individuals, as well as extremely proficient in twin-engine and, later, four-engine aircraft.

We also taught the new pilots to transmit twenty words a minute in Morse code on a radio telegraph machine. We didn't have the regular radio telephone that we have today. Each plane had a radio telegraph operator, but our management felt that the pilot should also know how to use all the equipment. To call on the maritime analogy again, you can't be a master of a ship unless you know the duties of all the other crew members. When the radio telephone came along, we dropped the radio telegraph operators (which was a big fight that I got involved in later on). With a throat mike, the pilots could immediately communicate without having to go through the radioman.

Our hiring and promotion procedures were organized on the European model, particularly along the lines of Lufthansa. We hired pilots only on the basis of flying experience; they didn't need to know things like celestial navigation when they came to us. We preferred to train them with our program and saw that they learned it before they were promoted. They rose in rank strictly on the basis of demonstrated and measured achievements, as shown on our mail-order examinations. But we paid them more because they were better trained, in addition to the fact that foreign duty was more demanding than domestic flying.[7]

Our pilots received salaries that were quite high for the Great Depression era. Since they had all the international problems that one doesn't have domestically, we always felt that their salaries should be higher than those of domestic airline pilots. A captain's salary was around ten or twelve thousand a year, and the copilots would get about six thousand. That made it one of the higher-paying professions. The flying personnel were also ahead of the administrative personnel in that regard: the pilots got more than the operations manager, even though they worked for him. The theory was that they wouldn't be physically able to fly beyond about age fifty. Also, we recognized that the pilots were the ones with the primary responsibility.[8]

At Pan Am, a great deal of prestige was attached to the position of pilot. Our pilots felt that they were far superior to other U.S. commercial pilots—and they were. They were better qualified, had more varied training, and dealt with more problems than the overland domestic pilots. Domestic airlines just flew a highway, back and forth, but our fellows had to be master seamen as well as pilots in those flying boats. That's why we started all those correspondence training courses. We also taught them all kinds of troubleshooting mechanical skills relating to the airplane, so they could direct repairs if they got stuck in some out-of-the-way foreign port.

Today, everything is handled by specialists. If there is trouble with the airplane, the pilot gets out and walks away, and the specialists get on board to find out what's wrong. It was entirely different back then; our pilots even carried coveralls with them. If they had trouble in another country, they would put on the coveralls and help the chief mechanic at the station. We had a special title for our top pilots: Master of Ocean Flying Boats.

Competition for our piloting jobs, with those salaries, was enormous. There weren't too many jobs like that around. But that's when hamburger was ten cents a pound, a fine house went for six thousand dollars, and income tax at that time was negligible.

Although the domestic airlines were unionized, we didn't have unions until the end of World War II, except for a small local union that came with the Mexican airline we acquired down in Brownsville. Our crews weren't interested in unions because they were getting such high pay.[9]

# Across the Pacific

*After the excitement in Cuba,* I was soon to find myself on the other side of the world, across the Pacific Ocean. But before that happened, my Harvard interlude began in October 1933 and lasted about eight months.

I had decided to go to Harvard Business School because it had become apparent to me very early in the game that I needed a lot more business training. I was given administrative leave, with the option of returning to Pan Am afterwards. However, I didn't want to spend the full two years the business course required, since in that length of time I would lose touch with what I had been doing. So I took four first-year courses, which were mandatory, and sat in on four second-year courses for which I wasn't allowed to get credits. They didn't want to set a precedent of students doing the whole two-year course in one year.

It was very hard work, but it was well worth it; I'll leave it at that. In addition, I made some contacts at Harvard that were useful to me later on. One was the professor of labor, Sumner Slichter, who became a good friend of mine later when Pan Am went into negotiations with unions after the war.[1]

While at Harvard, I talked with several other companies that were much more established than Pan Am and offered higher salaries and benefits. I did think about skipping out on Pan Am, but I made up my mind to stay with them because I couldn't imagine that any of those other companies could ever be as much fun.[2]

In June of 1934 I finished up at Harvard and went back to the New York office. Although I had less and less to do with engineering, I was still officially assigned to the engineering department headed by André Priester. The first job he put me on was the planning for the trans-Pacific route. I joined a group that had been developing a master plan for starting the route. It was supposed to be ready to begin operating immediately, and Trippe wanted us to be flying the route, at least experimentally, in 1935.[3]

We had already tried to get a trans-Atlantic route through to London, or by way of Bermuda to Portugal, but the British still wouldn't let us in because they didn't have airplanes good enough to compete with ours. They feared that the air traffic would soon all be in the hands of the Americans. When we began to plan the trans-Pacific route, the British wouldn't give us landing rights going into Hong Kong, either. The ports of the old British empire and all its former steamship coaling stations were simply denied to us. "Not forever," the British said. "Just until we become competitive."[4]

We did the initial planning for the Pacific operation in New York— everything from plotting out the routes to ordering the shore launches and all the other necessary details. But our headquarters for charting the route was in San Francisco, and eventually I found myself working on the West Coast for months at a time.

Since planes couldn't fly all the way across the Pacific Ocean even from Hawaii in those days, we had to find places to refuel along the way. We settled on three islands that luckily were U.S. possessions; Wake, Midway, and Guam. In order to prepare Wake and Midway Islands for use as bases, we would have to absolutely transport everything we needed by ship. At Midway there was nothing but a radio station and a few Americans, and at Wake there were just land crabs. We even had to bring in a small hotel with rooms for the air crews and passengers. We had to have a dock, and in case an airplane should have to be pulled up for repairs, we had to build a ramp, because we couldn't use the soft, sandy beach. In order to create a safe landing "sea strip" for our seaplanes, we had to blast out all the coral heads that were in the bay; they could rip the bottom out of a plane. John Borger and Bill Taylor were among the young engineers who helped build these island stations.[5]

Our station startup group was quite a big team and even included experts on food, because places like Wake and Midway had to ship in all their own food. There were supplies for just about every modern necessity, and a lot of the luxuries.

We finally got all the arrangements made, and the first freighter went out in mid-1935, sailing without a hitch to the islands. By the time the ship arrived, we had people living in tents while we built permanent quarters and put in ramps and buoys for the planes. Finally, we had enough of an airport completed. We also had spare-parts depots with engineers and mechanics all the way along the route. Our building and airports department, headed by Captain Odell, was in charge of the supply job, and his people did a fantastic job, particularly with limited funds.[6]

Early in the game we had set up a radio station. But even with that in place, we had to have a backup for sending signals to the planes. As our pilots said, "What if the radio fails when I'm somewhere out over the Pacific?" If they came down somewhere near Wake and their radio failed, they wouldn't have enough fuel to return to Hawaii. We decided on bright flares, which would be shot up from the ground. If the plane was overdue, the ground crew would start shooting up flares. In the daytime, we could shoot up smoke shells that went up one to two thousand feet with a mortar.[7]

The Coast Guard had the right kinds of flares, but they used an elaborate flare gun that cost twenty thousand dollars each. We were short on funds; in fact, we had very limited capital to set up the whole operation. So I went to a fireworks plant in Indiana and told them about our problem. They said that they could build the same kind of magnesium parachute flares for night use without the expensive gun. They were rocket launched and burned for about five minutes as they floated down. You could see them from a great distance because the magnesium was so brilliant when it burned. Their parachute smoke flares for day use worked the same way. The five minutes would give a pilot a pretty long time to adjust his route. The weather was usually good out there, and you could see for miles.

We knew without asking that we could never get these flares approved by the Civil Aviation Authority, so we never asked them to approve it. As in Latin America, we didn't have the money or the time to wait for the government. We just stocked them as emergency backups and experimented with them. Later, when I was out on Wake in the middle of the winter, we tried them out. I had seen the fireworks people in Indiana hide behind trees in case the things blew up, so I hid behind a tree too when they were first shot off. They didn't work too well.

We talked to some of the Navy men stationed there who had fired magnesium flares in World War I, and they taught us how to use them. The flare was like a mortar shell. You could fire it by lowering it down into a mortar tube; there was a pin at the bottom that would ignite the shell when you pulled a string. That's all there was to it. Pull the string and up it went. Or you could just drop it into the tube and off she'd go. It was just a homemade, crude mortar, but it worked. They were never intended for routine use but only in emergencies.

Luckily, we never had to use them there in an emergency, but we later did use them in the Philippines for landings at night. Manila Bay was full of all kinds of boats floating around in the dark of the night with no lights on them, and somebody had the bright idea to use aerial flares to light things up. It helped a lot. The ground crew fired the mortar off the company's launch. When I went out to check on what they were doing, they were casually dropping the shells into the tube to fire them, cool as could be. There weren't any trees to hide behind out in the bay, but they weren't even worried about an explosion. The whole area would be flooded with light, just like daytime, making landings relatively easy. Then our plane would taxi into the Navy base, where they let us use one of their ramps.[8]

I also got the job of obtaining the launches for the islands. The budget was very limited, so I finally settled on a New Jersey-type sea skiff hull that was designed for carrying small cargo loads. I had Ford Kermath engine conversions installed because, when I contacted Ford, they said they'd take those engines back in trade later, even though we'd be using saltwater cooling in the Philippines, San Francisco, and Honolulu.

At Guam, the International Telegraph Company had a fairly large open sea boat, and the Marines had ships resupplying them from the Philippines. But on Wake, there was nothing. So we got a much larger boat, a regular ocean-going tug, since we would have to tow in all the supplies. The supply ship couldn't get into the harbor and would have to offload cargo onto a barge. We had to do the same thing at Midway; in fact, at Midway the harbor was even worse. The entry to the bay where our station was located was blocked with coral, so we had to wait until high tide when the barges could surf over the reef on a big wave.

All of this was an awful lot of work. But after the Pacific route really got going about a year or so later, we were able to give up the freighter mode of supply and carry the supplies in by air. We even got into growing vegetables in water tanks out on those coral reefs. It's now called hydroponic farming. The present method was developed from Japanese techniques for American occupation forces, but we did it earlier. There was some fellow in the United States experimenting with it, and we flew him out there to put the tanks in place. We also had contracts with food companies for special kinds of frozen packaging well before freezers came into use. The logistics were enormously complex. I was amazed at how the experts we hired were able to solve such tough problems.

Putting the system in place cost a lot of money, and Trippe made us squeeze every penny. He could raise only so much, and the banks wouldn't lend us any more. I do know that Pan Am borrowed money from all of the big New York banks, and one of Trippe's means of securing a loan must have been his fleet of aircraft. Loans were secured by equipment trust certificates. As I recall, the Boeing 314s had placards in the cockpit stating that they were owned by some bank. This method of financing was most unusual in the airline industry at that time.[9]

When Trippe and his associates decided to explore the Pacific routes, they had already talked with the major aircraft companies that wanted to develop big flying boats. The planes we had on hand, three Sikorsky S-42s and three Martin M-130s, were not ideal airplanes for the routes because we had to install extra fuel tanks in the cabin, and we intended to use them only during the route development phase. I was right in the middle of working out the technical specifications with the manufacturer, and we figured we could never carry passengers with the fuel under the floor. We had been negotiating with Boeing for a new plane and, after looking at the competition, we decided that Boeing had the best proposal for a large flying boat that would carry fuel in outside tanks rather than down inside the hull.[10]

In October of 1935, the year before the scheduled *China Clipper* service began, we ran a test flight to Manila using a Sikorsky plane. Later that year, we sent out a big Martin 130 four-engined flying boat, and Priester and I went out on that trip. We took off from San Francisco to survey the entire system, before beginning scheduled passenger flights.

I remember our departure vividly: the Martin was very sluggish on takeoff, and it took us an interminably long time to get up to air speed and off the water. This was the Martin's first flight over such a distance, and we found it to be just too heavy, so heavy it couldn't carry any load to speak of. Also, it didn't have enough room for fuel in the wings in order to make the full flight, so it had to carry fuel in the hull under the floor.

We had the chief engineer from Boeing on board. He really didn't want to go, but he and his people were in the process of designing the successor to the Martin 130, and we wanted him to see what the operating conditions were on this route. His name was C. N. "Monty" Monteith. He was formerly an MIT professor in aerodynamics, and he wrote the aerodynamics textbook that everybody used in those days.[11]

The longest part of our trip was the flight from the West Coast to Honolulu, going westbound against the prevailing winds. It was about twenty-four hundred miles, at a cruising speed of 130 mph and an approximate flight time of eighteen-plus flying hours. We operated in a long-range cruising mode with low throttle for maximum fuel conservation. We had figured out scientifically the most efficient speed, by slowing the engine down as much as possible without creating too much drag and stalling.[12]

In Honolulu, Pan Am put on a big reception for us, a native Hawaiian dinner with hula dancing girls. But Priester sent us all home early. He went around and got everybody out of there right after dinner because we had to leave early in the morning in order to get to Midway. If the crew was suffering from aching heads, we would have had a choppy takeoff.

We landed at Midway with no major problems. To get there, the navigation wasn't too difficult because you could see a string of islands in the daytime, and you just followed that chain. All the way there we were flying into westerlies, the everpresent prevailing headwinds. Then we went on to Wake, with the radio directing us, so we didn't have any trouble with its location, either. The compound there was about half built, and a diver was still dynamiting the coral heads, preparing a landing area for the flying boats.[13]

Our next destination was Guam, where we were received by the U.S. military unit stationed there. They took us to dinner with the governor. We left Guam just before dark, and that's when trouble started.

I was very happy to have my best friend in the company, Ed Musick, as the pilot in what was to transpire. He was one of the first pilots to be hired by Pan Am, and I met him on my first trip to Miami. We hit it off right away, and he became a very good friend. In our free time we saw a lot of each other and particularly enjoyed playing tennis together. While I was in Havana, which was on his regular route with a layover in Cuba, we started playing squash at the Athletic Club, which we continued frequently on his visits to New York. He was the best pilot with whom I have ever flown, always very calm, and never one to get excited in the worst emergencies. The whole pilot group looked up to him, and he became our first chief pilot. On the many trips I flew with him I always made an excuse to go up to the cockpit in order to be with him and exchange ideas about the instrument panel, the planes in general, and what would make them better.[14]

Once we took off, we climbed to a cruising altitude of about ten thousand feet, where we ran into a light, soupy fog that required us to fly on instruments. We were in the fog for about an hour and a half and had no weather reports to help us because the Japanese had just started coding all their forecasts. We were concerned about typhoons, which originated in the islands to the south of our route, in the area now called the Philippine Sea. If you knew precisely when one of them had blown through those islands, you could figure about when it would cross your course. But we didn't have a clue.

When we were about halfway to the Philippines, a typhoon hit, and the effect was indescribable. I was up in the cockpit when suddenly we were slammed by the heaviest rain and highest winds I had ever experienced in my life. The plane started jumping all over the sky. Even though we were at ten thousand feet when it hit, we couldn't possibly get above it; the storm was too high. Ed shoved on full takeoff power and we still couldn't hold altitude; we were going down at about five hundred feet a minute, and we couldn't see anything. We didn't know if we would just fly right into the ocean.

The windshield of the plane was so obscured by the heavy rain that it was like flying under water. The plane rolled and pitched all over the sky, and we kept losing altitude. Then, at about eight hundred feet, about a minute and a half off the ocean, we broke out into the clear. At that same moment we got the help of lift from the ocean surface on the wings, and we were able to level off.

The first thing that struck me when I looked out of my window was that the waves below were like mountains—tremendous waves, with the tops being blown right off because of such high winds. At that point the navigator, who was taking drift sights, yelled to us, "Hey skipper, we're going backwards." And it was true; in that powerful wind, we were actually flying backwards! Was I ever glad that I had developed the drift sight for our airplanes in order to tell which way the wind was blowing. This enabled Ed to keep the plane from being blown off course. It was a telescope-type instrument that had horizontal and vertical scales. You'd drop a flare at night or a smoke bomb in the daytime and then take a sight on it.

We were going down again, but when we got down to just above the water, we saw that we could level off and even go back up a little. From the direction of the wind, we figured out about where the center of the storm was, and that it was rotating counterclockwise, so we knew we had to reverse our course. No one but Ed could have done it. He started, very gingerly, to turn us around, getting one wing down, as he eased the poor battered craft in a wide circle and finally got the wind on our tail. The navigator figured the wind speed was somewhere around 170 mph, and we were right in the middle of it. So we rode it around, traveling in a circle with the wind behind us, until we finally headed toward the Philippines.

Our speed was usually about 135 mph, but now with that high wind on our tail we were going so fast that we got to Manila only a little less than an hour late!

I spent the whole storm up with Ed. When we first broke out of the typhoon I went back to the main cabin to see how everybody was doing. I found Priester sitting there, buckled in and pale, and Monty Monteith, the chief engineer from Boeing, looked white as a ghost. He wasn't buckled in, and he was in a daze. The ceiling was stretched cloth, and there was a dent in it where he had flown up and his head had crashed into it. He was fumbling around near his mouth, and I couldn't figure what he was doing. Then I remembered that he was a cigar smoker. Since we wouldn't let him smoke, he had a habit of chewing on a cigar during flight. He'd chew them right down to a stub. I asked him what was the matter, and he said, "I can't find my cigar." Then he sort of gagged and said, "I think I swallowed it!"[15]

The same storm hit us again two nights later, while we were staying in the Philippines. We had to check the plane all night long and keep it headed into the wind. We had finally decided to let it ride out the storm on the water, tied to a buoy, so that it could swing with the wind. We put big planks on the wings to break their lift and kept the engines going on idle to turn the propellers during the worst of the storm. We had local people in boats out there trying to keep floating debris from hitting us: all kinds of junk was floating around, including fishing boats with nobody in them. At one point a big, tuglike boat floated by with nobody aboard. It just missed us.

It was a long, hard night, and when we saw the plane still afloat and undamaged at dawn, we considered it no small miracle. We finally collapsed, exhausted, into our beds at the Manila Hotel. That night the local people gave us a big, friendly reception.

During that time in the Manila Hotel, I learned something we later used in Africa, in 1940, when we were setting up the trans-Africa service and malaria had killed several of our employees. I noticed there were no mosquitoes in my hotel room, even though there were no screens on the window. I asked the manager about it, and he pointed to the ivy that ran all over the outside of the hotel. "You see those little lizards running around on the ivy? They eat all the mosquitoes." The man who set up the arrangement was a Filipino, who brought in local lizards and soon had them running all over the hotel. He also would fill up any footprint where water could collect, since these would create a breeding ground for mosquitoes.

We stayed there for five days, recovering from the typhoon and checking out the airport. Our route stopped there because we didn't have rights from the British to land in Hong Kong. Later we got rights from Portugal to land in Macao, which fixed the Brits; it was only a short ferry ride from that island to Hong Kong.[16]

After resting up, we headed back towards the States. With westerlies pushing us most of the way, it was a much faster trip going home. We made a lot of quick stops on the way, checking on what was in short supply at our refueling stations. Finally, we flew into Honolulu and then the next day landed in San Francisco without incident.

I remained in the San Francisco office through early 1936, helping the operations team with a million details for setting up a maintenance base and other preparations for the Pacific operation. We did this in borrowed space at the Navy base across the bay, and since the bridges weren't built then, I had to take a ferry boat out there each day. John Leslie, the operations manager in San Francisco and an aeronautical engineer, did most of the developmental work.[17]

At the base, we developed the long-range cruising technique so that we could carry the maximum number of passengers on the Boeings. We had to do all the mathematics the hard way, with pencil and pad. There were no computers in those days for the complicated calculations necessary to figure out optimum cruising speed. But the principle was simple. As the airplane burned up fuel, you could slowly reduce the power to a certain point for maximum range. During the war, we taught that same technique to the military.

The new Boeing, the 314, was due to be delivered in 1936 but was delayed until 1939, so the M-130 was modified for the first trans-Pacific passenger flight on October 21, 1936. This modified M-130 was christened the *China Clipper.*

In the meantime, we ran mail flights, which gave us a guaranteed income. As in Latin America, we couldn't have survived without the mail contracts, since we didn't carry enough passengers worldwide to justify the operation.

Later, in setting up the route to Australia, we had a conflict with the military that could have been serious. There was a tiny island called Kingman's Reef about halfway between Honolulu and Australia, but there were no charts available for it. We wanted to make it a fueling stop, so I called a friend at the Navy Department, and he said, "Oh, I can get you a chart." He came up with a chart classified as Secret, and said, "Don't say too much about this, because this chart is the only one showing the depths around Kingman's Reef." We checked the chart and saw that our planes could land and enter the inlet with no difficulty. So we sent a freighter out there, loaded with supplies and a big ramp. Soon our airplanes were landing in the inlet, refueling, and then going on from there.

About six months later, the captain of the Pan Am freighter told Clarence Young, our manager in San Francisco, "I didn't have any chart of Kingman's Reef when I went out there, so I drew one up." He said he had taken soundings from a small boat, and he produced a chart. He wanted to get a little credit for his enterprise. Clarence sent the chart over to the Navy Department. When they took it and superimposed it over their own chart, they found that the two were identical!

I got called to Washington by the Navy Department, and they said, "You're involved in something pretty serious. You have copied a chart of Kingman's Reef, which is classified as Secret." I answered, "I didn't copy it; the freighter captain created it." They insisted that someone must have gotten hold of their chart. I told them, "I don't know how the captain did it, but Pan Am is the only one using the chart, so I suggest that it would be better if we just forget about it for now." Fortunately, the Navy decided to let the matter drop.

One of the S-42 planes with inside fuel tanks cost the life of my good friend Ed Musick. This happened in January 1938, and I barely missed being with him. He was the pilot through the Pacific typhoon, and he and I always flew on test flights at the factories. We were scheduled to go to New Zealand and Australia on one of these experimental flights, but at the last moment, I was called to Washington on some complications with the Civil Aeronautics Administration, the government's aviation regulatory agency, and because of the meeting, I couldn't go with Ed. The plane subsequently blew up near Suva, Pago Pago, in the Samoan islands, when they were dumping fuel. Pieces of the plane were scattered all over the ocean. The crash investigators decided that the dumped fuel was sucked back through the wing into the cabin and ignited by the spark of the telegraph key. But this was never conclusively proven.

In any event, when Ed had taken off from the island an engine wasn't running properly, and he had radioed that he had decided to dump fuel and come back. He knew that he could get into some pretty heavy swells when he landed, so he wanted the aircraft to be as light as possible coming in. He had dump valves on the outside tanks that would come out and release the fuel. He and I had tested that dumping arrangement at the Sikorsky plant when we first bought the airplanes, and we'd never had any trouble with it. But on this flight, he telegraphed that he was going to dump, and then a few moments later there was silence.

The New Zealanders thought so much of Ed that they put up a monument to him at the headland where you first come in from the sea and called it Musick Point. He was a great guy, and it was a terrible loss to all of us.

We continued to be troubled about what had caused Ed to crash. So one day down in Miami, after making a lot of test flights, we flew an S-42 at close to stall speed and dumped fuel. The fumes came pouring into the cabin. It hadn't happened at normal cruise speed, which we'd always used at the factory in tests. But at close to stall, a backdraft brought the fumes right into the cabin. The Sikorsky design engineers flew with us on the test flights, since they were naturally concerned about the airplane and had never accepted the explanation of the crash investigators. Some of them had offered a theory that static electricity had ignited the fumes. But I never believed that.[18] Anyway, the Sikorsky engineers were reluctantly convinced that the backdraft had caused the problem. They redesigned the fuel dump chutes so that they projected several feet beyond the trailing edge of the wing and installed them on the existing airplanes. We ran the tests again at close to stall speed and didn't have any more suction of fumes into the cabin.

# A Base in Newfoundland

*While I was in San Francisco* helping to clean up problems with the Pacific route, we got word from the British that they were going to have their Empire flying boat ready in 1937 to run test flights across the Atlantic to Canada. They said that we were welcome to run test flights to England at the same time, provided each plane made the first flight on the same day, taking off at exactly the same time. I suppose they wanted to make sure the British did not lose prestige. I was assigned to work on setting up these flights and transferred back to New York.[1]

The first thing I had to do was to set up a base of operations in Newfoundland, at a place called Botwood on the north side of the island. A few British freighters came in there, but it was a godforsaken place. Once I got to Newfoundland, I caught a narrow-gauge train that was supposed to go from St. John's to the other end of the island. We were about halfway there when the train stopped in the middle of nowhere, and all the passengers were told to get off. I sat in the station for a long time. Finally, someone told me that I could get a lift from the mailman. He came along at about eight o'clock in an old ramshackle car, and he drove me down to Botwood.

When I got to Botwood there was no place to stay. The one inn in town was used regularly by the workers of a railroad that brought iron ore down to the docks, where it was put onto ships. Ordinarily, it had a few extra beds, but I was told that they were all taken up by a group of British engineers who were putting in a radio station and a weather service for their new DeHavilland test planes. So I didn't have any place to sleep. However, there was one general store in town, which carried everything, including furniture. One of the show windows had a bed in it, and I made a deal with the manager of the store to let me sleep there. I slept in the window (with shades drawn) for several nights until finally something opened up at the inn. It was a bed in which several railroad engineers slept. One was on night duty and slept in the daytime. I could use the bed at night.

Once my bed situation was settled, I went to work. Right away I was faced with the problem of what to do with our plane when it arrived; there was no place to dock it. So I approached a local Newfoundlander who built fishing boats, a wonderful guy. He said sure, he could build something for me. I sketched the big barge I wanted, which we would anchor offshore. Then we would transport passengers and equipment back and forth with a motorboat. The British had a fine motorboat that we could use, along with lots of other equipment there.[2]

As in Latin America, I found the British to be very cooperative. Their team handled the weather service, so I didn't need to worry about that aspect. At the dock, Imperial Airways, the predecessor of British Overseas Airway Corporation (BOAC), did all the work. Some British people down there weren't doing much, so I got together with them, and we set about building a barracks where we could put up our crews. Meanwhile, the Newfoundlander finished the barge for me. We towed it over and anchored it in time for the first planes.

When Pan Am's plane took off from Botwood on the first flight on July 3, 1937, the British plane would take off from England. The two were coordinated by radio, and everybody would get the joint publicity for the first transatlantic commercial flights.[3]

A special train with its own diner came up from St. Johns, bringing the Canadian governor general and his whole staff; he wanted to be there for our takeoff and the British arrival. On the night of the crossing he gave a big dinner up at the radio shack for all of us, with fancy food prepared in his private dining car. He was a really great guy. Earlier in the day I was finishing up some splicing on some big lines that were thrown out to our plane to haul it into the ramp. He insisted on helping, saying, "I was in the Navy. I know all about this." It turned out he was a retired Navy admiral. Then he got his whole staff together, sitting on the floor splicing rope.

I had already taken the governor aboard our plane with Harold Gray, who was the plane's captain. (He was later head of the Atlantic division, and, later still, president of the company). I had told Harold that the governor was coming, and when we arrived he had his air crew in their blue Navy-style uniforms lined up on the float at attention and saluting. The plane inside was in picture-book shape, all fitted out with seats and elegant dining facilities, though there were no passengers for this first trip. The governor was very impressed. This was in sharp contrast to the British plane that arrived the next day with its whole interior pulled out because of weight problems.

We were up all that night waiting for the radio reports from the planes. Pan Am landed in England right on schedule, but the British plane, the *Short,* proceeded to get lost. They were close to the southern coast of Newfoundland, but even with radio directional finders, they didn't know their location. They had to wire in for directions. Finally, a radio station in Canada was able to pick them up. They then came north, and once they hit the island, they didn't have any trouble finding Botwood. After the schedule started, Dr. Andrew McTaggart-Cowan, a Canadian member of the North American planning committee, set up a weather forecasting station. Surrounded by ice, it received coded data from Britain, Iceland, and Greenland.

The next day the governor went aboard their plane, and that was a disaster. The crew members were all disheveled, and the plane was dirty and greasy. The governor told me later that our aircraft was up to the highest British navy standards. He was very impressed with Pan Am and its organization. He said, "That British Airways *Short* was a disgrace." It was clear that he was discouraged when he considered the poor level of competence the British had put forth, and I guess he sent back a pretty sharp report on the poor British chaps. But in fairness, they had a problem with that airplane. It had just barely enough range to make the trip, and after that it was never used for scheduled transatlantic service. Imperial had been flying between New York and Bermuda, but even on that relatively short trip one airplane went down at sea due to carburetor icing. That ended British transatlantic service until 1941, when they bought three Boeing 314s from Pan Am. Pan Am began service from New York to Bermuda in the spring of 1937, paving the way to opening a southern route to Lisbon, Portugal, in 1939.

We ran several more test flights after that, and then we closed down for the winter. Our planes simply weren't well enough equipped for the travails of North Atlantic winter flying; it would have been an impossible operation. We had only primitive de-icers that were installed on the wing edges. Later, there were heated edges that worked much more efficiently.

I took an amusing journey while I was in Newfoundland that shows the independence of people working for the airlines back then. I had heard about a giant airport that was being built at Gander, and I decided to go see it. To get there, you took the seaplane launch across the bay to a dock on a stretch of desolate land. There were no roads, just a railroad track. They had a hand car by the side of the roadbed, which you put on the rails and then pumped your way a couple of miles down the track to the railroad station. There, you waited for a train to Gander. The airport site was on a plateau, covered with forest. They were just getting started, bulldozing trees and everything else out of the area. The Canadian workmen were living in railroad cars on the side track, and working conditions at the airport site, especially in winter, were brutal.

Boy, they were a tough bunch! I was invited by the manager to join them for dinner, and after dinner there was a big party, with lots of heavy drinking. Toward the end of the party, when they were really feeling good, the radio guy came in with a radiogram from the British Air Ministry in England, asking whether the airport would be ready in August for them to fly in a new four-engine landplane they had developed. Well, the manager hit the ceiling. It was already June; they were just getting started, and all they had done so far was cut down a few trees. He sent back a radiogram: "Re your signal. August what year?" He said, "That'll fix those dummies!" And he was right: there was no further word from the British.

# Opening Up Alaska

*In late 1932,* Harold Bixby, one of Pan Am's vice-presidents working out of New York, called me in to see him.[1] Bixby announced, "We're buying up three or four airlines in Alaska. We want to start routes up there, with the idea of eventually going on to Tokyo via the shorter Great Circle route, over the top of the globe."[2] The Alaskan airlines were flying small single-engine planes without instruments or regular schedules. Pan Am planned to send a Sikorsky amphibian and some Lockheed twin-engine Electras up there in order to open up scheduled flights from Seattle to Juneau. Planes could land in the water at Juneau because the bay never totally froze over. You had to put a lot of grease on the hull bottom to keep the loose ice from sticking during takeoff, but it opened up the possibility of operating all year round.

Then Bixby said, "First thing, we've got to do something about the pilots up there. A lot of them are old-timers, and they've never had any instrument training. They all fly by the seat of their pants, following the rivers and the mountains. They even fly the dog-team mail up there." What he meant was that the bush pilots would bid on the contracts for mail ordinarily delivered by dog team, landing in the snow on skis. The biggest contract flier of dog-team mail was a small airline run by a bush pilot named Joe Crosson. Pan Am bought out his airline, and now Crosson was to be manager of our new Alaska operation.

One of our first tasks would be to train pilots to fly with instruments. In 1935, Wiley Post and Will Rogers crashed in Alaska, and Joe Crosson was sent in to fly their bodies out. Alaska was a flat, snow-covered country, very deceptive for flying without instruments. Because of all the snow, it was difficult to judge altitude visually. You had to rely on your altimeter or you'd fly right into the ground. Poor Wiley Post had only one good eye, and he wore a patch over the other one. While this patch may not have been a problem elsewhere, in Alaska it was. He was used to judging altitude by the size of things like trees or buildings. Up there, he had nothing but endless white. He did have his altimeter, but apparently that wasn't enough.[4]

The bush pilots all flew out of Fairbanks. None of them flew into Anchorage because they were all scared of the power of the Alaskan Railroad, which was run by the U.S. government. The Alaskan Railroad made it clear that they wanted to carry all the freight and passengers between Fairbanks and Anchorage, and they didn't want any commercial airplanes flying back and forth on that route. Since the government controlled the mail contracts, you did what they said—or else.

Bix wanted me to go up there to set up the Alaskan operation. So I flew out to Seattle in early 1933 to meet Joe Crosson, who came down from Alaska to pick me up. Joe was one of the real old-timers up there, even though he came from Oklahoma and his mother was a full-blooded Indian. As I was getting ready, I said, "Joe, what am I going to do with those tough old bush pilots up there? I know what their attitude will be: 'Here's one of those smart-aleck guys from New York, coming up here with all that money to buy us out while we do all the work.' They don't know that I'm just a farm boy myself and got into this business by pure chance."

"You're right," said Joe. "And I'll tell you what: There's going to be a big reception in Juneau at the governor's mansion to celebrate the first mail flight between the continental United States and Alaska; it'll be held just at the time we get there. You've got to do something at that party to establish the fact that you're not a stuffed shirt like they think. Otherwise, they'll all give you the cold shoulder."

When he said that, it reminded me of when I first transferred to Miami, and what a challenge it had been to get the people there to accept me because I was from the main office in New York. Thinking about Florida reminded me of canned rattlesnake meat. I said, "Joe, if I could get some canned rattlesnake meat, I think I can solve this problem!" Joe gave me a stunned look, but I was already halfway out the door at a dead run. I went down to a big delicatessen and, sure enough, they had rattlesnake meat. So I got a couple of jars, and we took off for Alaska.

We landed in Juneau and went straight to the governor's mansion, where the celebration was due to begin soon. As luck would have it, the governor's daughter was a very close friend of one of our pilots. We went in through the back door of the mansion just before the party, and Joe introduced me to her. I told her of my need to hit it off well with the pilots, and then I let her in on my plan involving rattlesnake sandwiches. I had to get her cooperation, and luckily, she was quite a girl and thought it was a great idea.

We got into the kitchen and took all of the labels off the jars. Then we gave the jars to the people preparing sandwiches, telling them it was fancy chicken for canapes. The fact is, it looked just like chicken. So they made up little sandwiches with this stuff on them and they started passing them around, announcing, at my suggestion, that this was the latest thing in New York nightclubs. Soon, everybody was gulping down rattlesnake.

After I met the governor and a few of the other important people, I came out to the kitchen, where Joe was hiding out, a little nervous. Just then one of his friends came into the kitchen and said, "You guys had better get out of here. Somebody just told the guests that it's rattlesnake meat they've been eating and, boy, that crowd is furious!"

We took off out the back door, raced down to the airport, and flew up to Fairbanks as fast as we could. I didn't go back to Juneau for several weeks, until things had quieted down. I learned that while a lot of people appreciated my joke, there were others who didn't think it was funny at all. I don't know if it was true, but there was one story that some of the old ladies went to the hospital and had their stomachs pumped out. Apparently, it brought the party to a quick end. But the governor thought my little joke was very funny; the fact that his daughter was in on it might have helped a little. But it sure broke the ice with the bush pilots.

While things were cooling down in Juneau, Joe flew me over Pan Am's Alaskan routes. We went out to Nome to look at the facilities and planes there. They were all single-engine cabin planes, some on floats but most of them on wheels. When they had to go out for a snow or ice landing, they put on skis.

It was very interesting, flying with Joe. He'd fly along the mountains, and you could see mountain goats running along the ridges. We went up to a mining post there called Burwash, and that's where the natives always brought out bear stew for us. They thought it was a delicacy, but to me, it was god-awful stuff. It tasted as if it had already turned bad, but I had to eat it to impress the Alaskan bush pilots.

Then we went to Fairbanks, a fascinating town. In all of Fairbanks, there weren't any paved streets, even though it was supposed to be a big city. Fairbanks was right on the river, and they had an annual "icebreak celebration," which consisted of a dogsled race from Juneau to Fairbanks to see who would get to Fairbanks closest to the time of the ice breakup.

Among the many remarkable people I met in Alaska was a girl who competed in that dogsled race. She was a nurse, and some years before she had cared for the retarded son of one of the big U.S. drug company families. They lived in the family lodge just below Juneau, and when the boy died, they gave her the lodge and all the land around it. It was a beautiful place, and she trained her dog team there. She later moved to Colorado, to one of the big ski areas, where she took tourists for dogsled rides.

While in Fairbanks, I went over to Joe Crosson's house for dinner one night, and after dinner he and his wife, Lillian, volunteered to take me back to the hotel. It had been raining a lot and the roads were full of mud holes. He turned down a side street toward the hotel, and I noticed his wife getting real mad. I didn't know what the problem was, but I soon found out, because we got stuck about halfway down that street—right in front of a whorehouse. We were in the red light district, on its main street where all the brothels were. Joe was making sure I saw all the sights!

Joe kept trying the starter to get the engine going again, with no success. But we weren't there more than a minute when the door of a brothel opened and a woman who looked like the madam came out and walked over to the car. "What's the matter, Joe?" she said. "Are you stalled? I'll get the girls out and we'll give you a push." And that's exactly what she proceeded to do. This bunch of shady ladies came running out, pushed on the car, and quickly had us rolling on our way. That's the kind of small, frontier-type town Fairbanks was in those days.

Another unusual thing that happened in Alaska brought me in touch with the Eskimo culture. While I was traveling the route, somebody had given me a pair of mukluks, or Eskimo boots, and at the hotel I noticed a terrible smell in my room. It turned out that the Eskimos always tanned their boots with urine! And in that hot bedroom—well, it took two days to get the smell out of there.

After I completed my inspection flight of all the routes and existing bases with Joe, I returned to meet our pilots. My major concern was their lack of instrument-flying experience. Without instruments it would be impossible to keep to a schedule. When I discussed the problem with them, their first reaction was, "We've been flying this way all our lives, and we're not going to change our ways now. We're too old for that." Most of them were in their forties and fifties and had been up in Alaska for ten or fifteen years doing seat-of-the-pants piloting, and doing it exceptionally well, too.

I told them about Pan Am's plans for Alaska, that we were going to give them multiengined aircraft and that we were going to fly on schedule, at least most of the time. We wanted to fly from Juneau to Fairbanks and Anchorage if possible, delivering passengers as well as mail along the way. Then I explained the logic of Pan Am's training objectives. They knew all about Link trainers, the special planes without windows for teaching instrument flying, but they still said that even with the training they couldn't learn to fly with instruments. Listening to their objections, I soon saw that we were getting nowhere. I said to come back the next day, I had to think it over.

There was another big problem. Even if we did try to teach them instrument flying in the Link trainer, I knew that as long as they were flying in Alaska, the next time they went up flying, instead of following their instruments, they would just look for the nearest mountain range by which to navigate. So I told them the next day, "I think you can all learn instrument flying. It doesn't make any difference what your age is; it isn't that difficult. But I don't think you're going to learn up here in Alaska, where the landscape is familiar. To really concentrate, you've got to get out of this environment. And you're going to have to fly in really bad weather. The only place where we can guarantee such weather is between Brownsville and Mexico City, because there's hardly a day when you don't go through a layer of clouds coming and going. You have to fly on instruments anywhere from half an hour to a couple of hours every trip. So what we're going to have to do is transfer you all down there for a year. We'll pay all expenses for you and your families, and meanwhile we'll bring in some of our Pan American pilots who know instrument flying, to temporarily cover these routes until you return." Well, it was obvious to them right away that Pan Am could have just fired all of them out of hand. But that wouldn't have been a good idea, not only out of fairness but because these men were admired and respected people in Alaska. All hell would have broken loose if we'd fired them, and Pan Am didn't need the bad publicity. When I finished talking, there was some murmuring, but I finished up by saying, "Think it over."

One of the pilots, Al Munson, came up to my room to talk to me. He was the oldest pilot in the group, and he'd been in Alaska nearly as long as Crosson. He said, "San, I can never learn to fly that way. I'm too old. I never had no education."

"Al," I said, "you don't need an education for this. It's just a matter of practice."

He thought about that and said, "Do you really think I can do it? I've almost decided to quit."

"No, don't quit," I said. "Take the training, and later, if you think you can't make it, you can always quit then."

"I've been flying all my life," said he, "in and out of these valleys. I've always flown by sight; I can't imagine flying on instruments over these mountains in a storm. It's always so safe. You get down in the valley and fly underneath the storm. The mountains coming into Juneau used to terrify me as a young pilot. You come down to Sitka, and then you come in through a mountain valley to Juneau. But there is an old trapper up there in a hut who was taught how to use a radio. He'd call in when he could see clear sky in both directions. You can't turn in that valley, so when you get in there you have to keep going on through." In 1947, Munson was killed when, flying on instruments, his DC 4 crashed into one of those mountains.

Al wasn't the only one with doubts. Others also had complaints, and the thing that stuck in their craws the most was that younger pilots, with much less flying experience, would be teaching them. These old-timers had been flying all their lives, and they first learned on some rough dirt field. They were a different breed of men altogether; practically none of them had had much education. Yet they were rough and ready, as well as honest and straightforward. They were great guys.

Following the meeting, a lot of them talked about dropping out of the training program, but finally they all joined and did spend the year in Brownsville. They all did very well, and I think they appreciated it when they got through, although it hurt their pride a bit to have to learn a new way to fly. Once they accepted the fact that they had to do it, because we couldn't run a scheduled airline without instrument-rated pilots, the year went smoothly. The training included Link trainer instruction on the ground, practice in the hooded single-engine plane in the skies around the field, and then flights to Mexico City and back, where they had to fly the airplane on instruments until they finally felt comfortable with it.

The Brownsville Air Corps base was where instrument flying actually had started, several years before. It was developed by a couple of Air Force pilots for military training; they were the first ones to equip an airplane with a black curtain over the windows and load it with instruments that showed the altitude of the airplane. After we acquired the Brownsville-Mexico City route, we found that occasionally a plane would lose altitude in the overcast, falling out of the sky and coming out of the dive over Tampico. It turned out our pilots got disoriented in the fog and couldn't keep flying. So we got those two Air Corps pilots to set up an instrument training program for us.

While the Alaskan pilots were in Brownsville getting trained, I went to Seattle to work out the details of the Alaskan route with Joe Crosson, who stayed behind as general manager. After I went back to New York, I saw Joe when he came there, as he often did on business visits. It was amazing to me to see how someone like Joe, who lived for long stretches in the woods, reacted to crowds. One time I took him to a Columbia-Yale football game. It was at Columbia's stadium, and there was a huge crowd all around us. Looking over, I noticed he was getting pale, and I thought he was getting sick. "What's the matter?" I asked.

Joe gasped, "I can't stand this crowd. Would it be all right if we left?" He didn't like New York City, either; it was too big and crowded. But one pleasant experience we had together was a trip to the Central Park Zoo to see the polar bears. Joe had found two tiny abandoned bear cubs on one of his flights and brought them home. They were raised in the house as pets. When they were about the size of large dogs, Joe was worried about what to do with them and gave them to me. They were much too large and inappropriate for a New York apartment, so I offered them to the Central Park Zoo. The zoo was delighted and built quite a large cage with big rocks and running water. At this time Joe hadn't seen them for a few years, so we went to have a look. They were huge. As soon as we drew near, they recognized Joe and rushed to the edge of the cage to greet him. On telling the story to the keeper, he let us in. In their enthusiasm, the bears almost mauled Joe, but he called them by name and seemed to be enjoying it as much as the bears. We stayed a long time, and Joe seemed utterly happy; in fact, we stayed until closing time.

The Alaska program was ready for operation in about one year. Before I returned to New York, we put several new Lockheed Electras on the route. The Electra was a sleek-looking, twin-engined craft that could carry mail and up to ten passengers.[3] Before they came, we carried a few passengers in the old single-engined planes, but not many, because when our pilots got back after that year in Brownsville, they were still very apprehensive about carrying people through any really bad weather with just one engine.

# Luxury Passenger Service to Europe

*In the spring of 1939* we took delivery on the new Boeing 314 flying boats, developed for use across the Atlantic and Pacific Oceans. They were big four-engined craft, normally carrying from thirty to fifty passengers, and the first was christened the *Yankee Clipper* by Mrs. Eleanor Roosevelt on March 3, 1939. We had ordered a total of twelve planes, which became our entire over-the-ocean Clipper fleet. We operated them through New-foundland when going to England, and they crossed the Pacific from San Francisco.[1]

All passengers sat in first-class sleeping compartments, like a train, with upper and lower berths. The first two compartments were dining rooms, and the fare included fancy meals. It was a surprisingly luxurious experience, all things considered. Once the plane left the U.S. territorial limits, cocktails were served.[2]

We had at least two stewards on every flight to attend to food and drink; the number varied with the passenger load. It was quite a technical accomplishment to keep the food tasty. We finally decided to cook it ashore before the plane left, then put it in special thermal compartments to keep it warm. The big disadvantage with the 314 was that the cabin noise was considerable. Once the plane got underway at cruising speed, we actually gave people ear plugs to use.[3]

The 314 had an upper deck with bunks in an open area behind the cockpit, so the crew didn't have to sleep down with the passengers. The cockpit area was quite spacious, with room for the navigator, one or two radio officers, and two pilots. Later, the navigator also had to be a qualified pilot. The crew members worked a maximum of about twelve-hour shifts. In the rear of the cockpit, there were doors opening into the wings through which the flight engineer could climb to make minor adjustments to the four engines. We had great hopes for that setup, but it turned out there weren't too many things we had to do to the engines in flight, so the idea was abandoned on later aircraft.[4]

Since these flying boats made an ocean crossing much quicker than going by ship, there was quite an increase in our passenger load. Our flights became popular over both oceans, but with the limited ability to eliminate icing on the wings in the early forties, we had to close the northern Atlantic flights during the winter months. But we soon got to work on the southern Atlantic route, which was scheduled to have two refueling stops: one in Bermuda and one in the Azores. The second stop presented special problems, since there was no protected harbor at Horta, our landing place in the Azores, and our planes would have to land in the open sea. Once down, there was a breakwater and our planes would have to taxi behind it, which was sometimes difficult in heavy seas. Early in the planning stage we saw that before our planes left Bermuda, we would need to have expert wind and wave forecasts. There were limits beyond which the plane ran the risk of stoving in its bottom on the waves. So we trained the local Azores manager in meteorology, wave forecasting, as well as radio telephone so that he could change the flight schedule if necessary. A lot of people thought we were crazy to change the flight schedule according to local weather conditions, but the arrangement worked pretty well. While this was in use we never did have a major difficulty.[5]

By the spring of 1939, I had spent a lot of time out in Seattle at Boeing, getting ready for the first delivery of the 314 flying boats. Bill del Valle, an engineering representative, and John Borger, his assistant, were out there with me, and they handled all the technical details. In May we started receiving the flying boats and were planning our first passenger service to Lisbon, Portugal.[6]

I had recently become engaged to Betty Gay Symington, and at the last minute the survey flight was scheduled on the same day as my engagement party. I missed the party because I had to go out on the preliminary flight to Lisbon with the chief federal inspector for the Civil Aviation Authority. It happened that the inspector, Bill Noah, was an old friend of mine, and since he had to give final approval to the route, my bosses decided that I would be the perfect Pan Am person to accompany him. It interfered with my private plans, but I wasn't given much choice in the matter. It was important that I accompany him on the trip so that any last-minute snags could get fixed immediately. Dr. Ross McFarland from Harvard also came on the trip, to look into passenger and employee health factors on long-distance flights. Over the years, he drew up very helpful health standards that became mandatory for all flight personnel.

As the federal inspector, Bill Noah had to critique all of the plane's sea landings for safety considerations. In Bermuda we landed and took off for him in about three-foot waves, which went fine. Then we flew on to Portugal, and once again, the landing went off perfectly. Both Bill and I were delighted with these successes, and Bill approved the route. Then, since there was some talk about Pan Am possibly flying to France, we decided that as long as we were over in Europe, we might as well fly on to Marseilles and get his approval for that route, too. We landed on a big lake just outside Marseilles, and Bill and I went into town to the U.S. consulate so he could send off a cable to Washington with his approval.

It was very important that the cable get to the U.S. immediately. This was a Friday night, and on Sunday Pan Am was planning to send off its first passenger flight. That gave us Saturday for the cable to hit the desk in the State Department for approval, but the people at the consulate said not to worry, it would be there in a few hours. Bill had a friend in Switzerland, so he said goodbye and took off for the Alps. Unfortunately, I didn't get any address for him there; I didn't think there would be any need for it, since he was going to reappear Sunday night for our Monday return flight.

That Saturday night I began getting telephone calls from Pan Am management. "Where's the approval?" the anxious callers wanted to know. They hadn't received it yet! They were going crazy in New York, because this flight had been widely publicized, and there was to be a big ceremony in connection with the takeoff. After all, it would be the first passenger service across the Atlantic. And it was due to happen the very next day.

They put me on the phone with the CAA people, and I talked to one of the head men there. I told him I had been to the consulate with Noah on Friday night, that he'd wired off his approval to Washington, and, as I had a copy of the message, I read it to him. I said that I was sure it had gone out but that I didn't know where it was now; somebody obviously was asleep at the switch in the State Department. At first, the CAA bigshot said, "You'll have to hold up your flight—we can't approve it unless we have direct word from Noah." But finally he gave in: "Well, if you'll send us a copy of the message you have, along with a written statement that you personally saw it sent at a certain time, we'll approve the route." So we got it approved on that basis.

My visit to Marseilles occurred just three months before World War II started. Right near where we docked the airplane was a big aircraft factory that made fighters and bombers for the French Air Force. The manager of the plant took me on a tour of the place on Saturday, and I noticed that about half the workers were working and the other half were playing cards. When I walked over to where a large group of workers was gathered, I found that the main work being done that day at the factory was on a broken bicycle. In America, we had heard a lot of talk about the possibility of war, and I asked some of the plant workers about this. They said, "Oh no, there isn't going to be a war."

I talked to the managers at the factory about that, and they said that while they believed there was going to be war, they couldn't get this point across to the workers. The unions had loaded them up with coffee hours, coffee breaks, the right of workers to play cards during breaks, and other such perks, and it was impossible to keep them on the job. So there was a general feeling of hopelessness among the managers. It struck me that the French would have no ability to resist an attack if the performance of those workers was typical. As it turned out, that's exactly what happened.

When Bill Noah got back from Switzerland, he and I flew home. Bill was very upset about the goof-up. He blamed himself for sending it over the State Department wires, saying that he should have sent it commercially, because everybody knew the government communications were poor. "I should have sent it by Western Union," he moaned. I finally calmed him down by pointing out that Pan Am got the approval in time and that the plane had taken off on Sunday with the first load of passengers, right on schedule.

The passengers on that first flight were a strangely mixed bag of celebrities, government officials, ordinary paying passengers, and a group of the usual "first" people who wanted to go on the first flights of all our different routes. When the plane landed at Bermuda for refueling, the passengers were allowed to go ashore for a couple of hours to stretch their legs. Many of them went sightseeing ashore, and in each case, newsreel cameramen were with them, grinding away to record their every move.[7]

I did not go on the survey flight to England via Gander, Newfoundland, because I was scheduled to get married on August 11, 1939. They couldn't force me to bail out of that personal event. However, when I was up there in 1937, I had stayed at a lodge on the Gander River run by a Scotsman, a wonderful man, and I had gotten to know a Nova Scotian

Indian who was a fishing guide. I suggested to Betty Gay that we take our honeymoon up there and do a little salmon fishing. She agreed, and the morning after the wedding we went up to Nova Scotia.

We flew to Nova Scotia on the regular flight to Europe, which stopped at Botwood. Pan Am had just started carrying passengers through there. You had to take a narrow-gauge railroad for a few miles to get over to the Gander airport, which was still under construction two years after the British had demanded immediate completion. They were landing smaller planes from Canada, but none of the transatlantic planes. From there we went over to the lodge on the Gander River, where we had a wonderful time, although the Nova Scotian guide didn't think much of taking a woman along on a fishing trip.

After the fishing trip, and after checking Gander Airport to see a few planes, Betty Gay and I got back to Botwood and caught the plane on its return trip from England. We went down to the lounge and met Eddie Rickenbacker, the president of Eastern Airlines.[8] He was just coming back from a trip to Berlin. All the way back to New York, Rickenbacker talked about his trip to Berlin, and he insisted that there was not going to be any war. He had seen everybody important while he was there, and Goering and Hitler had each personally assured him that they didn't want war.

# The Beginning of World War II

$O$n September 3, 1939, three days after the plane ride with Rickenbacker, war was declared in Europe. The Germans tried to make it look as though they were the ones who were attacked by the Poles—as though they would never start a war, and as though they were just defending themselves.

I suspected there would be a war eventually, but I didn't think it would happen that soon. We were all taken by surprise. There was a blitzkrieg strike against the Poles, then things quieted down in the spring. It was called the phony war period—which wasn't phony to the Poles, of course. Then the Germans started bombing London in 1940, and Pan Am eventually had to stop flying to Southampton. It was too dangerous. After that we combined the two routes and ran all our services through Lisbon, which became the only transatlantic destination. We had quite a few flights each week, but then there was such a demand, with people escaping from Europe, that we were running daily flights. We had ten or twelve aircraft in our fleet of planes, and since there usually were a few out of service for checking and maintenance, we probably had seven in the air most of the time. They would turn right around and return the same day.[1]

Lisbon at that time was the bustling city of Europe. Under the repressive rule of the dictator, Salazar, there was law and order, and Lisbon had become the hub of social entertainment for those who could afford it. There were opera, flamenco, bullfights, and all types of social activities. Every nation had its intelligence people there, and as the only neutral port city, it was constantly flooded with people from the far corners of Europe, many of them wealthy aristocrats or high up in government circles. Lisbon was a nest of spies, filled with rumor and intrigue. In the best restaurant a bunch of Germans with the swastika insignia on their sleeves might sit down at the table next to you; over there would be the British ambassador; nearby, the French attaché; everywhere, people of every nationality quietly having dinner. All the top people would show up, and, despite the strange mix, everybody acted quite relaxed. You would never have known there was a war going on.

The British had set up a connecting night flight between Lisbon and Southampton in their four-engined landplane. Airfields in England operated at night with no lights. One particularly memorable casualty of that service was Leslie Howard, the famous actor who had appeared in the movie *Gone with the Wind.* He died on a London/Lisbon flight that was shot down in 1943. Someone told me that the Germans intercepted his plane because they knew he would be on that flight.

People from all over Europe came to Lisbon as refugees. Once there, they would try to get on a flight to the States, and we had long waiting lists. The refugees were mostly British and French, but there were even some from Germany, both Jewish and non-Jewish. So ours was a vital service, and our government was eager to keep it going. The passengers also included spies for both sides going back and forth on secret missions.

Among the refugees were many prominent people who drove down from Paris, including ex-Premier Renault and his mistress. He arrived with over five million dollars in illegal francs. They couldn't get on, because we could take only thirty-five to fifty people each trip, and you had to wait your turn. So they rented a big palace outside of Lisbon and enjoyed the good life until their turn came. They were on our standby list, but given the military situation, we had some "must-ride people" who came ahead of them—generals, diplomats, and some mysterious important civilians. We had many very wealthy standbys, who, once they got to the States, lived on New York's Park Avenue until the war was over.

When the U.S. became involved in the hostilities, there was discussion about flying across the Atlantic at night with all the plane's lights turned off. We decided against it because we weren't military, and we figured that if we were all lit up, they wouldn't shoot us down. We had seen that a brightly lit ship at sea could get through without being attacked. It was the oddest thing, when a convoy was all blacked out, to suddenly see one of those neutral Swedish hospital ships come blazing down through the convoy, all lit up like a Christmas tree. And it worked for our planes as well.

Our government reserved a number of seats for U.S. military people on every flight. I was on a transatlantic flight one day, and an Air Corps general also was on board. He went up to the cockpit and was watching the navigator at work, using the octant and then reading his chart. Finally the general came back to the passenger section and said to our Pan Am group, "My God, the Air Corps doesn't have anybody who can navigate!" He later got hold of Trippe and told him that we had to train hundreds of navigators for the Air Corps right away. This request developed into an operation that took up quite a bit of my time during the war. I was given the assignment of starting up the program and coordinating Pan Am's involvement with the government's requirements.[2]

That order hit us like a ton of bricks. We were a business organization and were not prepared to suddenly start up a Navigator Training school. We had no facilities, and we had no personnel to do the teaching. But we got right to it and leased a building at the University of Miami. This was in 1940, and President Roosevelt wanted us to train navigators in thirty days!

Of course, the crucial question was, Who was going to teach these people? We had a crackerjack chief navigator, Charlie Lund, who several years before had actually been a ship's captain. He was a lifetime navigator, so we put him in charge of the training. He was called the dean and was quite pleased with that. Then we had to come up with about twenty people who could be instructors. But we had no surplus airline navigators we could move off the commercial flights.

I suddenly thought about the U.S. Merchant Marine Academy up in New London, Connecticut. They were graduating students all the time, and while they weren't air navigators, they were navigators. They knew the stars, they knew the sky, they knew celestial navigation. The academy happened to have a brand-new graduating class, and we got permission from the government authorities to have some of those fellows released so they didn't have to go into the service. We hired about twenty of them as navigation instructors and rushed them to Miami.

We next put drafting boards and sextants along the sides under the windows of some obsolete twin-engined Commodore flying boats. We could carry twelve students in each plane. A periscope went up through a hole in the ceiling for taking star shots. For thirty days we trained the instructors; then, the instructors started training the students. But it was the blind leading the blind. Charlie Lund realized that we had to do something drastic to improve the situation. He wrote out complete, day-by-day courses for the school and mimeographed them, one set for each of the teachers. It spelled out exactly what to do, including both course content and necessary materials, for the whole thirty days. That was how we were able to train navigators so fast. Once it was operating, the school took in about sixty young men every thirty days.

The Air Corps set up their own navigation schools with our graduates as instructors. That was a great idea, since we couldn't possibly train the thousands of navigators they were going to need. They brought in young air cadets undergoing training in piloting, navigation, and bombardiering. The instructors themselves had only thirty days training, but eventually the entire program was lengthened to six weeks.

Remember Jimmy Doolittle's raid over Japan? Their navigators were all our graduates. That raid was a great morale booster for Americans. Militarily, the value of it was worthless, but it certainly startled the Japanese. They couldn't believe we'd pulled it off. And we needed a victory desperately in those dark early days of the war.[3]

Another way that the military used Pan Am and the other commercial airlines during the war was for providing a massive air transport service to carry the troops. We were also the main transport for rest and recreation leave (R & R).

The government put a freeze on all the airlines regarding hiring personnel and buying new aircraft while the Air Corps was being organized. We were called down to Washington for a meeting to organize cooperation with the government. The presidents of a number of airlines were there, and they picked out four or five of the operating heads of airlines and sent them off into a private room to discuss how we could best implement the government's request. As Trippe's representative, I was part of this group. Rickenbacker, the president of Eastern Airlines, began telling us his ideas. We should set up a program, he said, whereby the airlines would run the whole Air Transport Command as a civilian agency. Its people would be in a special uniform but wouldn't be militarized, and the government would give us access to all the airplanes and personnel we needed. But we would run it. That way, it would be run efficiently, he asserted. He claimed that if the military ran it, it would be very inefficient. He had a point, but his proposal was impractical, because we would be expected to run our regular commercial schedule at the same time.

After a break, our group met again to discuss what we would report back to the full organization. Jack Hurlihy, the United Airlines operations vice-president, who was chairman, right off the bat said Rickenbacker's plan was impractical. "It would be a complete mess to organize," he said. "What we should do is hold what we have in the way of aircraft, if we can, and then contract it out to the Air Corps whenever they want to use it. If the Air Corps wanted fifty DC-3s, the airlines would come together, pool their resources, and make a one-time contract for that limited operation."

His point was, quite rightly, that we couldn't get new commercial mechanics in wartime, and there would be no way for us to expand. We wouldn't be able to get factories to make airplanes for us, since they were all controlled by the military.

The group secretary wrote it all down, then Hurlihy asked me, as the only underling, to present our comments to the full group of presidents. I said I'd do it; I thought Hurlihy's plan was the only sensible thing to do. Let the military run their own air transport and make individual contracts with the airlines to fly for them. So at twelve o'clock we went back to the airline presidents, and I read the report. Rickenbacker was sitting right across the table from me, and he said, "Son, that isn't the kind of report we wanted. We wanted to take over the whole thing."

And I said, "I'm just reporting for the key major executives of the domestic airlines, and this is what they decided. That's what I'm reporting." Rickenbacker didn't look too happy; I imagine he had expected it would be just an affirmation of his ideas.

The American Airlines president, C. R. Smith, had a sense of humor. He was sitting down at the end of the table and he called out, "Keep it up, son, you're doing fine!"[4]

Shortly after that, the military people, headed by Air Corps Chief General Hap Arnold, marched in and sat down, and the general said, "Before you present your report, I want to tell you right off the bat that we are going to run the Air Transport Command (ATC). It's too massive to be run any way but by military rules, military pay, and military people. We can't run it under private enterprise conditions." His words took the wind right out of our sails. It was clear that the military didn't want to hear our report. He just announced right at the beginning what he was going to do. Finally, he said, "I want to get your cooperation, as good Americans, to work out a method for coordinating your existing services and our new division. We'll take some key executives out of the airlines and militarize them and have them work in the Air Transport Command." C. R. Smith was commissioned on the spot as a brigadier general and became second in command to General Harold George. Smith brought key people in from the airlines to aid him and made them all colonels. ATC was paralleling the ground and sea transportation, ferrying trucks, jeeps, and tanks as well as men to the front lines. This made for a much faster network than had previously existed.[5]

# Pan Am Enters the War

*By 1940,* after eleven years with Pan Am, I had fallen into the role of troubleshooter for the company. When there was some job that demanded emergency attention or had unusual twists, I'd be called in by Trippe or some other executive to jump on it. Before the war, Pan Am was still a relatively small company with only a handful of top executives, many of whom had started in the company in the late twenties. Although Pan Am had an organizational chart on which my boss, André Priester, headed what was called the engineering department, we were all generalists before the war and were expected to use our problem-solving abilities in many different areas. We were given the outline of a problem and then expected to solve it on our own initiative.[1]

Pan Am had developed considerable expertise as an international carrier. In the spring of 1941, just before the U.S. got into the war, I was called down to Washington by the government for a major problem concerning the British war effort. I was told that Churchill had contacted Roosevelt because the Germans had driven the British troops almost back to Cairo. Churchill was afraid that the Germans were going to destroy the British forces in Africa. The Royal Air Force planes, tanks, and other ground equipment were short of emergency parts, and there was no way to get replacements to them. He asked Roosevelt to set up a civilian airline across Africa that could fly materials to Dakar, on the west coast, and then inland. Churchill wanted it set up within thirty days. (They always picked thirty days for these things, regardless of how feasible that might be.) So Pan Am Airways Africa, Ltd. came into being.[2]

In this way, Roosevelt had a World War II airlift well before Pearl Harbor. In order to create a chain of airfields to link the United States across the Caribbean to Natal, Brazil, a private company could serve as an unofficial go-between, since the United States was not yet at war. Pan Am was asked, and it built forty fields and bases at a cost to the United States of twelve million dollars.[3] This aerial lifeline sustained the British and soon the American forces in distant theaters of war. These same bases enabled Pan Am to leave the flying boats for land carriers in 1943. Because of the original contracts, Pan Am was able to hold title to these airports even though paid for by Uncle Sam until well after the war.

I met with officers from the Air Corps, which was coordinating the operation for the president, and they presented me with the problem. Everyone knew it was only a matter of time until the United States entered the war, and we were all required to support the war effort. So I said, "First, we need planes. What are you going to start us off with in the way of planes? Pan Am does not have a single extra plane. If we have to use our planes, you'll have to designate which of our routes are less important to you, so we can use the planes in Africa." After that meeting, they got in touch with various government agencies.

When I returned the next day, they said, "We can't designate any unimportant Pan Am routes; all your routes are essential. We'll take the planes away from the domestic airlines. People can use the trains."

I said, "Well then, we'll need DC-3s, which easily convert to cargo planes," and the Air Corps agreed. Of course, the domestic airlines were furious, but they had to comply, and they assigned us about twenty DC-3s.[4] It took four or five days to strip them and equip them as cargo planes. The next question was, Who would fly them? The military people didn't seem to realize that a commercial airline doesn't have a whole lot of extra pilots standing around, waiting for something to do. They acted surprised that we had nobody to spare. I explained, "We'd go broke if we did that; because of the draft, we couldn't find anybody to hire."

Then one of the Air Force officers said, "We have a class of air cadets graduating next week down at Randolph Air Force base in Texas. We couldn't order them into Pan Am, but they could volunteer and then get out of the service."[5]

I thought it would be risky to put civilian personnel into a combat zone, but the government was determined to set up the airline, and graduates of the Air Academy would be an excellent source of pilots. I said, "We would have to give them additional training, and that'll take time. So in order to get the African service rolling immediately, we'll put your graduates on as copilots on our South American and Central American routes. Meanwhile, we'll pick out the most experienced of our present copilots, promote them to Pan Am captains, and send them over to Africa. Then, after some on-the-job training, your graduates will be available to take over the planes in Africa." They agreed to the plan.

The class was graduating a couple of days later, so I went down to Texas and met the colonel commanding the academy. I told him about my mission and gave him a letter from the chief of the Air Corps, General Hap Arnold. It authorized the release of up to sixty of the class on a volunteer basis, who would then be employed by Pan Am for a very important government mission. I said, "I can't tell you anything about it. It's a top-secret assignment, but I need to try to recruit some of your graduates immediately."

The colonel answered, "At nine o'clock in the morning we'll have them all in the assembly hall for you." At nine on the dot, the cadets marched in. The colonel got up and said, "Gentlemen, something very unusual has happened. The Army has authorized up to sixty of you men to volunteer to go to work for Pan Am on a very important top-secret government project. I'm not authorized to order you to do it, but I *am* authorized to have someone tell you about it." I then told the student pilots that I represented Pan Am, and I would process the applications of those who were interested. At this point the Colonel interrupted, "If you're not interested in this proposal, you might as well leave. You don't have to sit through this whole thing." Nobody left. The colonel stared at them, then laughed and said, "Here I've been pumping Air Force morale into you guys, and now you all want to leave. I ought to be ashamed of you guys, but if I were your age, I would probably do the same thing." I suppose the fact that it was so secret and couldn't be talked about sounded rather glamorous to those twenty-one-year-olds.

I explained, "I'll have to interview each one of you and look at your records. Those I choose will report immediately to our headquarters in Miami." I spent the whole day processing applications, staying overnight to finish. I hadn't realized there would be so many applicants who would be interested in the mysterious assignment. They all had good records and high marks in flight and instruments, so it was a difficult choice. The next day, the whole class graduated and got their wings and lieutenant's bars, but sixty of them would soon turn around and resign their brand-new commissions.

We set up a training program in Miami to get our candidates integrated into the copilot's seats on our regular Latin American routes. Those fellows had had very little twin-engine experience when we got them.

They had just completed the first phase of training and were at the point where they would be deciding whether they wanted to fly bombers or fighters in the second phase. It was quite a jump up to the DC-3.

We also set up an airport construction company to build airports for the new company, with a string of them from Miami through South America and then into Africa. A fellow from a subsidiary construction company had invented a method of hardening the ground surface quickly by using some kind of an asphalt-mixture injection system. Instead of digging down to put in the foundations of runways and then pouring concrete on top, this injection did the whole thing, so they were able to put in the runways very fast. The runways held up pretty well; they were certainly good enough for two or three years of war. In fact, when I was down in South America quite a few years later, they were still in use by the local carriers.

Although we didn't get Pan Am Airways Africa completed in thirty days, it took less than sixty days to get the new airline going in Africa. There was a great deal to do, including hiring ground personnel, setting up landing fields, and putting together an organization to support the airline. To avoid German fighters, we had to fly the planes all the way down to Brazil and then take the Ascension Island route across the Atlantic. The air route in Africa left from Accra, Ghana, or Lagos, Nigeria, on the west coast and went across central Africa to Khartoum, Sudan, and then up to Alexandria, Egypt. Khartoum had a good airport with paved runways, but elsewhere we built relatively small airfields. One reason we picked the DC-3 was that it could land on grass runways.

We sent George Kraigher, our operations manager in Brownsville, over there to manage the whole thing. George hated the Germans; he had fought against them when he was a Serbian pilot during World War I. He wanted very much to get into the service, but he was a little long in the tooth for active duty. So we put him in charge of the African operation. He was ideal for the job because he could improvise and had a lot of experience running one-man operations with rough conditions in Central America.

We had to have airport managers who were trained in meteorology to run these airports. At this time, the civilian air services had a pressing need for trained pilots and maintenance crew people. Because the draft had begun in September of 1939, no good people were available. We would have to train airport managers from scratch. I heard that an interim graduating class was about to come out of Yale University, so I interviewed a bunch of those fellows and hired about twenty of them as airport managers, enough to take care of the whole route.

I sent them to Miami, and the old-timers down there were outraged. They couldn't teach college kids. But I said, "Give them a chance; they will learn fast." They set up the courses so that the trainees worked alongside our own managers, and in four to six weeks they were ready for Africa. Everybody had their doubts, saying the college kids were too young and inexperienced. But they did a bang-up job! This was an example of how things happened during the war: people said we couldn't do something, but we went ahead and did it, usually quite well. However, I wasn't surprised at the success of these kids because of the education they had had.

In the first few months, the ground personnel and some of the pilots began to get malaria, so the Army's surgeon general sent a malaria expert over there. That was a waste of time, because all that guy did was come back and recommend putting in dams and hospitals. It was impossible! At one point I had the opportunity to tell the surgeon general about the famous malaria remedy I learned in the Philippines. I said, "I saw malaria licked in Manila with lizards." He told me to go ahead and get some of them.

I got a hold of a friend who had contacts with a professor at the University of Chicago. The professor had spent many years in the Philippines and was considered one of the top experts on malaria. The three of us met in New York, and when I asked the professor to take on the African malaria problem, he was eager to go. He was patriotic and wanted to contribute to the war effort. I told him about the lizards at the Philippines Hotel, where they didn't even have screens to stop the mosquitoes, but unfortunately those lizards were not available in Africa. So I asked him, "If you were over there, what would you do? We have to have somebody improvise an answer right away."

He replied, "Yes, something can be done." And he laid out his ideas, one by one. He said, "The personnel have got to have screened quarters. From sunset to sunrise, they must wear mosquito-proof helmets and boots whenever they are outside, because that's when mosquitoes are around. You've got to train the people on how to avoid them. And then there is a chemical that will have to be sprayed on any standing water around the places where they're living." We sent him to Africa, and there was no more trouble with malaria, even without the help of lizards.

When the U.S. entered the war, I asked the Air Corps about taking over the African airline operation. They said the military was still too disorganized, but they'd take it over later. So we ran it for another year or so, although we were lucky if we broke even on the costs. However, given the war conditions over there, we had a very good safety record.

When the Air Corps finally militarized the airline, they offered commissions to all, both ground personnel and the pilots, if they would stay with the airline. They had a choice of taking a commission and staying in the military, or not. All but one of those young fellows that I got from Yale to manage the airports signed up and took commissions, but most of the Pan Am pilots, including the Air Force cadets I had recruited, left the African airline and elected to stay with our company.

Once the U.S. forces were involved, we delivered P-40 fighters to the U.S. Air Corps pilots stationed with the British in the desert. The U.S. government would send the planes in crates to Accra, Ghana, by fast ship, and there we would assemble them and ferry them across Africa to Khartoum.

My younger brother Jack was in the Air Corps. He had just graduated from primary training when they sent him over to fight in the desert, flying one of those P-40s. The Allied troops were still in bad trouble, and he was stationed out in the desert for months at a time. It was horrible: dysentery, sand flies biting, the blowing sand getting into everything. He had ninety missions, flying all the way up into Sicily and Italy. When he got out of the service he wanted to fly for Pan Am, but I told him, "I think that after the fighter experience you had, you'll never want to fly for the civilian airlines. It's too dull." I had seen so many former combat pilots come and go. But Pan Am hired him, and he stayed for around eight months or so. Then he said he couldn't stand it anymore, just droning around the skies.

After the African operation was running smoothly, George Kraigher, our elderly Serbian, finally got his wish to get into the war. The Armed Services wanted to use his knowledge of the Balkans, because at that time the Allies were moving up into Italy. George was made a colonel and was put in charge of a base in southern Italy where various types of airplanes were assembled to go on rescue and survey missions in the mountains. George himself would fly into the Balkans every month or so in a small plane to contact Mikhailovitch and Tito, our Yugoslav allies. Mikhailovitch was from the Serbian aristocracy; the British eventually dumped him in favor of the Croatian, Tito. George also had a sister in the Serbian mountains, a partisan who worked for Tito.[6]

George got to know Tito pretty well during his flights into Serbia. In fact, he was at Tito's birthday party in the mountains when they got word that a force of Germans was coming. It was bedtime, but Tito told all of them, "Don't take your clothes off, because we may have to leave on real short notice." George didn't think that sleeping in his clothes was such a good idea, so he stripped and went to bed. Early in the morning the German tanks started rolling through the village, and Tito's adjutant ran around waking everybody. George got up and started across the road holding his clothes, but then he turned and ran back. He had remembered a gallon jug of fine whiskey that he had brought up from Italy as a birthday gift for Tito. He finished dressing, grabbed the whiskey, and hurried off after the others. The tanks were already thundering through the town.

Tito and some of his people had escaped to a little inn down the mountain. George figured that he couldn't carry the gallon of whiskey such a distance, so he buried it under an old oak tree. He later told Randolph Churchill where it was, and Churchill found it and drank it all. Randolph, who was the British prime minister's son, had been assigned to Tito as a liaison officer. Tito had his headquarters out there in the mountains, with the Germans down below in the village, and George told me that Randolph would stroll around in broad daylight in his British uniform. The guy didn't seem to know fear at all.[7]

After George hid the whiskey, he joined Tito and his followers. They walked through the mountains to the nearest of Tito's encampments, where George's plane was parked in a small airfield. From there, he flew back to Italy.

While I was in Washington during the war years, the FBI kept trying to recruit me because of the years I had spent in Germany. Our Washington manager, Mrs. Ann Archibald, tried to get the FBI off my back, because I was working for the war effort through Pan Am. She knew her way around Washington and had a lot of contacts. Nevertheless, I was called to the War Department for a confidential meeting. They proposed flying me behind the German lines in France, where I would parachute down to spy on the Germans for them. After all, I spoke German, so they would never discover me. I pointed out that I spoke German with a pronounced American accent; they would spot this immediately and shoot me. Furthermore, although I didn't say this to the FBI, I didn't want to spy on them; the Germans had been kind to me when I was working in Berlin, and I still had friends there. But Mrs. Archibald finally managed to have me put on the list of industry people who were indispensable to the war effort, because I was in charge of the Pacific military transport for Pan Am, which was part of the Naval Air Transport Service. After this classification, I heard no more from the FBI.[8]

The Pacific military transport was run by Pan Am on contract for the U.S. Navy. After the African operation got up to speed, I moved on to help organize it. We put in place a transport service at our Pacific division in California that served Alaska and the Aleutians. We also set up a similar Navy contract service through the South Pacific islands and down to Australia and New Zealand.

All civilian plane manufacturing stopped. Pan Am and TWA orders for Constellations were taken over by the Army, as were orders for Douglas DC-4s from United and American. You couldn't buy anything but military transport aircraft, but Pan Am had no trouble getting what we needed since most of our passengers were top priority people, and there were plenty of them. In fact, we had an assured income from officials traveling overseas and actually more business than before the war.

All of Pan Am's significant work in the Pacific was done for the Navy, but I did have one personal encounter with the Air Corps. A general was put in charge of the invasion of France about a year before it took place, and he called me down to Washington. He wanted to take me onto his staff as a lieutenant colonel. He didn't tell me about the invasion of France, but it was pretty obvious there was going to be one since he was building up a staff to take abroad. He had been given full responsibility for the American part of the invasion, and he was getting ready to move over to England to organize the ground and ocean transport, as well as limited air transport.

I told him what I was doing and that I was considered essential to the war effort. I said, "It sounds to me like you're talking mostly about land transport with trains and trucks, and sea transport with ships, with air transport a much smaller part of the system."

He answered, "You're right. But you've been in transportation a number of years, and your name has been recommended to me highly, so I'd like you to come with us. I'm having a lot of trouble with the railroad and the trucking people; they don't want to let anybody go." He was quite upset about the lack of cooperation he was getting in acquiring key people.

I said, "Well, it isn't up to me, it's up to the Manpower Board, to decide that. They'll have to ask Pan Am whether or not they'll release me. I'll do whatever they decide." The Manpower Board turned him down. I recommended a friend of mine, Whit Knapp, who was a lawyer with Governor Thomas Dewey in his campaign against crime. Whit went down to Washington and talked with the general, and the general was very happy with him. But when Knapp went to Dewey and told him about the general's offer, Governor Dewey turned around and played politician on Whit by sending his secretary of state down to Washington to take the job.

Pan Am assignments kept coming at me; there never seemed to be even a single day's break between them. In about 1942, I was sent down to Brazil with a team to look over Pan Air do Brasil, because they were having a lot of crashes. The airline was a subsidiary run by the Brazilians, and they asked Trippe for help. The president of Pan Air do Brazil was a member of a wealthy family who had no knowledge of aviation. So I went down with a team of specialists. I had a chief pilot, Joe Chase, along with me to check the quality of the pilot training, as well as an engineer to check all their maintenance procedures. When Chase arrived in Brazil he was arrested for nonpayment of income taxes from a previous assignment years ago. Brasil had just installed an IBM card check system for tax evaders, and Chase's card popped up when he went through immigration. We quickly paid the taxes.

We went through the whole airline organization, figured out the problem, and wrote a report on it. They weren't being careful enough in flight operations procedures and, frankly, they were doing stupid things. For example, they were flying at night between Rio and the Amazon with no lights or beacons. The pilots were getting lost and crashing into the jungle. We made a lot of recommendations and sent back some instructor pilots to retrain them.

During a good part of that time I was away from home, and it was a pretty hectic schedule. I became completely exhausted. Like everybody in responsible positions during the war, I faced a twelve- to fourteen-hour day. I first started feeling tired on getting back from hiring those pilots at Randolph Air Base for the African air-transport operation. Immediately thereafter I was in Brazil for two days and two nights, and on my return I had gone as far as Washington when I was so tired I had to get to a hotel and go to sleep. I did not even have the strength to go on to my home in New York. After that trip I finally collapsed and was forced to take a leave of absence for some months before my next assignment.

# More on World War II and Its Aftermath

*During the war,* we generally worked very smoothly with the armed forces. Because of our extensive intercontinental experience, Pan Am was the American airline that did the most to support the war effort abroad.[1]

We also had some important things to teach the military. As an example, I was called down to the Pentagon in 1945 to meet with the chief of the Air Corps. He said, "We have a very serious problem. Many of the Boeing bombers that are bombing Tokyo don't have enough fuel left for the flight back. One of our men was talking to a Pan Am pilot, and he said that if you use the right power technique, you can extend your range. Is this true?"

Of course, it was not only true, but our use of this technique went back almost ten years to our earliest trans-Pacific flights. On the first flight I made across the Pacific we used this variable power technique. It is simply a matter of the relationship between weight and power. When you first take off, you are at maximum load. When you get nearer to your destination and are on the way down, you're thousands of pounds lighter. Our fellows worked out a formula whereby you could reduce your power every half hour or so to match the decreasing load and thus extend your range considerably. What was news to the general was a nearly ten-year-old fact to us.

I sent my chief flight engineer and a couple of his men out to Saipan. They adapted the rules to match the Boeing bomber and made some test flights for the military. Then they taught the military air crews how to use our special charts to adjust the air speed to the aircraft weight. The flight engineer entered the bomb weight and the fuel load, and then he would find the ideal horsepower. He had to readjust the cruising speed for each stage of the journey because of the prevailing winds. Then he would notify the copilot, who would change the engine settings on a regular basis. It made enough difference to eliminate practically all their landings in the sea caused by running out of fuel. It seems like such an obvious thing in retrospect; it's just too bad they lost so many lives before they found out about it.[2]

We had cooperated with the military many times in the past. As always with the government, we found it easier to work informally with local people rather than go through Washington. For example, when we started flying in Alaska, we went to the head Navy fellow at Naval Air Station on Sand Point, Lake Washington, in Seattle. They had a ramp to pull seaplanes out of the water, and they let us use it before we had our own setup. In return for their favor we would carry their mail up to Alaska and give their officers a ride now and then.

The Navy also let us use their facilities at the Treasure Island Naval Base near San Francisco, and we operated out of there for a long time when we were developing the Pacific refueling bases at Midway and Wake. In the late thirties, when it looked as if there was going to be a war, the Navy was able to put Marines on both islands. We gave the Navy all our charts so that they could get their ships in, and it was a valuable chapter in civilian-military cooperation.

Before the war we were involved with a subsidiary company in China, the China National Aviation Corporation, or CNAC. It had been based in Peking, was moved to Hong Kong, and then we moved it to an inland city, Kunming, where Chiang Kai-shek was stationed. Our regular flights across the Pacific connected with CNAC flights into China.[3]

Pan Am also supported the Highball China Express, from Miami through India and over the Himalayas to Kunming. The Highball China Express, officially Pan American Air Ferries Ltd., was the brainchild of a Pan Am pilot named John Steele. He dug up a lot of old-time barnstormers like himself, most of them over draft age, and others who had been rejected by the draft due to physical conditions. Financed by Pan Am, Steele then set up this amazing airline that ran from Miami to Brazil and then to Ascension Island and across into India before crossing the mountains into China. Later it was run out of Miami as a completely separate operation.[4] After the war and the dissolution of [Ferries Express,] we took a lot of the Ferries pilots into Pan Am, including Al Ueltchi. After becoming Juan Trippe's personal pilot, Ueltchi eventually founded Flight Safety, Inc. and became a millionaire.[5]

Civilian pilots were flying across the Himalayas between China and Burma in DC-3s. "Over the Hump," it was called. They sure lost a lot of planes on that run, and to have been in the China-Burma theater is considered in the flying world something very special. We were losing planes constantly, and not only to enemy fire. The planes were also going down covered with ice. Icing equipment had been around for quite a long time, but it wasn't very effective at that altitude. They didn't have heated wings in those days, and the ice would form a ridge over the boot. Before long the ice built up to the point at which the plane could not fly.[6]

An American named Chennault was working for the Chinese airline before the United States entered the war. He formed the Flying Tigers, a civilian group of pilots that was later brought into the U. S. Army Air Corps. His P-40s were painted like sharks, and they became famous for knocking off Japanese Zeroes like mackerel in a net. The operation was all done on a shoestring, since they began without a big military organization behind them. Before the group was brought into the Air Corps, Pan Am helped out Chennault's buccaneer operation.[7]

The China operation was headed up by William Langhorne Bond. Once established in China, Bond wired us that he needed an operations manager out there. I had a pilot named Chili Vaughn who was well educated and had a good deal of experience, but I had grounded him because he couldn't pass his electrocardiogram; his reading was typical of someone who might have a sudden heart attack. He was very upset, so I said, "Well, how about this job in China? You understand, you're not going there to fly airplanes, you're going to run operations." He said he would take it, and he went out there and functioned as manager for several years. Then, when the situation really got rough and Japanese fighters were shooting down a lot of the CNAC planes, he ran out of pilots and put himself back in the cockpit. He was back to the States a year later on leave, and he happened to mention to me that he was flying a regular schedule. He said he figured that it didn't matter under war conditions. And I had to agree, so I kept quiet about it. After the war he became operations manager of the Atlantic division and lived into his eighties.[8]

The Japanese began to intercept our radio messages telling who was aboard the planes, and they would shoot down flights carrying prominent Chinese military and government officials. The Chinese officials got wise to this, and they booked themselves on several planes at once in order to fool the Japanese spies. Once, we had a Chinese general who had done exactly that; he was booked on a flight flown by a Chinese friend of mine but wasn't in fact on board the plane. When it got over the Yangtze River, the plane was jumped by five Japanese Zero fighters, who shot it up badly. The plane, full of Chinese passengers, headed down toward the river, and at this point my friend yelled just before they hit the water, "Don't put on life preservers—stay under water! They're going to shoot at anybody they see floating!" He knew that the Japanese presumed the general was aboard and would try to kill all crash survivors.

Out of about twenty-four people, my friend was the only one to come out of the crash alive. Despite what he had said, they had all put on life preservers, and the Japanese shot them while they were bobbing around. My pilot friend survived because every time the fighters dove on them, he would go under the water. He finally made it to shore, completely exhausted, and then after passing out struggled back to his base. The plane was sunk in the Yangtze, but the Chinese, who were geniuses at make-do engineering, retrieved it despite constant Japanese patrols in the area. Using local villagers who operated a mammoth rig of long poles and crossbars, they pulled the plane to the surface, took it apart, and got it back to Hong Kong, where they rebuilt it.[9]

Our affiliate airline in China was truly what my old boss would have called a "chop suey" operation. Pan Am remained part owner of CNAC until after World War II, then sold out to the Chinese government just before the Communist takeover. Bond stayed with CNAC until it went completely into Chinese ownership in 1949.[10]

We brought similar affiliates into being in many other places as we spread out around the world, both before and after the end of the war. We had them in Brazil, Argentina, Costa Rica, Mexico, Colombia, Venezuela, and Cuba. They were feeders for our regular flights. In most cases they didn't have any money, so we financed them, gave them some old planes, and helped them start up their service. Then, when countries started nationalizing toward the end of war, Trippe changed the policy regarding affiliates and began selling them to the various nations. One of the reasons for this policy change may have been that the Civil Aeronautics Board required us to reduce our holdings in these affiliates to less than fifteen percent.

After the war, John McCloy went to Germany to become that country's U.S. military governor and high commissioner, from 1947 to 1952. I was subsequently offered the job as his assistant because I spoke German and had spent a year over there working for Lufthansa. McCloy thought I'd be fine for the job, but I turned it down; I didn't believe in occupying another country. I'd read about the occupation conducted by the Allies after the First World War, and I didn't see how that occupation had solved anything; in fact, considering what later happened, it may have made things worse.[11] Pan Am did become involved in the German occupation in a roundabout way. Along with the British and French airlines, we flew part of the Berlin airlift. The Western half of the city was kept going with supplies from the West. It was a great demonstration of the capabilities of aviation.

In June 1950, Pan Am got an urgent call to go to the Pentagon the day before the North Koreans attacked the South Koreans. All the airlines were represented at the gathering, mostly by their presidents. But Trippe would never go to such meetings, so I was there in his place.

A general of the Air Transport Command called us to order, and I could see he was extremely worried. He said, "We're losing this war in Korea. We're being driven back into the sea." He told us that the main reason they were being driven back was because their light cannon could not damage the North Korean tanks. "If we're going to save our troops from being driven into the sea," said the general, "we're going to have to get bazookas and ammunition over there immediately. They have to be flown over, right from the factory in Kentucky to Korea." His next words came as quite a surprise to me; he said, "We've got to do something quick, and we're not getting any help from you civilian airlines. The worst of you is Pan American."

I immediately raised my hand and said I had been on the telephone that morning with our San Francisco office, and I told him that we would be sending out the first DC-4 cargo plane loaded with bazookas before midnight. The general stopped, taken aback, and he sent a colonel to check. Then the general went on about how they had to have hundreds of commercial airplanes going to Korea as soon as possible. Just as the group was telling him he was going to get the necessary planes, the colonel came back and whispered to the general, who said, "It's true. Pan American is ready to go." It was gratifying to know that Pan Am was doing precisely what was needed, especially after the general's uncalled-for reprimand. But the general never apologized in public for what he'd said, and by that time I was quite annoyed. He came to me at the coffee break and apologized to me privately, but it seemed to me that after a public insult an apology isn't an apology unless it, too, is made in public.[12]

When the General found out that domestic airline four-engine planes couldn't cross the Pacific nonstop because they couldn't carry enough fuel, he was quite upset. He immediately sent a colonel off to order extra fuel tanks to retrofit commercial DC-4s. The general thought he would have the planes fitted with extra tanks in about a week. I stood up and said, "If I might suggest, I know something about retrofitting airplanes with extra tanks, and it isn't going to be done overnight. You have all sorts of fire safety problems. If I were handling this resupply, I'd get an aircraft carrier loaded with a hundred airplanes and sail full speed toward Korea. Within a few days you'd be within range for them all to fly in." He thanked me for my suggestion but went on to plan for retrofitting the planes.

Later, a friend of mine in the military said, "You look pretty worried, San. Don't be; it's always chaotic like this in the military. But we always win the war!" Of course, that time we didn't win. The military was terribly inefficient and they couldn't even find the fuel tanks in their depot to retrofit our planes.[13]

Our forces were in deep trouble in June and July of 1950. The military finally did get a carrier underway with planes loaded with supplies for Korea. Maybe somebody else thought of the idea I had suggested, even though the general ignored me. It was the obvious thing to do.[14]

# IATA: Labor Relations and Policies

*In 1945,* the top executives of the Western countries with airlines met together in Montreal to form the International Civil Aviation Organization, ICAO. Trippe went to it with our lawyer, John C. Cooper. During the meeting, Cooper called me and told me to get up there immediately to represent the technical side for the United States, as only government and military people were present. I went to Canada with our chief pilot, Sam Miller, and got the technical people from Trans-Canada there as well. From this the International Air Transport Association, IATA, was formed to help international cooperation in technical, traffic, and legal areas.[1]

The first IATA technical division met on November 5 and 6, at the Lexington Hotel in New York City. John Cooper was chairman of the executive committee, and my boss, Andre Priester, was vice-chairman. There were two representatives from each of the following: Canada (TCA), South America (Panagra), England (BOAC), the United States (Northwest, Trans World Airways, American, and Pan Am), France (Air France), and Norway (Royal Norwegian Air Transport, which later became SAS). As other countries formed airlines, they joined the organization.[2]

Cooper suggested that Stan Kryczkowski, a Polish aristocrat who had been a high official in the Polish airline but had escaped to Canada during the war, would make a good secretary general for the association. So Stan became our very able leader for many years to come, and a very good friend to me as well.

The IATA technical committee met twice a year in different countries, and attending these meetings became one of my major responsibilities. I remember many arguments through the years, and really tough decisions that were reached by mutual agreement. Utter chaos would have occurred if IATA had not been able to arrive at mutually acceptable rules and regulations to standardize such things as air controller language, airport procedures, and training. The IATA system now operates in every international airport throughout the world and is an excellent example of the possibilities of international cooperation.[3]

After the war, Pan Am started up its pilot training schools in San Francisco, Miami, and New York. We now provided even more inclusive training, teaching such things as international law and other sophisticated subjects. We applied the concept that the aircraft captain is like the captain of a ship.

Then somebody told Roosevelt that Pan Am was a subsidized U.S. mail carrier and only had one small union in Brownsville. That caused trouble, because Roosevelt was a great union booster. He got hold of the Secretary of Labor, Frances Perkins, and told her to inform us in no uncertain terms that if we wanted to stay a government mail carrier, we had to get unions. We pointed out to them that according to the Wagner Labor Relations Act, it was illegal to coerce us in such a way. But that didn't cut any ice with the White House, so we had to start dealing with unions late in 1944.[4]

The government told us that we should go out and promote unions among our employees. We soon got into massive union negotiations, and I went back to Harvard to get advice from my labor professor there, Sumner Slichter. He gave us a lot of help on how to write those first labor contracts so as to keep out of trouble as much as possible. Basically he showed me how to simplify the contracts. He said, "The union will still have a contract, but this is the time to keep it simple, because eventually it'll get as big as a Sears Roebuck Catalog."

During the war, it became impossible to get any new pilots; the military had taken them all. Our policy had been to assign newly hired pilots as navigators and radio operators, but as we promoted them we needed to replace the navigators. So we hired 4-Fs, men who had been rejected by the military for medical reasons but were in general good health. We sent them through our navigation school down in Miami and then put them to work on the airplanes.

We made it very clear that they were being hired only for the duration of the war, because of the pilot shortage, since our preference would be to continue to have new pilots initially serve as navigators and radio operators. But after agreeing to the terms of employment, they subsequently aligned themselves with a union and fought us for tenure. I was given the job of working out an agreement with them after the war. The need for navigators was rapidly decreasing anyway, because navigation aids and instruments were so much improved. A pilot would take a sighting once in a while to check his position, but it really wasn't necessary. Besides, the planes were now going much too fast for old-fashioned navigation. Because time in the air was shorter, we needed only two or three people on a big airplane, instead of the four or five necessary earlier. So we had a big row with those wartime navigators because they had agreed to leave at the end of the war, and we didn't need them anyway. They had joined the Transport Workers Union (TWU), a very aggressive union in New York City. When we held them to the agreement that the employment was only for the duration of the war, they threatened to call a strike and include our mechanics, who were also members of the TWU. We had no labor relations department at that time, so I was given the job because of my knowledge of operations.

The head of the TWU was a tough old Irishman named Mike Quill who always carried a cane called a shillelagh. He was an astute man, and, although he had little formal education, he helped us solve the navigator problem. To hear him talk, you would think he was completely unreasonable, waving his shillelagh around, but then he would take you off to one side and work with you. He made deals behind his men's backs, but he must have thought that was the only way to solve complex and emotional problems. He was an unexpected ally in bringing about a settlement for Pan Am and often got me aside during negotiations. "We don't want this radio operators' union," he said. "They aren't worth our while. It costs us more than it's worth." Mike trusted me. If what he had told me had gotten back to the navigators, he would have been in real trouble.

He then said, "The problem is that you folks don't want to give a little money." When I asked him how much, he answered, "Just a few thousand dollars per man. Think it over. For a reasonable bonus, I think we can sell these fellows on dropping the whole thing. They can be gradually phased out as this new radio telephone comes in." The new radio telephone would be operated by the pilots.

I took it up with Trippe and told him, "I think we should give these men a bonus if they will quit. A bonus is pretty reasonable, considering their job is being phased out anyway, and they did work for us all through the war." Trippe recognized that it would save us a lot of money in the long run. So we settled on a bonus of something like two thousand dollars per man, which took care of the problem.[5]

I found it amazing how that Irishman and I got the mess settled so quickly. How much better than all the usual fighting around the table and threats of a strike. Quill just took me aside and gave me a suggestion to carry back to my boss, which resulted in a prompt settlement.

Mike was quite a character. He had a big Cadillac, which his chauffeur would drive to the union meetings in Long Island City. The chauffeur would park behind the building, since Mike didn't want the union men to see it. One night, after we had discussed the problem of the radio operators, he said, "I'll drive you in to the city." He took me around to the back of the building, and there was the fancy chauffeur-driven Cadillac waiting for us.

Our mechanics were trained on the job under a master mechanic, and they all belonged to the same union, the TWU. There was also a very small A. F. of L. local in Brownsville, Texas, representing the mechanics there. We had no other unions at that time. But they were coming.

At Pan Am, as with every other company in the world, labor costs were one of the foremost concerns at all times. Sometimes, however, these matters took a peculiar course. When the war started, the pilots who flew for our new affiliated airline in Africa weren't as interested in extra pay as they were in a good life insurance policy for their families. Pan Am already had pilots' insurance policies for fifty thousand dollars, so we agreed on a war-risk policy of three hundred thousand dollars, which covered all injuries or causes of death. After we decided to set up such coverage, we couldn't get a single company or group in the United States to write that insurance, so we had to go to Lloyds of London. London was under heavy bombardment by the Germans, so our contract must have looked pretty good compared to local policies. When we wrote them about our requirements, they wired right back that we were covered. I was very surprised. A happy footnote: As I recall, we never lost a single crew member.

We liked to think of ourselves as being far ahead of the times, but one way in which Pan Am lagged behind was on the issue of female employees. We never hired women as pilots at any time during the war, despite the pilot shortage. Women were used by the government for transporting bombers and DC-3 and for other noncombat duties. In fact, qualified female pilots formed the WAFS (Women's Auxiliary Ferrying Service), under Nancy Love. They delivered for export or training everything the Air Force had, and they were soon joined by the WASPs (Women's Auxiliay Service Pilots). These were women who had received further training and were organized by Jacqueline Cochran. Women as well as men flew coastal patrol and also search and rescue missions for CAP (Civil Air Patrol), an auxiliary of the Air Force. My friend, Nancy Tier, was active in this service from the start, and in 1986 she became the first president of the International Women's Air and Space Museum. For the duration of the war, both the Navy and the Air Force commissioned private planes and boats to serve on anti-sub patrol.

In the early days, we had male stewards on all of our international flights. Back then the stewards had to do all kinds of heavy manual work, such as unloading the baggage. In many places we only had two flights a week, so we didn't have big ground crews. Also, at our first airports, we had some pretty primitive sleeping quarters, which, by the social rules of those days, wouldn't have been proper for women. It wasn't until after the war that we began to hire women.[6]

Another interesting story about Quill involves my first meeting with him. He had already organized the mechanics, and we asked each of our divisions to send one man to be its union representative. We met in Vice-President J. Frank Gledhill's office in the Chrysler Building. Frank was chief purchasing agent between Trippe and the manufacturers, but in the early union problems Frank was in charge of labor relations.[7] I was usually involved, due to my experiences in operations until a separate labor relations department was finally set up. He had asked me to attend because there was a certain problem concerning work rules that he knew was going to come up at the meeting. After I got there, all the union representatives marched in, along with Mike, holding his Irish shillelagh. The last few men who walked in were four or five blacks from Miami, representing the aircraft cleaners, who all were black. There was a brief period of absolute silence, and then some of the white union leaders from the South started to walk out of the room. Frank jumped up and yelled at the whites who were walking out, "We're not going to negotiate with any of you white guys if you don't let these black men in; they represent their men the same as you do."

At that moment, old Mike started pounding his shillelagh on the desk and said, "Now folks, lets all be calm." Mike managed to get the white union members to accept the blacks, so the meeting started. Mike was well ahead of the law on race matters, but of course he had several thousand dues-paying blacks in his union. The next day we reserved a room in the Lexington Hotel because Frank's office was too small. At lunch time we all went down to the hotel dining room. The head waiter came over to the blacks and asked them to leave. Can you imagine: they were part of the conference, but they couldn't even eat there! Mike Quill got involved again. He threatened to leave the hotel, but the hotel manager didn't budge—in fact, he said they'd cancel our meeting room if the blacks didn't leave the dining room. They could eat anywhere they wanted to, but not in his hotel.

At that point the blacks told Mike it had all gone far enough, and not to worry about it. They left the dining room. But that incident shocked me: In 1946, in supposedly liberal New York, black delegates to a meeting were not allowed to eat in the same dining room with whites.[8]

Mike always accented his Irish brogue. I think he went over to the Old Country and practiced it, so he could use it at meetings. I don't know why, but he took a liking to me, maybe because I was a little different from most business people he dealt with. I accepted him as an equal, and I'd listen to what he had to say. But he was as capable as any top businessman and probably could have switched jobs with the best of them.

Years later, after we started working on the 377 Stratocruiser, we had trouble with the pilots' union. The size of the planes made it look as if it would cut down on their jobs. When we had to decide on something, we would get the chief pilots together in order to discuss any ideas they might have. One time in Miami we were discussing the cockpit layout and the size of the crews on them, and there was quite a difference of opinion. When they couldn't agree, I wasn't going to override them. I said, "Look, I've taken this hotel room for the night. You guys can stay here until you reach an agreement." They finally agreed on three-man crews on flights over eight hours.[9]

But the pilots' union wasn't a big factor at that point. Scott Flower, one of our chief pilots, never did join the union; he had been with us long before it came into being. The union pilots had confidence in him, and they seemed more interested in what the pay scale would be than in the number of pilots on board. However, those big airplanes were a threat to the pilots if they were flown with just two pilots. Theoretically, one 747 flight equaled about three 707 flights.

The manager of the Miami office came up to New York to see Trippe and told him that it was going to cost millions to change planes to handle a three-man crew, and it was a waste of money. He also attacked me for supporting the idea. Trippe called me down to his office and said, "We've been talking about the idea of having a three-man crew on our planes. It would be a big problem from a cost standpoint."

I replied, "Yes, that's true. But you're going to have to spend it one way or the other, and it'll cost you a fortune if you have to change the arrangement afterwards. Better to do it in advance, since the government is going to make us do it anyway." I had confidential information from friends in Washington that the Federal Aviation Agency was about to announce that they would require a three-man crew.[10]

The other airlines accused me of influencing the Washington regulators after our pilots had decided on a three-man crew. But I didn't influence them at all. They went out to Boeing, and, after looking at the problem pretty thoroughly, they made up their own minds.

The regulations required that you have either three pilots or two pilots and a flight engineer. FAA never required the third man to be pilot-qualified, but their intention was to phase out the flight engineers. The regulations permitted us to continue to use the flight engineer in place of the third pilot, provided we demonstrated that we were trying to make the change. We promoted as many engineers as we could to pilots, and the others were gradually retired or moved to ground work.[11]

Another problem we had with the pilots concerned retirement age. Our pilots all joined the union after the war, and they were pressing us in contract negotiations to remove the age limits. The pension plans for pilots required retirement at sixty years at the maximum, which already was a little farther than we felt was safe. I got the airlines all together, through the Air Transport Association, and we agreed to go to the FAA and recommend that sixty be made the legal maximum. The unions wanted to take out any reference to a maximum age limit. They said we could have doctors check pilots and certify them. But we knew how inaccurate that could be. One of our pilots died of a heart attack right after he'd had a perfect electrocardiogram test. Because pilot pay was so high, it was a temptation for a man to continue to fly even after he didn't feel up to it any longer. Even before age sixty, we felt that pilots were getting overtired, so sixty was our absolute maximum.

Fortunately, Pete Quesada (General Elwood Quesada), an ex-U.S. Army Air Corps general, was part of the Air Transport Command. He had been sent down to help start the Cuban Air Force while I was in Cuba as an airport manager, and I had met him then. His response to the age limit was, "Oh hell, sixty's too high." It was fine for him to have that attitude; he was not a civilian dealing with the unions. Then he added, "In the Air Force, you can't fly after fifty unless you have a younger pilot in the aircraft with you." But sixty was only the absolute maximum. Any airline could put in a lower maximum, if they could persuade their pilots to go along with it.

So Quesada agreed to sixty. Otherwise, I don't think we would ever have reached an agreement. It came in the nick of time, because we were already getting pressure from our pilots' unions. Of course, the union then took it to court. But as I pointed out to Pete and all the others, this wasn't just a question of economics; we could probably save money the longer we could use these guys. It was the safety of the passengers that was most important. We didn't think that a man past the age of sixty should be flying a loaded passenger airplane. It was time for him to retire.

Later, Eastern Airlines and Rickenbacker made a big fuss. Although their operations manager agreed with Quesada on this joint statement to the FAA, when Rickenbacker heard about it, he refused to go along with the plan. I wondered if Rickenbacker opposed the plan because a man in that age group would be almost as old as himself; he was sixty-five or more at the time.[12]

# The Beginning of the Jet Age

*In the early years,* there was plenty of room in the top management for generalists—people who could work in many fields and not just a narrow specialty. As I have mentioned, it was this versatility which got Pan Am going in the first place. As far as I was concerned, it was an excellent way to make employees' lives more interesting. But after the war, management at Pan Am began to specialize. Although I worked on the initial union negotiations due to my business school experience and later got involved with international development, I became concerned mainly with flight engineering. A large part of my job consisted of the development and purchase of airplanes. I wasn't a generalist anymore, which I suppose became true of work throughout the United States. Many companies had become so big that you had to be a specialist to survive.

You might say that the jet age began with an idea that developed right after the war. Prop planes often needed short extra boosts for takeoffs, and some people thought we could use a JATO, or Jet Assisted Take-Off device, for commercial planes. We figured that if we could develop JATO so that it was safe, we could increase our payload. We made quite a few test flights in Mexico City, and, while it worked, the conversion was so expensive and difficult that it didn't prove out economically.[1]

In the early 1950s we became interested in the development of an aircraft that would be longer and larger, with bigger engines and greater range than the planes we were using. The manufacturer, an English company named Bristol, was promising us specifications that would offer even transatlantic capabilities. We had doubts that they could do it, because they first needed to design an engine that was big enough. We negotiated a contract that gave us the right to take a dozen of these big airplanes, provided they met our specs, but it didn't commit us to buy. We weren't willing to be committed on something so vague, although we were very interested in watching the development of that airplane. Up to then, no American manufacturers had gone into commercial jets; they were building jets only for the military.[2]

One of the earliest short-range jets, the De Havilland Comet I, wasn't really of much interest to us. And unfortunately, it had an ill-fated career, with a series of accidents. One plane exploded over Italy because of a defect in the design. Other problems caused the engine to explode. After only a few months of commercial aviation service they had to withdraw the plane from use and go back to the drawing boards to redesign it.[3]

In 1951, Trippe sent me and Frank Gledhill, Pan Am's purchasing agent, to Douglas Aircraft, where we were to meet the people from Rolls-Royce, a British engine manufacturer. They were looking into the possibility of converting our still-undelivered Douglas DC-6Bs to turbo-prop engines, a type of jet engine with propellers. I said, "Frank, this is ridiculous. We should get a pure jet engine instead of a turboprop. We've had enough trouble with propellers coming off our Boeing prop-driven airplanes. I'm allergic to propellers. We shouldn't have anything to do with them." We'd had three or four situations where the propellers cut loose, and that is why we lost an airplane down in the Brazilian jungle.

A key reason I didn't want to see any more big propellers was because Hamilton Standard, the propeller manufacturer, didn't possess the necessary techniques to find out for certain if there were cracks in them. After the Brazilian accident, I went through Hamilton Standard's shops and saw all these big blades being made for various airplanes. Over in a corner I spotted about a hundred blades with yellow marks on them. I asked one of the workmen what they were, and he said, "Those are cracked blades."

So I got the manager and said, "Look at these."

He said, "Yes, they are rejects from propellers made for your airplanes." And it was clear to me that if the percentage of known rejects was that high, they couldn't be catching all of them. We did switch to heavier, solid-aluminum blades, but that cut our payload considerably.[4]

In any event, the people from Rolls-Royce were very excited about our mission, since Pan Am had twenty or thirty DC-6Bs on order. Donald Douglas called in his engineers, and they laid out some sketches of ways to put the jet-prop engines onto the airplane. There was no question that you could modify the prototype—if you had the engine. We spent three days in talks with the Douglas engineering department, but in all that time nobody asked the crucial question: "When will the engines from Rolls-Royce be ready for delivery?"

On Friday, the third day, I finally said, "Look, I'm going crazy sitting here talking about something that doesn't exist and maybe isn't realistic. I think Pratt and Whitney can have a commercial jet engine ready just as quickly as this jet-prop adaptation. They're building them for the military now, and they can modify them for commercial aircraft. How long will it take?"

The engineers went out to discuss the time factor, and, while they were out, Donald Douglas said they couldn't have any engines before 1958 or 1959, since they didn't even have a prototype. Finally they came back and said, "It looks like we can start commercial deliveries of the airplane with the propeller engine in October 1959." And mind you, this was 1951. So the turboprop engine idea gave way to the full jet.[5]

When Gledhill and I met with Donald Douglas to discuss engines for the DC-6Bs, he still wasn't sure he wanted to get into building a jet plane. Most of his directors didn't like the idea; they thought jet travel was too much of a risk. Stick to propeller planes for passengers, they said. Their research and development people had been feeding them stories of problems with the military aircraft. Douglas personally thought they ought to go on to the next development stage, but he didn't know whether his directors would go along with it.[6]

In July of 1954 Gledhill and I were on another trip to Los Angeles when we got a phone call from Wellwood Beall, the chief engineer at Boeing in Seattle. He said, "Before you go back to New York, how about coming up to Seattle tomorrow? I've talked our people into giving you a ride on our new airplane. It's only been up once. I haven't been on it myself." We knew Boeing had built a prototype of a commercial jet, but we didn't know whether it had been flown or not. They'd built it with their own money, with the net worth of the whole company at risk. Of course, they had previously learned a lot from the military jets they were building. They used a basic engine setup in the wing, but they developed a different kind of fuselage, modified for passenger planes, with a sharp angling back of the wings that enabled the plane to reduce drag and fly much faster.[7]

Frank called up Trippe, who said, "Okay, go look at it." He wasn't too enthusiastic about pushing it too fast because we were taking delivery on all these new DC-6Bs. So we went up to Seattle.

Late in the evening, Frank called up an insurance agent at home. When I asked him why, he said, "Hell, I want some insurance if I ride on this damn airplane. I got you a million and me a million!" And so the next morning, bright and early, we went out to the Boeing field. The prototype had a typical commercial airplane shape, but it was bigger than a DC-6B, and longer.

There were mechanics crawling all over one of the wings. I went out to look around, and then came back and told Frank, "We aren't going to fly today. They've got an engine hanger that's busted, and that's going to take a while." On seeing the plane it occurred to me: weighing 124 tons, it was 124 times heavier than the first plane Bill Boeing built in 1916.[8]

We had dinner with Beall that night at his house. He said, "Howard Hughes called me up from somewhere in Florida. He had heard about our prototype and wanted an option on ten of the first airplanes, sight unseen. I told him to send a Hughes technical group up here and let us work up a contract; that's the standard procedure. Hughes was quite unhappy and said, 'If my word isn't good enough, then the hell with you,' and he hung up." Howard Hughes was the major stockholder of TWA. Beall then said that he knew Hughes was going to keep calling but that he would not tell him we were there.[9]

The next day we went out to the airfield again. Beall reminded us that he hadn't yet been up in the plane. We walked over to climb aboard the plane through a trap door, just behind the cockpit, with our parachutes on. Beall was a very portly fellow from eating too much for years, and it didn't look like he was going to fit through the trap door. So he said, "Hell, I'll leave the parachute off. And if that means I'd have to go out in the cold with no coat or chute on if we have trouble at thirty thousand feet, I guess I'll just stick with the airplane." There were a lot of laughs about that. So he removed the chute, tried again, and this time everything worked. We took off and climbed straight up.

I was particularly interested in hearing what the noise level was in a plane with jet engines, so I went up to the chief pilot and asked him to cut the engines back. That way we could tell how much was engine noise and how much was air noise. I hadn't told the engineers and mechanics with Beall about my request. When all of a sudden the engines cut off, they went rushing forward, ready to jump. But I found out that the engine noise was acceptable. With the addition of normal insulation, you would have a nice, quiet cabin.

We turned the engines on again, and I went back to explain what we were doing. We tried single-engine, two-engine, and three-engine flight; the performance was very good in each case. It could hold altitude pretty well even on one and two engines. However, the prototype plane didn't have much gross weight; fully loaded it would be a different story. The next thing we did was check the plane's performance on landings and takeoffs, which also went smoothly. What speed, what power! I had never had such an experience in my life.[10]

Trippe put a lot of faith in our judgment concerning the technical aspects of a plane, and he always backed us up. He was more concerned with the economic side. Would the jets be ready before the new DC 6Bs now on order wore out? And would Pan Am have the cash to purchase the jets when they were ready? We discussed the prototype performance and these other questions with Trippe on our return to New York. Afterwards, Pan Am decided to sign a temporary agreement with Boeing to assure us a first delivery position. It was a gamble, because once we signed we couldn't sneak away. If the planes met certain specifications, we were committed to buying them.[11]

Howard Hughes kept calling Boeing, but we had gotten the first delivery position. We ordered twenty-six planes. Hughes still had some options, but one of our lawyers, Henry Friendly, was concerned about an antitrust suit if Pan Am had such a corner on the jet market. Personally, I could never see it. It was a free market, and we weren't cornering it. There were still plenty more companies out there who could build jet engines; it would just take them a few months longer. However, this was during the 1950s, when General Motors and Dupont had been defendants in the courts for almost twenty-five years in antitrust suits.[12]

Furthermore, Boeing couldn't go ahead with the program unless they could get orders for fifty airplanes. They couldn't afford to tool up on just our order. It wouldn't even pay for their research and development. So we agreed to take only the first ten planes, and then Boeing could alternate sales between us and other airlines to make up the run of fifty.[13] On October 13, 1955, at the annual meeting of the International Civil Aviation Organization, Trippe announced that Pan American had ordered forty-five jets, between Boeing and Douglas. You could have heard a pin drop; it caught everybody by surprise. This was by far the largest order ever placed by an airline.

In an industry of our kind, where the chief players of the game all know each other, it's most extraordinary that our purchases didn't leak out. I'm sure some technical people in some of the other major airlines knew we were visiting Boeing and Douglas, but then everybody else was, too. Most people thought it would be at least five years before anything would happen regarding jets. In fact, the domestic airlines didn't want them, and they didn't think anybody else would have the nerve to go out and order untested jets with a whole fleet of undepreciated airplanes in operation.[14]

The next morning I had breakfast in Chicago with Bob Gross, the president of Lockheed. I was eating my cereal when Bob called the waiter over and asked for a newspaper. When he opened the paper, there was the headline: "Pan Am Orders 45 Jets." You should have seen his face; it turned pale, and he dropped the newspaper and said, "My God! You are always upsetting the apple cart. Here I'm just coming out with the new Electra turboprop, and at the same time, you will be starting service with these jets that are twice as fast!"

We had been using twelve two-engine Lockheed Electras that we had gotten in the 1930s in Alaska. In 1946, just after the war, we got some four-engine Lockheed Constellations, which were very successful. Lockheed was now working on a four-engine turboprop Electra, which the domestic airlines were buying, but it did not have sufficient range for nonstop overseas travel. Unfortunately, the turboprop Electra was a disaster, and it had a lot of serious accidents.[15]

After the announcement, we went out to Donald Douglas and he gave us a shock: he said his board hadn't yet approved construction of a jet, and he wasn't sure they were going to after all. On learning that Douglas might drop out, we went to Lockheed again and said we wanted a jet design from them, too. It was to our advantage to get designs from different manufacturers because commercial jets were a new, unproven product, and we knew that competition would make it a better product for everybody. Finally, Donald Douglas took the information to his directors, and, when TWA ordered twenty more Boeing jets, Douglas decided to go ahead with their jet plane. This became the DC-8. It was much more precarious for Douglas than for Boeing, with the B-52 experience of building jets for the military, but Donald Douglas was ready for the gamble and did it with the company's own money. Pan Am paid $245 million for this first jet fleet from Boeing and Douglas.[16]

Many of the domestic airlines initially said that they wouldn't use the jets, but soon they all started ordering them; I guess they were afraid of the competition getting ahead of them. Passengers would be getting a taste for jet planes on the international carriers, and they would want them on domestic flights as well. Today it is difficult to remember air travel before the jets.

Unfortunately, my boss, André Priester, who had had such a part in developing the jets, did not live to see them in the air. He died while chairing an IATA meeting in Paris in November 1955. The abrupt Dutchman was a man of few words, but a man with a keen mind. He was acknowledged as one of the best engineers in the industry, yet his brusque manner and way of dealing with people did not attract them. I reported to many different officers off and on within the company, but he was always my official boss. He was stern, formal, and demanding, but always fair and honest. I got along with him very well and in my estimation he was largely responsible for Pan Am's leadership in the technical field of aviation.

# Jet Travel Becomes a Reality

*The military had been* developing and using jet engines for years. There was a curious relationship among commercial airlines, the military, and research scientists at the universities during this period shortly after the war. The airplane manufacturers had their own engineers to carry out military research and production, but, of course, their engineers had contacts with the universities. They used the NASA test lab in California, and the lab got help from various West Coast schools as well as from the government. In addition, development of commercial airplanes had often followed military advances, and it would be fair to say that the military development of jet-engine technology provided an immense boost to commercial aviation. Although many changes were made, the same companies that produced the military engines went on to develop engines for commercial use. The United States government had again contributed to commercial aviation by subsidizing the original research and development for the military. A private company would never have been able to afford the astronomical costs.[1]

The airplanes built by Boeing and Douglas were quite similar in design. The two companies were perfectly willing to cooperate and exchange ideas that they didn't consider secret, so we all worked together. The only commercial jet engine then available in the United States was made by Pratt and Whitney. A British company, Wright, was building an engine in this country, but they didn't spend much money on it. I had been to Pennsylvania to see their test location, which was associated with the University of Pennsylvania. They had bought thousands of acres of land, and the fellow running it was a Wall Street financier. I got the feeling that he had more interest in the real estate value of the place than he did in the airplane business.

When we visited the Wright aeronautical test location in the fifties, they had improved the British design and had developed what they considered a state-of-the-art jet engine. I felt I should thoroughly investigate this engine, so I asked them to run some tests. The results didn't come close to the Pratt and Whitney test results; the Wright engine's RPMs were limited, and it didn't have the type of high-strength metal in the blades that would be necessary to withstand the high operating heat. Pratt and Whitney was already way ahead of Wright with air-cooled blades. Also, Wright's fuel consumption was much too high, and fuel consumption relates directly to how much payload you can carry.[2]

We didn't have too many problems with the Pratt and Whitney engine, although some of the early models for the 707 jet overheated when idling on the runway. The first Pratt and Whitney jet engines, the J-57s, were too small, so we got a commitment from them to build the JT-3D with an aft fan. However, we still needed longer range. Pratt and Whitney was testing a military engine, the J-75, for a high-performance fighter. Although the J-75 was classified because it had been developed for military, Gledhill was able to make a deal with Pratt and Whitney and the military to commit the engines to Pan Am.[3]

The original six 707s with JT-3D engines functioned well enough, but they were not sufficient for nonstop transatlantic flights. We usually had to stop at Gander, although with a good tail wind the plane could sometimes make the flight without stopping. We used these planes successfully in the Latin American division for many years, until they were replaced on the transatlantic routes by the long-awaited larger Boeing 707 with the J-75 engine.[4]

Scott Flower and John Borger did the acceptance flying. I went out to the West Coast with them, and Boeing formally gave us the keys to the new 707. We took off across the U.S., and it seemed that every air traffic controller in the country was talking to us. "What kind of airplane is that?" they wanted to know. "I can't keep you on the radar, you're going so fast; I picked you up in Topeka, and now you're already in Wichita! Are you flying a meteor or something?" We stopped at our Miami base, then Puerto Rico, and finally landed in New York. Why the roundabout route? We would not have to pay New York City or State sales taxes if the plane landed in New York as an offshore delivery.[5]

Pan Am was the first airline to go overseas to the Antilles, it was the first airline to cross the Pacific, the first airline to cross the Atlantic, and the first to go around the world. On October 26, 1958, it would bring in the jet age by flying the first scheduled trip by jet from New York to Paris.

Captain Sam Miller, a good friend of mine, flew that first passenger flight as chief pilot for the Atlantic division. To prepare, he made test runs to four European capital cities. The plane, being fifteen times as powerful, twice as fast, and twice as big as planes up to that time, needed a much more precise flight plan to manage the extra bulk and speed. Once we started flying these planes nonstop to Europe, the enthusiasm for air travel was tremendous, and we had long waiting lists. We decided to charter one of the first new planes to National Airlines between scheduled European flights. National flew the plane from New York to Miami and back, on a scheduled basis, advertised as the "first domestic airline to fly jets." This made TWA and American so mad that they took us to court. They said we were breaking the law by subleasing a Pan Am international plane to a domestic carrier. They didn't win; they had no basis for suing us, as planes were frequently chartered between airlines.[6]

The new 707s radically altered the face of Pan Am's worldwide system and simplified the logistics of air travel. We were able to cut down considerably on the fueling stations we had to have for the old prop-driven planes, both in the South Atlantic and the South Pacific. On the first flight I made in 1935 from San Francisco to Manila, we had to stop constantly; our longest nonstop flight was to Honolulu. As the jets developed, we kept getting more and more range from them. American transoceanic aircraft have always been superior to those produced anywhere else, and one of the secrets was that the U.S. companies developed a better blade metal as well as more efficient air cooling system for the blades.[7]

But then the jet age almost ended for us as suddenly as it started: Our pilots went on strike because no jet pay scale had been agreed upon. We offered them more money, but they didn't think it was enough. Then an interesting thing happened. I had been head of personnel relations for pilots since before the war, so most of the more senior pilots knew and liked me. One day some of them came to my house and volunteered to break the strike, but Trippe wouldn't okay it. He said there might be some violence, with bad publicity, and he probably was right. Members of Pan Am management, who were also pilots, tried to keep the system operating, and the union couldn't object to that. They kept the European flights going, which fortunately were limited to the six early 707s. As the intercontinental 707 model would not be available for a year, we had to provide crews for only these six airplanes. For navigators, we went back to a few of our wartime nonpilot navigators who were still working as navigation instructors. This allowed us to fly the airplanes without interruption while we worked out the jet pay scale with the union. Our management pilots did all the jet flying for almost six months.[8]

It was during this period in 1959 that we had a close call. Pan Am's administrative pilots were still manning the Atlantic schedule. One of our flights was coming back from Europe with a full load of passengers, and the crew was pretty tired. As they were coming into Newfoundland, Captain Waldo Lynch, the chief technical pilot for radio communications, went back to the toilet and left the pilot from the Pacific division at the controls. The man was so tired he fell asleep, and when Waldo felt the airplane lurch, he scrambled out of the toilet, crawled forward on his hands and knees, and got to the captain's seat to find they were into a dive. Waldo later said that the pilot woke in a daze after the plane started to dive. He didn't know where he was or what was going on. Waldo could see the ocean coming up at them, so he braced his feet on the floor and used all of his strength to pull the wheel back. The plane dove from thirty thousand feet to about five, when Waldo pulled it out just seconds before it would have hit the water.

They struggled into the Newfoundland airport with the passengers pretty shaken up. The FAA decided it was clearly the pilot's error, and he was so frightened by the experience that he quit flying, although he continued to work for Pan Am until he retired. We knew he was just tired, like a truck driver going off the road because he had been driving too long. Still, if the plane had crashed, it could have slowed down the whole jet age. We would never have known why; this was before the famous flight recorder (or "black box," as it was nicknamed)was required to include a locater beacon.[9]

Despite the FAA's decision that the near-crash was pilot error, we got Boeing in on the incident, because we felt that it had been too easy for the aircraft to go into a dive. It was on automatic pilot at the time, but the autopilot became disconnected without a warning indication. We were having a lot of trouble with automatic controls for the jet, but otherwise I had only praise for Boeing's plane, which had not been designed to withstand the kind of force generated by this dive.

We eventually got the pilot's strike settled, and, remembering that dive, we instituted special resting periods for the crew members. We also kept three pilots on each jet, and the FAA ruled that they could never leave either of the two pilot seats unoccupied.[10]

Once the Boeing 707 was operational, it became the world's prototype for subsonic jets. In Europe, since they had missed the boat on the subsonic market, the British and French decided to make a leap forward and beat out the Americans in the next round, which presumably would be the supersonics. They agreed that they should not compete with each other on this, because they needed their combined resources in order to build the best aircraft possible. So they negotiated an agreement whereby they would jointly produce an airplane called the Concorde. I couldn't see any profitable economics in the projected plane, but Trippe didn't want anyone to get the jump on him. He quickly took out an option in June of 1963 to buy the first three planes, but they never passed the safety and technical specifications that my department required.[11]

As technical overseer of any deals for foreign planes, I went to Europe several times to check the Concorde's development, although this took time from the more important Boeing 747, the jumbo jet, which we were working on at the same time. The French-British Concorde did not make economic sense, because it used gasoline when kerosene only cost twleve cents a gallon. The last time I went there to check the Concorde's progress, the price of fuel in France had risen to over a dollar a gallon. Technologically it is a fine plane, but it did not have enough passenger space to make it economically viable. I showed the French company my cost-effectiveness projections, which demonstrated that the Concorde could not be flown without a subsidy, a luxury which wasn't available in the United States. I suggested that they end production with the twelve planes already built and make a deal with the military to use them for high-speed transport to trouble spots or for moving high officials. Understandably, they were not cheered by what I said, but when England tried to cancel further work because of the mounting costs, the labor unions and the French government would not agree to stop.

The first time I went to the Dassault plant in Bordeaux, there were Mystere fighters all over the field, beautiful machines. I asked, "What are you doing with them? Are they finished?"

And they said, "Oh, yes; they have been bought by Israel. But the French government won't let us deliver them." I learned that the French were friendly with the Syrians, and had been for years, and therefore France was blocking the sale of any weapons to Syria's enemy.

The Dassault people also showed us a new business jet design they had come up with called the Falcon. It was a good small airplane, a competitor with the American-built Lear jet. When we walked into the hangar where they were building the Falcons, the employees all left their work and surrounded us. It turned out they wanted more pay, and they thought they might put heat on the management when potential purchasers were there. The company manager, Vallieres, pushed his way to the forefront, grabbed the union leader and said, "Look, if you don't get this thing over with right now, you're going to lose a lot of work for your men, because Pan Am is just about ready to walk out of here and cancel their contract."

We ended up ordering several Falcons and got a good price on them. When they subsequently informed us they were ready to begin delivery, I went over to Bordeaux with our chief test pilot, Scott Flower, to try out the first airplane. While Scott was up doing the test, the owner of the airplane factory, Mr. Dassault, called from Paris. He was a French Jew who had been sent to Auschwitz by the Nazi occupation and barely escaped the gas chamber. Before World War II, his name was Marcel Bloch, but he adopted his brother's code name from the French Resistance after the war. Dassault said that he wanted to speak to the Pan Am test pilot the minute he got down. As soon as Scott landed, he was put on the phone, and Dassault asked him what he'd learned about the Falcon. Scott told him there was just one major problem: the airplane had very bad stalling characteristics, and he did not think that the FAA would certify it that way. Scott had a list of about ten other minor things he wanted changed, but he liked the airplane overall. Mr. Dassault got the manager of the plant on the phone and said, "Get the list from the chief test pilot and do all of the things he wants." Just like that. The factory had to redesign the wing to correct the stall problem, adding a leading-edge device.[12]

Trippe told Dassault that he wanted the interior stripped out of the Falcon so that we could customize them for other buyers. Unfortunately, Trippe agreed to buy thirty-six Falcons a year, regardless of whether we sold them or not. This put us in the business of buying and selling airplanes. Such an arrangement was a novelty in those days, but nowadays, of course, everybody gets into everything. We were soon in serious trouble, because the customized planes weren't selling fast enough.

They were terrific airplanes. We called in the chief pilots of various corporate groups to fly them, and they were very enthusiastic. The airplane quickly became the quality item in the business jet market, even though it was more expensive than the competition. Then we ran into a recessionary business period, and the sales stopped. But the planes kept coming, one almost every week. We couldn't even find a place to store them. So I finally sent our purchasing manager to try to slow this automatic pipeline of airplanes to the point where we could get them as we needed them. I didn't know how enthusiastic the factory would be about that, but I knew we would go broke if the planes kept coming and nobody bought them. The Pan Am team negotiated with the Dassault company, and they agreed to slow down production depending on market demand. Did Pan Am make any money in the long run? I doubt it.[13]

There is an interesting anticlimax to this involving Federal Express. We had all these Falcons—I think there were about thirty of them—sitting in a field. One day our vice-president of purchasing, Howard Blackwell, came to me and said, "There's a fellow waiting outside who wants to see me about making a rent/purchase deal on a few Falcons. What should I tell him? He's a young guy who looks like he's just out of high school."

I said, "Let's have him in. I'd be interested in anything to get rid of those Falcons."

His name was Fred Smith, and he said, "I've got tentative contracts from several banks to transport canceled checks between banks in the big cities of the United States. The idea is to speed up the dead time when the money isn't earning them any interest. I can get access to several hundred thousand dollars to start with, but I can't buy the airplanes outright now. So what I would like to do is get them on a rental, with an option to purchase when the business takes off." By this time Howard was looking more than a little dubious. He thought this was just a fly-by-night kid with a hair-brained idea. But something told me there was substance to this fellow. I asked Smith what he would call his company, and he replied, "Federal Express."

I told Howard, "Give him a chance; we could do worse. What are we going to do with all of them anyway? They're just deteriorating out there in the field." But I never dreamed that Fred Smith would be so successful that within six months he would buy all thirty planes. He's a multimillionaire today.[14]

# The Jumbo Jet

*In 1966 we ordered* an even larger jet from Boeing, the 747 jumbo jet. All told, it took about four years from the time we set up our specs and signed the contract until delivery, which is remarkably quick for such a big airplane.

I was thinking of that plane the other day, after I saw a program on television about whales. The whales were the same shape as the mockup of the 747 we worked with in the early days. It looked just like a humpback due to the fact that the cockpit was placed high above the large cargo-loading doors in the nose of the plane. The wives of Pan Am's directors then added a spiral stairway and an upstairs dining room for first-class passengers. This stairway was quite a feature of the plane, and the press photographers loved it, using it to pose celebrities for photos.

We took a dim view of that upstairs lounge in the engineering department, because the staircase added several tons. It reduced our payload considerably, so we had to find ways to add more power. But adding engine power required ever-increasing weight. I was afraid we would end up with a white elephant, like Howard Hughes's Spruce Goose, the giant plywood airplane that never got off the ground. And how do you pay for it? The staircase made great advertising and was very dramatic, but only the engineering department thought about how many thousands of pounds of extra weight we would be lugging along that didn't pay for itself.[1]

One major problem with the 747 mockup was the cockpit design. We had a lot of new instruments and equipment, everything we could get that was the very latest thing. We had Boeing draft a typical cockpit and instrument placement, and then we tried out several versions of it. There was a big controversy among the pilots about switching from circular readings of knots, air speed and such, to a vertical reading. TWA wanted the vertical reading, but, after much discussion, we kept the circular instruments.[2]

The 747 was finally finished in December 1969, and it was superb. I retired in 1972, thinking that it was the best transoceanic plane that could be built for many years to come. It had all the safety devices known at that time, including triple inertial navigation systems that could take you from an airport on one side of an ocean to within a couple of miles of a point on the other side. It was fantastic when I remembered the early flights into Latin America only forty years earlier, when we had to fly by day and never knew for certain that we would hit our destination.[3]

The big new plane required a complete change in the ground-support system, and Boeing helped us in designing auxiliary equipment to provide the servicing of the planes. They even designed new passenger ramps and cargo loaders. There was nothing in the contract that required it, but they wanted to sell the airplanes to other airlines, and they figured that such equipment would help. They weren't merely selling a carrier, they were selling a total transport system.

Converting to jets required new ladders, the tractors had to be bigger, and you needed jet starters, which were particularly expensive. Then there was the elaborate fueling setup. Although the engines were very advanced, with much more efficient fuel consumption, one of these 747s took on thousands of gallons each time it was fueled. Conversion of ground equipment was a major expense, and we had only two years to complete the conversions before the first jets were delivered.[4]

The 747 had to have runways of at least ten thousand feet in length, which meant that a number of airports that were satisfactory for Electras, DC-7s, and smaller jets could not accept the 747s. The cities would not let us come in with these fast airplanes unless something was done about their runways. We got a lot of help on this problem from local agencies, and organizations such as the Port Authority of the City of New York helped to finance airport reconstruction. But in return they charged us heavily for landing fees. The costs did not stop with the planes, that was for sure.[5]

A number of airports around the world already had gone to ten-thousand-foot runways. In the early fifties, the technical committee of the International Air Transport Association (IATA) began setting up similar system standards for airport facilities worldwide. I had proposed ten thousand feet as a minimum standard worldwide in anticipation of larger, faster planes.

While IATA had no power to make airports do what we said, we simply said that unless they gave us ten thousand feet, we couldn't come in. Eventually, they all followed suit and put in the facilities we recommended. Then we got the length of ten thousand feet approved by the International Civil Aviation Organization. Even then, the new turboprop planes, when heavily loaded, were requiring ever-longer runway lengths. I remember coming into Johnson Island, between Hawaii and Tahiti, and the plane barely stopped before we reached the far end of the too-short runway.

Just as we started working on the 747, Pete Quesada, who had become head of the FAA, called me down to Washington for a meeting with some generals of the Air Force. Their plan was to cut costs by having a common airplane for both military and commercial air transport. On the face of it, that seemed like a pretty good idea, but practically speaking it wouldn't work. For one thing, the military had to have short-field capability so they could land in emergency situations, even on grass fields and short runways. That would have required building in extra-sturdy landing gear, thereby adding extra weight. By the time you got through, it wouldn't have been economical to develop one plane for such different purposes.

We had a long meeting, and those Air Force generals were adamant about going into this all-purpose-airplane business. However, I had visions of working with all that bureaucracy and what a nightmare it would be, with everything going through five echelons of experts before we'd be able to get authorization to move forward. But since I knew they were touchy about such criticism, I simply told them that the two kinds of transports, military and commercial, were just not compatible. "Your mission and our mission are very different," I said. "Your mission is to get into unprepared fields, behind the battle lines, and into small airports, but we don't operate that way. We have to scrape every pound off these airplanes and build them as light as we can to create a maximum payload, always consistent with the safety factor." Finally the generals recognized my point, and the idea was scrapped.[6]

We completely changed our method of purchasing airplanes in the case of the 747. In the early days we used to present the manufacturer with a book as big as a dictionary, containing all the details of how we wanted it, down to how the hinges on the doors should be made. However, when the 747 was being developed, our staff provided only technical consultation and a list of basic requirements. We worked out precise operating performance guarantees spelling out payload for distance, runway length, the various loads, gross weight, and climb to maximum altitude. Then the manufacturer would give us the figures specifying what they said they could do. We allowed them to vary from the specs by a small amount without voiding the

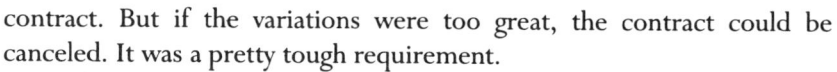

contract. But if the variations were too great, the contract could be canceled. It was a pretty tough requirement.

The FAA regulations covered the safety aspects of design, and the durability was covered by warranties from Boeing. Boeing spelled out in their warranty that the plane would be good for a minimum of fifty thousand hours at such and such a weight, plus specs on the durability of the airframe, the engines, and so on. But we had frequent meetings between the Boeing design groups and specialized technical staff from Pan Am and the other 747 customers. These meetings would occur at key decision points during the final design process, particularly prior to selection of competitive subcontractors for crucial technical systems in the cockpit.

In order to prepare our ground-crew personnel to service the aircraft, we sent the engineers of each division out to Boeing many times. Before we took delivery of the planes, a small group of our pilots and mechanics were trained out at Boeing so that they could come back and train the others.

Our greatest concern was safety with an airplane as big as the 747. Furthermore, with so many passengers on board, we didn't want the plane coming in like a hot-dog fighter plane. We wanted it to come in with some degree of cushion, so we had asked for an optimum air speed of about ninety-five knots for landings under normal conditions. But with one thing and another, approach and landing speeds had jumped practically ten knots before Boeing switched from the triple to the double flap. Finally, by lightening the load by three or four thousand pounds, we were able to reduce the landing speed.

The 747s worked out surprisingly well. At first everybody in the industry said that it was too big, that we would not be able to fill that airplane. Executives I knew at the domestic airlines said, "San, it's ridiculous. Why do you want it so big?" My response was that aviation was increasing in popularity, airports were getting congested, and we simply couldn't move enough people in and out of the airports in the smaller planes. By the time the planes came on line, we were having terrible travel delays at the airports. You could be as late as an hour landing in New York, and you would see twenty planes lined up ready to take off. Furthermore, the economics of size in the case of the 747 was twenty-five percent better—less cost per seat-mile than any other airplane ever built.[7]

Although people were skeptical at first, the 747 quickly became a most popular carrier worldwide, in even small countries. In fact, it seemed like the first thing a new Third World country got was a runway and a 747.[8]

# Personalities

*W*<sub>hoever said</sub> "What makes a life is the people in it" made a lot of sense. I was certainly fortunate in regard to the people I knew: those early aviation pioneers were remarkable men, outstanding in so many respects. Some became my close friends. Many of them were real leaders and had the vision to see that a worldwide air net was feasible. Equally important, they also had the ability to bring in the air age.

Probably Juan Trippe was the most amazing of them all. He was the son of a New York investment banker and became interested in flying when, as a young teenager, he saw a stunt pilot performing over Long Island. He attended the Curtiss Flying School in Miami, and soon after—while in college—organized the Yale Flying Club, which consisted of one plane with two open cockpits. After graduation he started Long Island Airways, with seven World War I surplus planes he bought at auction for five hundred dollars each. In 1922 people used to wait in line in order to take a short spin aloft. However, this was hardly enough for the ambitious young man. During the next five years he bought and sold several airlines. Then, in 1927, he became president and general manager of Pan American, obtained the postal permit, and started the first scheduled overseas air route to Cuba. From this small beginning he was able to create an airline that soon became a leader in world transport and travel and finally led the world into the jet age.

His mind was always working, and he was way ahead of most of his colleagues. He was a lone wolf, dreaming up big ideas on the fiftieth floor. Much of the time you didn't know what he was thinking about, but you could expect anything from Trippe. One morning he called me down and showed me a clipping out of the *New York Times* sporting section. It was an article on, of all things, ski lifts in Switzerland. "Look at that," he said.

"Wouldn't it be great if we had one of those cable cars running between the Pan Am building and the New York airports?" That's the way he thought—always something new. But he was also a man of enormous vision. Imagine starting a little airline in 1927, and by 1935 I was able to ride in one of his planes to China!

When Trippe retired, after many years as chief executive officer, Harold Gray was brought in to take his place. Poor Harold. He was a pleasant, reserved man and had come up through the ranks of Pan Am. He was one of our early pilots down in Brownsville, and he and I had become friends there. He was a good pilot, and primarily he was a good engineer. Then he became manager of the North Atlantic division. Because he wasn't a political type, he went through quite a bit of hassle from the corporate powers at Pan Am headquarters. When he was made president, and I congratulated him, he said, " You know what, San? I'd rather have your job than mine. I'm basically an engineer; you know that."

And he was right. Harold was very disappointed with how the presidency worked out. I used to see him occasionally in his office, and when I would ask how things were going, he'd say, "It's terrible. Trippe makes all the important policy decisions. I just represent the company at banquets and make speeches." Trippe was chairman of the board, and he was still the "grand old man," still at the wheel.

The fact is, Harold had no training in management, no experience in running a large corporation like Pan Am. But it must have been frustrating for him. Maybe that was why he developed the cancer that killed him not many years later.

Najeeb Halaby was the third president, and he was totally different from either Trippe or Gray. He was very outgoing and gregarious, and much more accessible than Trippe. He was a law school graduate, had been a test pilot for Lockheed, and then was head of the FAA. He was the only one I knew who could go to an aviation meeting and make a really interesting speech every time. But like Gray, Halaby didn't understand the running of a large business organization. He was a Lebanese, and probably because of that, he developed a friendship for the Beirut manager and gave him a large pay raise. He didn't realize that a company has to have standard wage scales, and raising one person's salary meant raising everybody's. But Jeeb was a good friend of mine: I was never afraid to tell him my opinion.

Halaby's daughter married Hussein, the king of Jordan. I was over in Lebanon, and I met Jeeb and his daughter at the hotel. He said, "My daughter is only just out of college, and I've already gotten her a job." It turned out that they'd flown to Damascus on a Jordanian plane and had found the interior of their plane very drab. When Jeeb was talking about it later with the Syrian airline manager and told him that his daughter had taken an interior decorating course, the manager hired her on the spot!

Later, apparently, Hussein boarded the refurbished plane and admired the interior. When he asked who was responsible, he was told that it was "some American girl." He wanted to meet her, invited her to the palace, and soon after that they were married. Supposedly she became his "chief wife," although I wouldn't know about that.

Eventually Halaby fell out of favor with the board of directors and was allowed to retire with a substantial sum. He was the first executive I'd heard of who had made a contract with a corporation before taking on the job. He explained it by saying, "I was in Washington long enough to learn that you had better protect yourself, because nobody's going to do it for you." After he left Pan Am, he set up an office in New York that specialized in representing the big oil companies dealing with the Arab world. He made a big success of it. Another person I think of often—and during the war years especially—was that quiet little man from Bavaria, sitting in a dark corner of a Berlin cafe, unwilling to talk with anyone. Who would have guessed that in a few short years he would become the leader my German friends—in fact most Germans—had been looking for to lead them out of the degradation of Versailles? And in that ten years he would become the most feared and hated man in the world?

I encountered many brilliant people in the airline industry, but the one who stands out as the most intriguing is Charles A. Lindbergh. As everyone knows, Lindbergh was the first person to fly the Atlantic in a solo flight. That was in 1927, the same year that Pan Am was started by Juan Trippe. Lindbergh flew the first Pan Am flight through Central America into Panama, in 1929, and became a consultant on airplane design for the company—not only on many of the early planes but also, later on, for all the jets. We worked together in this field for many years. "Slim" was his nickname in those days, at least among his close friends. He once told Trippe that he would continue to work for Pan Am, but only if he could report to me. I often used him to get ideas to Trippe, who always listened to anything Lindbergh had to say. He was one of the nicest people I ever worked with.

Slim was a humane man in the best sense of the word. His dream was to end the possibility of war. He always believed, as I did, that if people from different parts of the world could get to know and respect each other, then wars would be less likely—and he saw international air travel as the way this could happen.

Shortly before World War II, Lindbergh was invited to Germany to see the German air industry. Because of his reputation, they showed him a great deal of what they were doing and gave him a medal. He was distressed by the idea of the war that seemed to be brewing, and came home to start giving antiwar "America First" speeches. After a well-publicized speech he gave at Madison Square Garden, President Roosevelt called him a traitor to his country. It was ridiculous, but the bad publicity hurt him deeply and caused a great deal of public hostility.

I didn't know Lindbergh at that time, but I went to hear him speak. I wanted to know what he had to say. It was obvious that public speaking was not easy for him. He was very shy, and it took a lot of courage for him to say what he believed. He had a rather high-pitched voice, and in public speaking this became more pronounced because of the tension he felt. No matter how often he spoke, he never got over this—the topics he spoke about were too emotional for him.

But in spite of his hatred of war, he loved his country. Once the United States entered the war, he immediately went to Washington to offer his services as a consultant. President Roosevelt offered him the post of chief of the Air Corps, which meant being directly accountable to the commander-in-chief (the President himself). Lindbergh wouldn't accept it. He realized that Roosevelt wanted to keep him under control, and he couldn't accept that. He wanted the freedom to speak out about things as he saw them. "If you're a three- or four-star General, heading the Army Air Corps, you keep your mouth shut" was the way he described it to me later. He knew that Roosevelt didn't want him going around talking about things that might involve sensitive politics. Eventually Slim felt that it was his duty to enlist, but by that time he had spoken so much against the war that he was not allowed to serve.[1]

Trying to find a niche where he could use his knowledge to help fight the enemy was hard: he finally went to work for one of United Aircraft's subsidiaries. They were building fighter planes in the Pacific, and his job was to test them.

Slim was a great morale builder for the native workers on those Pacific islands. They loved to see him coming. He would sit down and eat with them, his sleeves rolled up, treating them as equals instead of the "high rank stuff" they were used to. He just asked them how things were going and would let the mechanics tell him what they could about the airplane he was about to fly. He actually flew some combat missions, although he didn't plan it ahead of time: if he was up testing a plane and happened to run into a Japanese fighter, he would probably shoot it down![2]

Slim was an extremely private person, and he lived a simple life. He said that he had too much money, most of which he made on the sale of his books, and, in fact, he worked for years as technical consultant to Pan Am for only one dollar a year. He had a beat-up old car in which he traveled all over the world. In order to save expenses on hotels, he would sleep in it, even though he was over six feet tall. When I asked him how he managed to sleep in such a small space, he took me out into the parking lot to show me how he did it. He had turned the front seat around, laid it out flat, and then stretched out an air mattress for sleeping. Even though he'd been told that this was dangerous, especially in places like Arabia where there were marauding bands, he always did it. He loved to travel.

Since both of us were involved in the development of commercial jet planes, we worked closely together. We would travel to the factories and talk with the engineers to check on the new designs. We talked about everything on these trips and got to know each other pretty well.

Slim was a practical joker. One of the project engineers on the Pratt and Whitney engine had a brand new car and was quite proud of the mileage he was getting. Slim decided to have some fun. Without telling him, he put a gallon of gas in the engineer's tank every day for a week—and then began siphoning it out instead. A couple of weeks later we had lunch with the owner. "How's your mileage?" Slim asked.

"The strangest thing happened," the engineer told us. "I was getting way over what the dealer said the car would ever get. I told him I was getting sixty miles to the gallon, and he said it was impossible. Then all of a sudden, it dropped down to where I was getting only twenty-five miles. There must be something flat wrong with the engine—I don't get it—I'm stumped."

We all snickered, and Slim said, "Do you want me to go down and check your car out?"

The engineer caught on then. "You bums," he said, but he laughed too. Slim loved doing things like that.

Initially, both Lindbergh and I hoped that through aviation, people around the world would get to know each other better, and that through increased worldwide understanding wars would become less likely. It was a dream for both of us. But there came a time in the late fifties and early sixties when we both became disillusioned. The United States was in Vietnam by then. Our being there didn't make any sense to Slim. For a man like him, with his belief in peace and his desire to play some role in bringing peace about, it must have been very painful.

He became an increasingly private and, I would say, mystical person. It may have been a reaction to his disappointment in human nature. He turned from hoping that people would get along in the world to a much more pessimistic outlook. I talked to him about it once. "I don't know that I can contribute anything useful to the world," he told me. By then he had become interested in animals and primitive tribes. "Maybe I'll get a clue from there as to why everybody is fighting all the time," he said.[3]

I think that Lindbergh's books reflect the underlying spiritual approach to life which he had. They remind me of St. Exupery's beautiful books about flying. Both men had a religious feeling for flight, for transcending the earth and all its limits. Earlier, Slim and I used to talk about the Olympic idea of transforming human combat into sports, so that people could release their aggressions without slaughtering each other. We talked about that quite a bit, but Slim foresaw that even the Olympics couldn't be kept out of politics for long. In the end he became discouraged about the human race in general. He thought that the earth was in terrible danger and saw no hope of change. In some ways I agreed with him, but my feeling has always been that politicians start wars, not people. I never found a country where the people weren't basically decent and friendly. I feel the way Will Rogers did: "I've never met a man I couldn't like."

# Conclusion

*Just as the nineteenth century* produced the Industrial Revolution, I think history will mark the twentieth century as the time when there was the revolution of air travel. By the turn of this century, the automobile had been invented, but no one had yet managed to lift off the ground. When the Wright Brothers accomplished this feat in 1903, a new age began. It's incredible to think how quickly, from the Wright's small, flimsy plane, engineers have developed the present gigantic jet, which can fly five hundred people. It's a thrill for me to realize that I was a part of that revolution from its earliest beginnings.

Before the air age arrived, we had all kinds of prophets of doom- and nay-sayers—people who just couldn't imagine what was emerging. I used to know some of them. Before World War II, in the 1930s, I was in a debate at Columbia University with a friend of mine named Ed Warner. He was a professor of aerodynamics at MIT and later the first head of the International Civil Aviation Organization. When I presented sketches of a thirty-nine-seat airplane we planned to have built for Pan Am, he got up and said, "An airplane that big will never work." Then he went to the blackboard and started writing elaborate formulas. Finally he stopped and said, "There, that proves it."[1]

Well, it didn't prove it to me. I didn't understand it. But he said that it proved there was a maximum size planes could be, and they couldn't get any bigger than that. The limit he described wasn't much bigger than the planes we were flying at that time; in effect, he "proved" that bigger planes weren't possible. It reminded me of the old joke of the scientist who proved that bumblebees couldn't fly because their wings were too small for their body size. We went ahead anyway and signed up for the bigger plane. And, of course, it flew.

Looking back over forty-four years spent working for the airline industry, I can't imagine any activity in which I would rather have been involved. Even allowing for the frustrations we had in dealing with the unions after the war, it was nevertheless tremendously rewarding and gratifying to have been a part of what finally became the jet age of air travel. It was a lot easier, though, to deal with the engineering problems of a triple flap than to have to mess with a bunch of union leaders.[2]

I particularly like to remember my assignments as airport manager in various locations in Latin America. I was a real generalist then and had to do everything. In those early days, Pan Am couldn't afford to have more than one person in one place, and that person had to handle the passengers, the airport, the accounting, and of course the airplanes. I even had to try, as I've mentioned, to handle revolutions! What I liked best was learning about each country as I stayed there, and about the people who lived there.

Those early flights to Latin America were very exciting. You would take off from Miami, and the plane would fly so low that you could really see the country, as well as schools of fish when you were flying over the sea. Flying low was the most efficient way to operate, and since all the planes were seaplanes, we always had a place to land if we needed it.

On a typical flight you would land on the water in the late afternoon somewhere in Central America and take a room in the local hotel for the night. Then you would go out and eat in some native inn. You would get up at daybreak to the sound of exotic, beautifully colored birds, and take off soon after sunrise. Then you might be flying over the Amazon jungle, looking down on every kind of wild animal. It was an unbelievable fairyland.

At the twice-yearly International Air Transport Association (IATA) meetings, the leaders in aviation from all the countries in the world would gather. They would meet, get to know each other, and the world would seem like such a small place. I often shudder to think of what aviation throughout the world would be like without the rules and regulations we set up: every airline at every airport following the same specifications as to runway design, language, landing and takeoff rules, and so on. We would often have long, drawn out discussions and arguments before we could come to the 100 percent agreement that was necessary.

Wives were invited to these meetings, and once the children were old enough to leave, Betty Gay would often accompany me. Then we would quite often stay in the host country for a short vacation. One trip that I remember particularly was with Knut and Esther Hagrup from Scandinavian Airlines (SAS). We met in Copenhagen, Denmark, then went on to

Stockholm and then to Oslo. From there, after a stopover with the Hagrups, we went up the coast of Norway by air, stopping at each town and city along the way. Since Knut was an important official in SAS, later president of the company, we were hosted by the mayors of each town we passed and were entertained royally, all the way up to the Russian border.

And there was another great advantage gained from getting to know couples from other countries. Three of our five children went to IATA families' homes for summer visits, and in other years children from abroad came to stay with us. Invariably they would comment on how similar life was in both countries. That confirmed in me what I have always believed.

But as I look back on all the experiences I have been describing, I think the biggest thrill was when I saw those jumbo jets come into service. It seemed to me then as though the airplane had reached its peak, at least as far as commercial aviation was concerned. Airplanes might get a little bigger, and perhaps a little faster, but I don't think they will change much in the coming years. I felt that 1972 was a good year for me to be retiring. The commercial jet age was just beginning, and the world was growing smaller all the time. For me this seemed to say that there was hope for a better world. I have always believed that the people of the world would be friendly if they had a chance to know each other, and if their leaders would only allow it.

*Sanford B. Kauffman's identity card which he was required to carry at all times in Berlin 1928.*

*The Junkers F-13, a single engine four-seat, short-range airliner. In the late 1920s, when Kauffman was learning the ropes at Lufthansa, the F-13 was the most widely used aircraft in Germany.*

*The Junkers G-31 Trimotor parked on the ramp at the Berlin airport. The G-31, another aircraft Kauffman worked with during his stay in Germany, was unusual for its low-wing configuration. Comparable in size to the better-known Ford and Fokker Trimotors, the G-31 could carry fourteen passengers.*

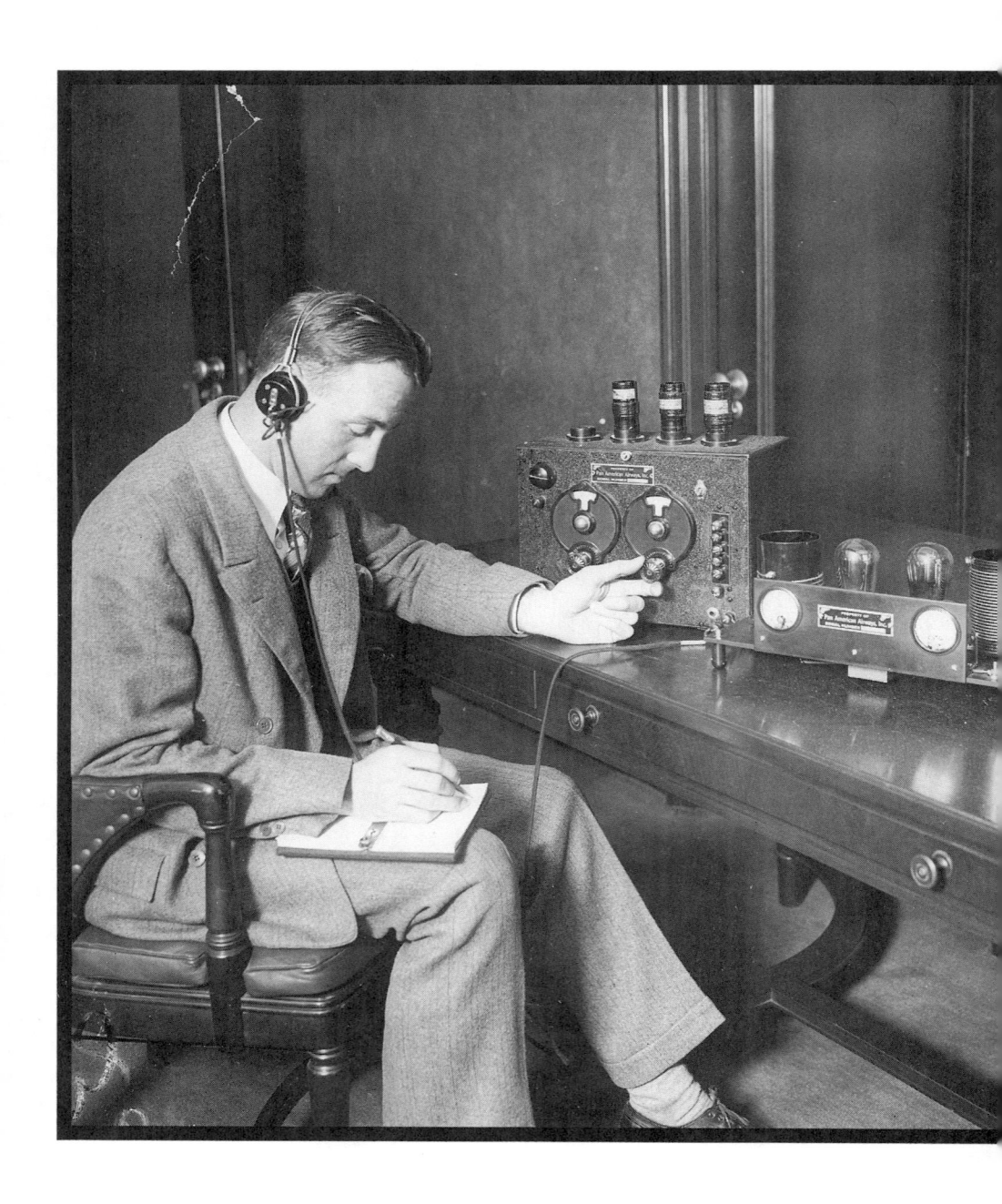

*Ed Musick at Key West circa 1927 with PAA's second Fokker F-7 Trimotor, the General New (named for Coolidge's Postmaster General.) Note that neither Musick nor his unidentified assistant (probably a "plane captain"—copilots were not yet in use), wears a uniform, but they do wear neckties, a psychological ploy to reassure nervous passengers that these airmen were not daredevils.*

*Hugo C. Leuteritz, the electronic genius behind so many of PAA's technical innovations in radio navigation and communication, circa 1928.*

*S-38 being loaded with mail, the only cargo that made profits for PAA during the early days. An unknown ground employee hoists the mail sacks to the veteran PAA pilot Basil L. Rowe, circa 1927-29.*

*Snapshots by Kauffman of domestic PAA facilities: lights (above), fire protection facilities (left), and hangar (below), circa 1929.*

An S-38 amphibian as it looked on land during standard passenger boarding (date and place unknown). Note that three PAA employees assist a mere two passengers in boarding.

An S-38 amphibian prepares for taxi, probably in Miami, circa 1929-32.

A PAA Ford Trimotor at Cristobal, Canal Zone, boarding passengers, circa 1929. The unimproved runway surface—rough gravel—did not contribute to smooth landings.

A Fokker F-10 over Miami, circa 1929-30. During that era, many passengers preferred to fly Fokker Trimotors rather than the similar Ford aircraft, because they mistakenly believed that the Fokker's wooden wing would float after an emergency landing at sea. PAA's publicists encouraged this misbelief, by implying that Fords flew only over land routes, although this was not in fact true.

*PAA male steward with in-flight lunches for passengers preparing to board a Fokker F-10, probably in Miami, circa 1929.*

*Interior of a Fokker F-10 configured with ten passenger seats, circa 1929-31. The steward sat on a bench at the rear during landings and takeoffs, a practice that would shock safety-minded modern flight attendants.*

*Publicity photo of the interior of PAA's new combination seaplane-landplane passenger station in Miami, circa 1929.*

*The PAA passenger station in Havana, Cuba, circa 1929, had the reputation as the best-equipped PAA facility outside the United States.*

*Kauffman's employee pass with the traditional PAA logo.*

B-14—75—12-32

# PAN AMERICAN AIRWAYS SYSTEM
## DIVISIONAL FLIGHT PASS

No.

*PAA*

1933

**𝒫ASS**

UNTIL DECEMBER 31, 1933
S. B. Kauffman
Asst. to Operations Mgr.

as

over **Caribbean** Division only, or as otherwise ordered by one of the undersigned officials, if signed by the employee named above, and subject to the terms and conditions on the face and back hereof. Not valid unless countersigned by the Division Traffic Manager.

NON-TRANSFERABLE

COUNTERSIGNED BY

PAN AMERICAN AIRWAYS, INC.

DIVISION TRAFFIC MANAGER

BY

DIVISION MANAGER

*Snapshots taken by Kauffman of the primitive facilties of United States airlines during his 1931 trip to his new duty station in Central America.*

*A typical United States airline terminal, circa 1931, Austin, Texas. Probably the Universal Divide of American Airlines, during the trip Kauffman describes.*

*PAA office at an undetermined location, circa 1932. This combination hangar-waiting room illustrates the primitive conditions passengers encountered during this era.*

*PAA's most elegant passenger facility, at Miami, with the Fokker F-10 parked in front, circa 1932. Note the two male flight attendants in their short-waisted jackets.*

*The famous Ford Trimotor, backbone of PAA's fleet of overland aircraft when Kauffman worked as a station chief in central America during the early 1930s.*

*As a station manager in Central America in the early 1930s, Kauffman would have managed some or all of these PAA personnel at various times as they passed through his out station.*

*Standing before an S-38 amphibian during an inspection tour of Central American facilities, circa 1932, are (left to right) Copilot Bennett Boyd, Mr. and Mrs. George L. Rihl (Rihl founded PAA's Mexican affiliate Compania Mexicano de Aviacion and later became an important subordinate to Juan Terry Trippe), Captain Ed Musick and radioman/plane captain William Ehmer.*

*A Sikorsky S-38 amphibian, the plane that earned PAA's first significant profits, beginning its takeoff run, circa 1933, probably in the Caribbean. This picture illustrates the problem of restricted visibility owing to spray that many pilots (including Lindbergh) thought made the S-38 dangerous.*

*A Sikorsky S-42 seaplane at Botwood, Newfoundland, 5 July 1939, at the time of the trans-Atlantic proving flights. Note the refueling/service barge to which the aircraft was tied. These barges were used at many PAA remote stations.*

*A Sikorsky S-42 on beaching gear being towed by a tracked vehicle designed specially for PAA as a "beaching tractor." Note that this was a pure seaplane, not an amphibian. NC 16736 was nicknamed Betsy by PAA personnel—a more homely and enduring name than the official name Clippers. Photo probably taken in Bermuda, circa 1937.*

*An all-purpose service barge, used by PAA worldwide to fuel and service seaplanes where there were no ramp facilities, circa 1937.*

*An S-42 alongside a passenger boarding ramp in New York, circa 1935.*

*An S-42 passenger boarding, circa 1935, at an unknown location, the copilot, as was usual, supervising loading.*

*A British Empire-class flying boat (the Caledonia) at Botwood, Newfoundland, after landing on the inaugural westbound trip from England. Note that it is tied up to a standard PAA service barge. PAA supplied ground support for Imperial Airways, even though the seadrome was in Canada, circa 1937.*

*Captain Ed Musick arriving at Manila, November 29, 1935, saluting dignitaries as he goes ashore.*

*Captain Rod Sullivan, one of the pioneer trans-Pacific pilots (left), with Flight Engineer Chauncy Wright, with a Martin M-130 seaplane in the background, circa 1935.*

*Wedding photo of August 11, 1939.*

*Kauffman (fourth from left) with other Boeing and PAA officials, inspecting the B-707 prototype at Seattle in 1954.*

*Kauffman (right) with Juan Terry Trippe, circa late 1940s or early 1950s, unknown location, typically at his elbow, ticking off points on his fingers.*

*The family in 1953: (left to right) Sanford B., Lelee, Bob, Ricky, Ginny, Pam, Betty Gay, and Peggy.*

*Kauffman accepts the keys for the first commercial jet, the Boeing 707, from Boeing official Bruce Conally (left), as PAA sales representative Klein Mitchel (right) looks on, 1955.*

*Corporate publicity photo taken during 1956 B-707 labor contract negotiations for both ground and flight personnel. These protracted negotiations resulted in substantial pay increases, but so bright were PAA's prospects when jetliners were introduced, that a degree of levity was possible.*

*Kauffman at the International Air Transport Association meeting in Amsterdam, May 12, 1958.*

*Bill Del Valle, PAA's resident engineer at Douglas Aircraft during the 1959 proving flight of the DC-8.*

The "other" jetliner—a Douglas DC-8, circa 1961.

*Kauffman (center) as Chairman of IATA (International Air Transport Association) in 1959 with Stanislaw Krzyczkowski (left) the Secrretary General of IATA and Knute Hegrup (right) Vice Chairman from SAS, the Scandinavian airline. Held in Berkeley, California in 1959, it was the first airline jet conference.*

*Sanford with Betty Gay, IATA Meeting, November 1964.*

# Notes

✈ *Pan Am Pioneer: Germany 1928*

1. The Professor Benson alluded to illustrates a fundamental problem for all memoirists such as Kauffman, who are reconstructing their past from memory, rather than from notes, diaries, or documents. Since Kauffman gave no first name, and there is a daunting list of Bensons in the *New York Times Obituary Index,* and there is no hint of other biographical information on him, it seems pointless to trace Professor Benson. His only real importance, historically, was that he introduced Kauffman to Otto Merkel, whom we shall meet shortly.

2. Otto Junius Merkel (1879-1955), born into a wealthy and prominent Bremen merchant family, became interested in the commercial possibilities of flight prior to World War I. He organized *Deutscher Aero Lloyd* airline in 1923, one of the immediate predecessors of *Deutsche Luft Hansa,* the German flag carrier which came into existence in 1926 and persists to this day (Lufthansa)—the world's oldest continuously operating commercial airline. Merkel was a member of the airline's executive board from 1926 to 1929. He later served as chairman of the Lufthansa Supervisory Board. See R. E. G. Davies, *Lufthansa: An Airline and Its Aircraft* (Rockville, MD.: Paladwr Press, 1991), 8; Joachim Wachtel, *The Lufthansa Story, 1926-1984* 3d ed. (Cologne: Lufthansa German Airlines, 1985), 147.

3. Kauffman's ideas on the subject of Hitler's financial backing touch upon one of the most bitterly debated questions about the rise of Nazism. Did Hitler derive his primary support from ordinary people, or was he the creature of a dark conspiracy of upper-class businessmen? Kauffman seems to favor the latter argument, but the best evidence is that wealthy industrialists did not begin supporting Hitler until he had already captured a political base among the German

middle classes, and his rise to power was assured. See Henry A. Turner, Jr., *German Big Business and the Rise of Adoph Hitler* (New York: Oxford, 1985), xi-xxi.

4. Was Kauffman's potential lunch partner actually Adolph Hitler? The circumstances are right, in that Hitler lived in Munich and was indeed a vegetarian. Hitler was also known to be reclusive in his social habits and so would not have welcomed an American stranger as a table partner. But Hitler would probably not have been alone in public at the time Kauffman claims to have seen him. After the 1923 Munich *putsch,* and his release from prison, Hitler was a celebrity who never went anywhere without an entourage and bodyguards. Nor was Hitler ever a member of the Reichstag. Hitler never held any official position in Germany until he became chancellor in 1933, and he could not have been in the Reichstag, for he was not yet a German citizen and hence was ineligible for election. Although Hitler renounced his Austrian citizenship in 1924, he did not immediately achieve German citizenship, and he faced the possibility of deportation throughout the 1920s. He did not become a German citizen until shortly before attaining power. See John Toland, *Adoph Hitler* (Doubleday, 1976), 220-21.

5. This business takes on the coloration of a John Le Carré spy thriller. The German authorities who made trouble for Kauffman over his ROTC commission were almost certainly conducting a calculated ploy, on the part of a German intelligence agency (of which there were several), to recruit a spy. That Kauffman was willing to give up his commission must have encouraged them to think that he was potentially recruitable.

6. Clearly, somebody in the American embassy realized that German intelligence was trying to recruit Kauffman as a spy, even though he himself apparently did not. Kauffman's abrupt refusal to engage in spying at the behest of his own government probably had something to do with the old-fashioned notion that spying, even for one's own country, was dirty work unfit for a "gentleman." At the time Kauffman found himself enmeshed with espionage, Henry L. Stimson, Herbert Hoover's Secretary of State (who would later become Secretary of War in Franklin D. Roosevelt's cabinet), curtly rejected efforts by U.S. agencies to engage in spying during the interwar years. In 1929, when Stimson learned that War Department code breakers in the celebrated Black Chamber were routinely reading diplomatic cables, he stopped funding the operation, calling it "a highly unethical thing." He later declared: "Gentlemen do not read each other's mail." Godfrey Hodgson, *The Colonel: The Life and Times of Henry L. Stimson, 1867-1950* (New York: Knopf, 1990), 203.

7. Wilhelm "Willi" Messerschmitt (1898-1978), an aviation genius whose name is synonymous with the superb aircraft he designed for Hitler's Luftwaffe. The most famous Messerschmitt was the Me-109, a single-seat, single-engine fighter that ranks as one of the premier combat aircraft of World War II. Willi Messerschmitt also developed the Me-262, the world's first fully operational jet fighter-bomber; had Hitler been smart enough to realize its potential, it might have altered the outcome of World War II. See Robert Wistrich, *Who's Who in Nazi Germany* (New York: Bonanza Books, 1984), 208; Ronald Lewin, *Hitler's Mistakes* (New York: William Morrow, 1984), 91-93.

8. Street brawls between Nazis and Communists were quite common, but to a naive young American, they must have seemed exotic indeed. In June 1932, as Hitler neared the verge of power, there were 461 pitched battles in Prussia alone, which resulted in eighty-two deaths and over four hundred wounded. The level of violence was so strong because the Nazis and Communists, especially in the 1920s, were competing for the loyalty of the same constituency—workers and lower-middle-class tradesmen aggrieved at Germany's economic situation. See William L. Shirer, *The Rise and Fall of the Third Reich* (New York: Simon & Schuster, 1960), 165.

9. Clarence Young (1889-1973) was and Iowa aviation entrepreneur who later became head of Pan Am's trans-Pacific division (1934-45). In 1926, Young was hired to manage the aviation activities of the Philadelphia Sesquicentennial Celebration, which consisted of air races, exhibition flights, and a demonstration passenger air service between Philadelphia and Washington, D.C. Young's success in this job won him an appointment as director of air regulation with the new aeronautics branch of the Department of Commerce. In 1929, he became Assistant Secretary of Commerce for aeronautics in the Hoover administration, a post he held until the Republicans lost the presidency in 1933. Juan Trippe hired Young in 1934 specifically to inaugurate Pan Am's new Pacific service. Young resigned from Pan Am in 1945 after an unspecified "difference of opinion" with Trippe. He served as a member of the Civil Aeronautics Board (1946-47) and then returned to work for Pan Am in 1950, after patching things up with Trippe. He retired from the airline in 1959 at the age of seventy. See William M. Leary, ed., *Encyclopedia of American Business History & Biography: The Airline Industry* (New York: Facts on File, 1992), 521-24.

10. The individual to whom Young was recommending Kauffman was André A. Priester (1891-1955), a Dutch citizen who got his start in aviation with Royal Dutch Airlines (KLM), in his native country. Attracted by career opportunities in

the U.S., Priester emigrated in 1925. He subsequently made contact with his countryman, the famed aircraft designer Anthony Fokker, who recommended him to the Philadelphia Rapid Transit (PRT) company, which was sponsoring an experimental airline between Washington, D.C., and Philadelphia as part of the Philadelphia Exposition of 1926. Young was Priester's boss in Philadelphia. While managing the PRT airline during the five months of its existence, Priester met Juan Trippe, who hired him as Pan Am's chief engineer in 1927. Priester's English was poor, a major impediment to his work, as Trippe had apparently complained to Young. Kauffman's language skills were thus key to his being hired by Trippe, initially to interpret for Priester. See Leary *The Airline Industry,* 380-81.

11. Kauffman mistakes the official names of the military organizations involved here.] By terms of the Versailles Treaty ending World War I, German military aviation was severely restricted. Secret organizations and "aerosports clubs" did indeed surreptitiously train pilots for military purposes during the 1920s, as Kauffman points out, but there was no *official* Luftwaffe until March 1935, when Hitler formally announced its creation in defiance of the Versailles Treaty. See A Galland et al., *The Luftwaffe at War, 1939-1945* (Chicago: Henry Regnery, 1972), 7-11.

12. One can only speculate that somehow German intelligence got wind of Kauffman's refusal to spy for his country and took this as a sign that he would be willing to spy for Germany. By implication, the German offer of a military commission would have compromised Kauffman and made him vulnerable to blackmail in the future. The Germans had to know (even if Kauffman did not) that accepting a foreign commission would, under U.S. law, be potential grounds for loss of American citizenship. So the Germans had nothing to lose by making the offer, while Kauffman had a great deal to lose by accepting it. Belatedly aware of the predicament in which his obvious pro-German views had placed him, Kauffman decided to get out—fast! His decision in this case was at least more fortunate if not more shrewd than Charles Lindburgh's in 1938 when in Lindbergh accepted a swastika-emblazoned medal, the *Verdienstkruez der Deutscher Adler* (Service Cross of the German Eagle), from Hitler, the cross was actually pinned on his lapel by Luftwaffe chief Herman Goering. German intelligence operatives were clever manipulators of foreigners who displayed pro-German sentiments. See Leonard Mosely, *Lindbergh: A Biography* (New York: Doubleday, 1976), 232-35.

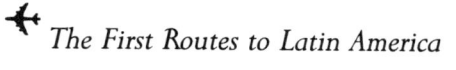

# The First Routes to Latin America

1. Cornelius Vanderbilt Whitney (1899-1992), whose intimates called him Sonny (a nickname he eventually came to hate), was often confused with his cousin, John Hay "Jock" Whitney (1904-1982), who also served on Pan Am's board. Sonny Whitney and John A. Hambleton (1898-1929), scions of East Coast "establishment" families, often were referred to in the society press as "sportsmen." Both had been Army aviators during World War I, and both were fledgling financiers trading upon their families' connections as they made their way in the world during the early 1920s.

Although Trippe came from lesser familial and financial stock, he was by no means poor and ran in the same social circles as Whitney and Hambleton. Trippe and Whitney, although not intimate friends, had been classmates at exclusive private schools as children and again at Yale. In 1923, Trippe briefly operated Long Island Airways using surplus Navy seaplanes. He was both president and chief pilot. The airline whisked the wealthy to and from their vacation homes and Manhattan, gave sightseeing rides, and attracted professional interest from Trippe's social chums, Whitney and Hambleton. Their experience with this air passenger service, plus Trippe's argument that aviation had vast potential, persuaded Whitney and Hambleton to back Trippe's aviation ventures financially. They are often listed as cocreators along with Trippe of Pan Am, and in truth each played more than a passive role. Whitney served on the airline's board, but his reputation as a dilettante and playboy hindered him. Trippe always had operational control of Pan Am, except for a brief period in 1939, when Whitney replaced him as Pan Am's CEO, a job for which he proved unsuited.

Hambleton, had he lived, might well have supplanted Trippe as the guiding spirit of Pan Am. A "golden youth" right out of an F. Scott Fitzgerald novel, Hambleton was rich, handsome, and athletically gifted. He dropped out of Harvard to enlist in the Army Signal Corps in 1917, just prior to U.S. entry in World War I. He became a fighter pilot with the fabled 95th Aero Squadron, participated in several bloody battles, and returned with a chest full of medals and the rank of major. Hambleton took an active role in Pan Am's pioneering phase, making aerial surveys of routes and possible landing sites in Central America and even serving as copilot for Charles A. Lindbergh on the airline's first airmail flight from Miami to the Canal Zone on February 4, 1929.

Trippe was in awe of Hambleton and often deferred to his judgment on aviation and business matters. A skilled pilot, Hambleton vowed never to fly in any airplane that he was not himself controlling. Although he often made an exception for Lindbergh, perhaps it was an omen. On June 8, 1929, Hambleton was killed in a private plane crash at Wilmington, North Carolina. He was a passenger. See Bender and Altschul, *Chosen Instrument,* (new York: Simon and Schuster, 1982) 60-64, 46-47, 58-59, 114-15, 151-52; Leary, *Airline Industry,* 345; R. E. G. Davies, *Airlines of the United States since 1914* (Washington: Smithsonian Institution Press, 1972), 49, 211, 381.

2. In a conscious decision to reassure passengers that pilots were professionals, the new commercial airlines began requiring them to wear uniforms in the late 1920s. *Aviation* magazine, the principal voice of the fledgling industry, advocated a variety of steps to enhance pilot prestige in order to "sell flying to the public." A December 1928 article titled "Passenger Impressions" warned airline managers that if airline personnel dressed in "grease-stained or rough and tumble clothing," passengers would disapprove. Since most early airline pilots had been in the military previously, they easily adapted to the wearing of uniforms. Pan Am, with its proclivity for hiring former Navy pilots, led the way with its distinctive white caps and navy blue double-breasted uniforms. See George E. Hopkins, *The Airline Pilots: A Study in Elite Unionization* (Cambridge: Harvard University Press, 1971), 16-17.

3. Because of its far-flung operations throughout the Caribbean, Pan Am was notoriously disorganized in the late 1920s. Charles H. Ruby, who later became president of the Air Line Pilots Association (ALPA) within the AFL-CIO (the union that represented Pan Am's pilots), worked for Pan Am as a mechanic briefly in 1929, just before Kauffman began straightening things out. In a 1979 interview, Ruby said of his experience with Pan Am: "They paid me a hundred dollars a month to go down to places like Haiti and hibernate with the crocodiles. The operation was pretty retrograde at the time, really a mess, and nobody seemed to be in charge." George E. Hopkins, *Flying the Line: The First Half-Century of the Air Line Pilots Association* (Washington, D.C.: Air Line Pilots Association, 1982), 216.

4. Among pilots in the 1920s, who learned their trade in the military, as barnstormers, or with the original Post Office airmail service, drinking was a problem airline managers like Kauffman had to control. The popular culture of the day associated drinking with flying. The image of the daredevil aviator, quaffing a last brandy before going out to meet his fate in the "Great War" of 1914-18, stuck in the public consciousness via movies and fiction. This imagery was quite persistent, enduring well into the modern era. "Something has kept these chaps young, and it isn't asceticism," *Fortune* declared in a March 1941 article titled "Airman." "When they play poker, they play all night. When they smoke, they

smoke too much. When they drink, their glasses leak." Because early pilots flew in mostly unheated, open cockpits, frigid temperatures contributed to heavy drinking. The conventional wisdom (which was, of course, physiological non-sense) held that alcohol consumption warded off cold. To pilots who were afraid of flying, alcohol was "bottled courage." So long as pilots flew only mail, airline managers tolerated the drinking. But with the coming of passenger service, Kauffman and others had a tough job policing the "alcoholic subculture" among pilots. Many pioneer pilots couldn't adapt, among them the legendary Jack Knight, the hero of the first transcontinental night air mail flight in 1921. United finally forced Knight to "retire" to a meaningless nonflying job in 1937 owing to alcoholism. Pilots eventually accepted that preflight drinking and airline passenger operations did not mix, but they joked about it: "Twenty-four hours between bottle and throttle, but only five minutes between throttle and bottle!"

Hopkins, *Flying the Line,* 103; editor's oral history interviews.

5. Although the airplane was an American invention, Europeans dominated technical progress through the first three decades of aviation history. Ironically, the defeated Germans began to lead in technical innovation shortly after World War I. Since the Versailles Treaty forbade Germany to engage in military aviation, German engineers and scientists poured their considerable talents into commer-cial airline development. Lufthansa benefited greatly and was arguably the world's most advanced airline throughout the 1920s and a great portion of the 1930s. See Christopher Chant, *Aviation: An Illustrated History* (London: Orbis, 1978), 164-88.

6. Aviation Corporation of America (AVCO) was the corporate holding company established in 1929 by two powerful Wall Street firms, Lehman Brothers and W. A. Harriman & Co., to exploit opportunities in the new airline field. Not only had AVCO invested in Pan Am, but it was also the parent company of American Airlines, one of the "Big Four." See Davies, *Airlines of the U.S.,* 99-108.

7. Kauffman's acquaintance with people like William McChesney Martin illustrates not only his talent for networking but also the interest of powerful financiers in the fledgling airline industry. This "takeover" of the airline industry by financial heavyweights caused enduring bitterness among pioneer airmen and barnstormers, whose bids on profitable airmail contracts (once the government began turning over the Post Office Air Mail Service to private contractors) were nearly always unsuccessful. See Davies, *Airlines of the U.S.,* 108; Hopkins, *Flying the Line,* 69 ff.

8. This pioneering, coast-to-coast air-rail line began operations in 1929 as Transcontinental Air Transport (TAT) and later became part of TWA. Passenger service out of New York westward was considered too dangerous not because of night flying, as Kauffman says, but rather because there were so few emergency landing fields over what pilots called the "hellstretch" across the Allegheny Mountains. There was no daytime service over this stretch, either, at the time of Kauffman's trip in 1930. See George E. Hopkins, "Transcontinental Air Transport," *American Heritage* 27 (Dec. 1975): 22-28.

9. One of several corporate entities that sprang up to bid on lucrative air mail contracts, Universal was formed in July 1928 by a group of Chicago, St. Louis, and Minneapolis investment bankers. It eventually became one of the key airlines in the merger that created American Airlines and was called the Universal division of American in January 1930. See Davies, *Airlines of the U.S.,* 101-6.

10. Founded in 1928 by two Oklahomans, brothers Tom and Paul Braniff, the airline flew single-engine Stinson "Detroiters," which carried five passengers and a pilot. It was essentially an air taxi operation designed to serve the booming "oil patch" in Texas and Oklahoma. After a highly successful few months serving the Tulsa-Oklahoma City corridor, Braniff expanded its routes to Dallas and Wichita Falls, Texas. In 1929, the Braniff brothers sold this first incarnation of their airline to Universal (AVCO), primarily because they did not have an airmail contract. In 1930, when Kauffman flew it from Dallas to Brownsville, Texas, it was known as the Braniff division of Universal. The Braniff brothers returned to the business in 1930; this second incarnation of their airline is remembered today chiefly as the trendsetter that hired artist Alexander Calder to paint its jets with avant-garde paint schemes in the 1960s and popularized its image with the advertising slogan "The End of the Plain Plane." Braniff was the first casualty of the Airline Deregulation Act of 1978, going bankrupt in 1982. See Davies, *Airlines of the U.S.,* 102, 133-36; Leary, *Airline Industry,* 78-80.

11. Thomas Elmer Braniff (1883-1954) was an Oklahoma businessman with heavy interests in insurance and real estate. His brother Paul, a World War I Army pilot, was Braniff's operations manager, while Tom (a nonpilot) ran the business side of the airline. Tom Braniff died in a 1954 private plane crash.

See Leary, *Airline Industry,* 73-77.

12. Mail was far more lucrative than passenger service in the beginning. Many early airmail operators got into the business only because of the mail subsidy, and they were frankly hostile to the idea of carrying passengers. In fact, Hoover's

Postmaster General, Walter Folger Brown, an Ohio lawyer, had to force the mail contractors to offer passenger service as a prerequisite for holding a mail contract. Brown shared President Hoover's belief that passenger service would eventually grow to the point that the airlines would become independent of the federal airmail subsidy. In 1930, they hit upon a scheme to force the airlines to purchase large, passenger-carrying aircraft (like the Ford and Fokker Trimotors): paying them according to the space they made available for carrying mail, rather than by the weight of mail they actually carried. Brown and Hoover also required airlines bidding on a mail contract to have multiengine aircraft, rather than single-engine, on the grounds that passengers would be more likely to fly in these larger, safer aircraft. But the airlines provided passenger amenities only grudgingly, as Kauffman found out on this 1930 trip to Brownsville. See Hopkins, *Flying the Line,* 69-70; Leary, *Airline Industry,* 82-89.

13. Lindbergh worked closely with TAT, the pioneering air-rail service linking New York City and Los Angeles. He planned the routes and selected the "changeover" points at which passengers transferred from plane to train for the night portions of their trips (Columbus, Ohio; Waynoka, Oklahoma; and Clovis, New Mexico), and he flew the inaugural eastbound passenger trip out of Los Angeles on July 7, 1929. Therefore, TAT's motto, "The Lindbergh Line," emblazoned on the sides of its Ford Trimotors, was more than mere advertising hype. When TAT was merged into the new TWA in 1930, the airline retained "The Lindbergh Line" logo for many years.

Lindbergh's connection with Pan Am was highly publicized. In 1928, he succumbed to the ardent wooing of Trippe, Hambleton, and Whitney and became Pan Am's technical adviser (a title he chose for himself), at a salary of $10,000 per year plus stock options, which eventually netted him over $150,000. Because Pan Am did not compete directly with TAT, Lindbergh saw no conflict in lending his enormous prestige to both simultaneously. See Hopkins, "Transcontinental Air Transport," 22-28; Leary, *Airline Industry,* 458-59; Bender and Altschul, *Chosen Instrument,* 113-14.

14. Although the military developed most of the essentials of instrument flying (through civilian contractors such as the Sperry Corporation), the airlines were obvious beneficiaries. Fog, low clouds, and reduced visibility were the greatest obstacles to "scheduled" airline service in the beginning. Improved altimeters and more accurate gyroscopic compasses and altitude indicators were necessary for successful flight in these conditions. The celebrated General James H. "Jimmy" Doolittle (who also held an engineering doctorate from MIT)

performed the first fully "blind" flight on September 24, 1929. Doolittle is justifiably credited with much of the engineering flight testing of blind flying, but on each airline there were individuals such as Ed Snyder who adapted these techniques to the special needs of their own airlines. See John W. R. Taylor and Kenneth Munson, *History of Aviation* (New York: Crown Publishers, 1972), 328-29.

15. The "pilot authority" issue has troubled aviation almost from the beginning. In 1919, the Post Office Air Mail Service pilots actually went on strike over a nonflying manager's authority to force a pilot to fly in bad weather against his better judgment. This issue was also a critical factor in persuading most airline pilots to unionize in the 1930s. Pilots complained that airline managers, in order to meet their schedules, engaged in "pilot pushing"—forcing them to fly in unsafe conditions. To this day, the motto of ALPA, which represents most U.S. airline pilots, is "Schedule with Safety." In the modern era, pilots have seen threats to their authority in the increasing "ground control" functions of the FAA. When the air traffic controllers' union (PATCO) went on strike against the government in 1981, this ancient antipathy was one reason the pilots' union supported President Reagan's decision to fire them. See Hopkins, *Flying the Line*, 18-30. (The details of the PATCO strike of 1981 are fully explored in my *The Line Pilot in Crisis: A History of the Air Line Pilots Association in the Era of Deregulation, 1970-1990*, scheduled for publication in 1995.)

16. The mystique of danger associated with flying meant that early airline passengers had, necessarily, to be an intrepid lot. Minor mishaps like this were quite common and perhaps added a touch of glamor to early airline flying.

Hopkins, *Airline Pilots*, 1-8.

17. The time-saving advantages of early airline travel were often inconsequential, owing to delays caused by mechanical breakdowns or, more often, bad weather. In the U.S., the bane of early airline operations was having to "train" passengers. Not only was it bad for aviation's image, but it also reduced profits. "Training" passengers was obviously not an option for Pan Am in the jungles of Central America. See Hopkins, *Flying the Line*, 34.

18. The Sikorsky amphibian in question was the twin-engine S-38 model, Pan Am's Caribbean workhorse during its early days. In 1928, when Pan Am acquired its first fleet of S-38s, it was the largest and fastest amphibian in the world, and it was arguably the safest commercial airliner in the world also. Owing to its ability to land on either land or water, it inspired great confidence among passengers. It was also relatively comfortable, if such a word could be applied to

the noisy, vibrating, nausea-inducing commercial aircraft of that era. To improve the S-38's water handling qualities, the hull was enlarged, so there was ample space for passengers. Trippe insisted that the S-38 be lavishly furnished, with wicker chairs padded with mock leather, and real mahogany trim. Depending upon the route, it carried either nine or thirteen passengers. On long, overwater flights, extra fuel had to be carried, which meant that passenger loads had to be reduced. It cruised at 110 mph and could maintain altitude on one engine, should the other fail. See Henry R. Palmer, Jr., *This Was Air Travel* (New York: Bonanza, 1962), 142-43.

19. SCADTA was the acronym for the Spanish initials of Sociodad Colombo-Aleman de Transportes Aereos (translation: Society of Colombian-German Air Transporters). It was formed in 1919 by Doctor Peter Paul von Bauer, a former Austrian pilot in World War I. Although Germans ran SCADTA, there were Colombian associates, and the corporation was chartered in Colombia. In the 1920s, SCADTA, with help from Lufthansa, became one of the world's most successful airlines. South America, with its jungles and mountains and rudimentary forms of ground transportation, was an ideal environment for airline operations. Should SCADTA be allowed to serve the U.S. market, it would have been a tremendous economic threat to Pan Am's profit potential. Von Bauer tried repeatedly in the 1920s to win the right to connect his Latin American routes with the U.S., but he was refused. This was less because of Trippe's influence (although he did everything he could to undermine SCADTA) than because the Army and Navy, concerned about the security of the Panama Canal, were uneasy about Germany gaining influence in an area of prime strategic importance. In truth, SCADTA was so much more experienced and had so much more access to Latin America, that Trippe was desperate to merge his fledgling Pan Am with it in the beginning. See Carl Solberg, *Conquest of the Skies: A History of Commercial Aviation in America* (Boston: Little, Brown, 1972), 74-77.

20. Many of the people involved in the Pan Am enterprise were what the 1920s called "sportsmen." Several of them had been Trippe's classmates at Yale. Grant Mason was different, however. An Iowan, Mason was pursuing the main chance in aviation before he teamed up with Trippe. In fact, Mason had originally been Trippe's rival and had actually chartered the name "Pan American" before Trippe formed his airline. Mason was an extraordinarily skilled negotiator who had secured a mail contract from the Cuban government in 1925. Trippe's influence and connections rendered Mason's mail contract all but worthless, so he swallowed his pride and became a Pan Am employee in 1927. Trippe placed

him in charge of negotiating landing rights with Latin American governments. See Solberg, *Conquest of the Skies,* 76-78.

21. The "chosen instrument" controversy troubled commercial aviation in the immediate post-World War II era. Trippe, who had conducted what amounted to his own diplomacy in Latin America prior to World War II, saw great possibilities in the postwar expansion of commercial aviation, and he wanted Pan Am to be free from the competition of U.S. domestic airlines seeking international routes. He waged a long and ultimately futile battle to make Pan Am America's only overseas airline. See Bender and Altschul, *Chosen Instrument,* 9-16.

22. It was an article of faith among pioneer airmen that aviation was not truly viable as a free-market enterprise owing to the demands of air safety. They feared that in an unregulated industry, irresponsible managers would jeopardize safety by skimping on maintenance, inspections, and crew training. They saw airlines as regulated public utilities, natural monopolies providing a service for which the public paid the costs plus a reasonable rate of return on invested capital. Competition, they believed, should be limited to nonessentials like in-flight meals and other passenger amenities. This fundamentally noncompetitive structure characterized the industry until passage of the Airline Deregulation Act of 1978. See Jean T. McKelvey, ed., *Cleared for Takeoff: Airline Labor Relations since Deregulation* (Ithaca: Cornell University Press, 1988), 1-7, 371-76; Hopkins, *Flying the Line,* 279-90.

## ✈ Stationed in Honduras

1. In the beginning, America's domestic "scheduled" airlines existed purely to fly mail, and they regarded passenger service as a nuisance. Since the government paid a fixed amount per "pound-mile," the most profitable aircraft were small, single-engine mail planes with no room for passengers. Consequently, in the 1920s only a few airlines offered even rudimentary passenger service. Boeing Air Transport (one of United's predecessors) flew the "Boeing 40," a single-engine open cockpit biplane, which could carry four passengers—if there was room after the mail sacks were aboard—in cramped, noisy conditions.

Things began to change with passage of the Air Mail Act of 1930 (also known as the Watres Act), which compensated airmail contractors by the "space-mile" rather than the "pound-mile." Herbert Hoover's postmaster general, Walter F. Brown (the Ohio attorney-politician who had managed the 1928 presidential campaign), engineered this change in order to wean the airlines from the airmail dole. Brown reasoned that by forcing the contractors to buy aircraft larger than

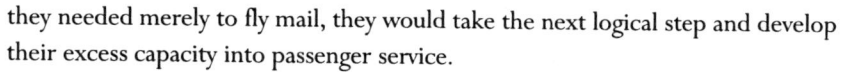

they needed merely to fly mail, they would take the next logical step and develop their excess capacity into passenger service.

Pan Am was different. Because of its long, overwater routes and the slowness and unreliability of competing surface forms of transportation, Pan Am flew large passenger-carrying planes almost from the beginning. Pan Am also had a reputation for being among the best at providing creature comforts. But as Kauffman notes, Pan Am's passenger amenities were far from perfect and won respect only because domestic airlines were so much worse. See Leary, *Airline Industry,* 20-23, 343; Hopkins, *Airline Pilots,* 100 (facing); William A. M. Burden, *The Struggle for Airways in Latin America* (1943; reprint ed., New York: Council on Foreign Relations and Arno Press, 1977), 3-7, 24-25.

2. Even if Kauffman himself didn't, other Pan American executives might have had underlying reasons for steering clear of the New York office. Juan Trippe was, by all accounts, a terror to his subordinates, and they were afraid of him. He kept them in constant turmoil with his brusque demands, peculiar decision-making, and mysterious mood swings. Consequently, junior executives found it wise to make themselves scarce, often conducting "field trips" or finding other work away from headquarters at the least provocation. See Bender and Altschul, *Chosen Instrument,* 102-10, 178-91, 294-98; Robert Daly, *An American Saga: Juan Trippe and His Pan Am Empire* (Random House: New York, 1980), 96.

3. Lest one think that Kauffman exaggerates the extent to which Pan Am "piggybacked" its way through Latin American in the company of sinister and corrupt forces, Bender and Altschul declare flatly: "Expediency was the moral imperative of the Pan American Airways empire builders, and they made no apologies for the means they used or the company they kept" (p. 127). Pan Am employees like Kauffman had the full, free use of United Fruit's facilities and services because of a deal the airline's financial wizard, Richard F. Hoyt, worked out between the two companies. A Wall Street insider who moved in the same social circles as Whitney, Hambleton, and Trippe, Hoyt also served on the boards of several other corporations that did business with United Fruit in Latin America. Hoyt made the deal that guaranteed Pan Am a monopoly of United Fruit's passenger business—one of the keys to the airline's early success. Bender and Altschul note, "Following Hoyt's dictum, Pan American rode the coattails of United Fruit, colonizer of banana republics and pioneer, in monopolistic concessions, for forty years" (p. 128).

Although critics of United Fruit's de facto imperialism often complained of Pan Am's cozy relationships, Trippe used his influence with the press and in

Washington to disavow any formal connection with the fruit company. These disavowals were in plain contradiction of the fact, which even casual observers noticed, that the employees of both companies acted as if they had a single employer.

So significant were Hoyt and his United Fruit connections that for a time he exercised power and influence that made him a formidable rival to Juan Trippe. Hoyt was even considered as a replacement for Trippe in the mid-1930s as the Pan Am board became concerned about his erratic managerial practices. Had Hoyt not died suddenly in March 1935, at the age of forty-six, he almost surely would have replaced Trippe when the board finally did oust him, temporarily, in 1939, in favor of C. V. "Sonny" Whitney. See Bender and Altschul, *Chosen Instrument,* 127-29, 180, 294-304.

## Jamaica and Haiti

1. The relatively small, twin-engined Sikorsky S-38, nicknamed the "Ugly Duckling," was the most successful aircraft designed by Russian emigré Igor Sikorsky. With its seaplane hull suspended beneath high, wing-mounted engines, elevated twin tail booms extending aft over the fuselage, and truncated "sesquiplane" lower wing, the S-38 was distinctive in appearance, resembling "a shoe tree onto which a wing had been attached." The S-38 was an amphibian, equally capable of operating from water or land, but it was more competent as a landplane. It normally carried two pilots and eight passengers (although that configuration varied), at a cruising speed of 110 mph. Sikorsky built 120 S-38s, with the first rolling off the production line in May 1928. Pan American acquired thrity-eight of these versatile aircraft, beginning in late 1928. Pan Am used them primarily to service the Caribbean "circle," a route of short hops and frequent stops (like the Jamaica to Haiti run), rather than the longer hauls to Buenos Aires and Rio. The S-38 was widely regarded as the airplane that made Pan Am's first significant profits. Pan Am retired its last S-38 in 1940. See Edward Jablonski, *Seawings: The Romance of the Flying Boats* (Garden City, NY: Doubleday, 1972), 31-43, 61-80; Davies, *Pan Am*, 12-13.

2. Pan Am had an inflated reputation for passenger service in the 1920s, mostly owing to Juan Trippe's skill at manipulating the news media. But like the domestic airlines, Pan Am's principal business was mail, not passengers, as Kauffman observes. When compared not to U.S. domestic airlines but to European air passenger operations, such as Lufthansa's, Pan Am was backward indeed.

Kauffman's comments about poor passenger amenities and consequent scarcity of customers came in late 1929 or early 1930, just as Postmaster General Walter Folger Brown began bludgeoning the domestic airlines into improvements. Using the leverage granted to him under terms of the Air Mail Act of 1930, Brown ruthlessly forced the domestic airlines to upgrade their passenger service as a prerequisite for holding a mail contract. Pan Am was not under the same kind of pressure from Brown as domestic airlines, because its long overwater routes already required it to fly the large, multiengine aircraft that made passenger service possible, and its contracts had been let in 1928, under terms of the Foreign Air Mail Act. But Pan Am won six of the seven Latin American routes, and its subsidiary, Pan American-Grace Airways (Panagra) got the seventh, even though it was not the low bidder in any case—in fact, it was the highest. So Pan Am was vulnerable to the same charges of political favoritism and insider dealing that would later taint the domestic airmail contracts let under the 1930 law.

The pressure Brown applied, including forced mergers of small operators with larger ones (so they could afford to buy larger aircraft), later became the basis of Franklin D. Roosevelt's celebrated cancellation of the airmail contracts in 1934. Alleging fraud, Postmaster General James Farley ordered the Army to fly the mail. It was a fiasco. A number of Army pilots were killed, thus giving opponents of the New Deal an emotional hook upon which to hang other criticisms.

Pan Am escaped cancellation of its contracts in 1934 on a fluke. Postmaster General Farley wanted to cancel Pan Am's contracts owing to Trippe's close association with the previous Republican administration, but the Navy (unlike the Army) refused even to attempt to fly the mail over such vast distances. There was also the problem of Pan Am's quasi-governmental status. Ralph O'Neill, founder of the New York, Rio & Buenos Aires Line (NYRBA), who lost out to Trippe and had his airline absorbed, declared in his memoirs: "Pan Am rode free and clear . . . for reasons said to affect foreign relations." It should be noted that Postmaster General Brown and President Hoover frankly admitted their goal of entrusting aviation only to well-financed entrepreneurs like Trippe. Brown declared publicly that he intended to exclude the "little guys" who could "only fly mail." The Air Mail Act of 1930, by Brown's interpretation, permitted him to do so. Despite all the uproar, including special Senate hearings led by future Supreme Court Justice Hugo A. Black of Alabama, subsequent court action exonerated Brown of all charges of malfeasance. Ironically, FDR's own aviation legislation, the Civil Aeronautics Act of 1938, closely followed Brown's plan. See Hopkins, *Airline Pilots,* 43-45; Leary, *Airline Industry,* 82-89; Henry R. Palmer, *This Was Air Travel* (New York: Bonanza Books, 1962), 124-25; Burden, *Struggle for Airways in Latin America,*

24-27; Henry Ladd Smith, *Airways: The History of Commercial Aviation in the United States* (New York: Knopf, 1942), 271-77; Ralph A. O'Neill, *A Dream of Eagles* (Boston: Houghton Mifflin Co., 1973), 313.

3. This passage deserves comment on two accounts: first, the difficulty of seaplane operations; and second, the problems caused by corruption. Although regal and romantic, the *only* advantage of seaplanes over landplanes was that they could operate in more places, providing calm water was available for landing and takeoff. The public wrongly believed (aided and abetted by Juan Trippe, on occasion) that Pan Am used seaplanes because they were safer. Early on, this might have been true, but by the time aircraft like the giant, four-engined "clippers" began operating, an open sea emergency "ditching" in a seaplane was only marginally better than a similar crash landing in a landplane. Neither was likely to survive intact.

Shortly after being hired away from his piloting job with Ford Motor Company by Pan Am in 1929, Roy Keeler discovered that the public had some peculiar notions about overwater landplane flights. "My first trips with Pan Am were Miami-Havana. I was hired because I was experienced with Fords, which Pan Am was going to use on that run. I flew the Ford to Cuba a few times, but then Basil [Rowe, the chief pilot at Miami] substituted the Fokker. It came out that passengers would not fly on the Ford because it didn't have floats. So Rowe put it out that the Fokker, which had a wooden wing [Fords were all metal], didn't have to have floats, because the wooden wing would float. So I had to get checked out on the Fokkers and we shipped our Fords to Panama."

Once land-based facilities became widely available during World War II, commercial seaplane operations were doomed, largely because of handling difficulties. Kauffman points out the rough water problem in this passage, but there were many other, more sinister problems associated with seaplane operations. The most potentially deadly was corrosion. The regular dipping of metal into saltwater took a frightful toll on the structural integrity of air frames and could lead to in-flight structural failure—usually without warning, and invariably with fatal consequences. In addition, saltwater spray ingested into engines during takeoff was very damaging and a constant problem. Hull design also caused headaches. In order to fly, a seaplane had first to rise up to what pilots called "the step," an aquaplaning position from which the bond of surface tension could be broken. The problem was that a hull shaped for water was aerodynamically unsatisfactory, and vice versa. Also, the hot, humid conditions under which Pan Am operated often meant that seaplanes did not have sufficient power to break the surface tension with the water and get airborne, except early in the morning or at night, when it was cooler. Night takeoffs in the inky blackness of a bay were inherently dangerous.

Nor was landing a seaplane any bargain. There was always the problem of floating logs in seadromes ripping the bottoms from seaplanes. Even worse, under certain conditions, a seaplane would "porpoise" terrifyingly, an alternating series of nose-up, nose-down oscillations that increased in amplitude until the seaplane buried its nose so deeply in the water that the tail section snapped off and came crashing forward into the passenger compartment. Under certain circumstances of adverse water and wind, a pilot could do nothing either to avoid or to control such a porpoise. Pan Am lost several seaplanes, with fatalities, because of porpoising.

The corruption problem was endemic in Latin America and the Caribbean. Culturally it was permissible and, in the case of foreign-owned corporations, almost expected. The extent to which corruption sapped the viability of the three major U.S. airlines operating in Latin America and the Caribbean, Braniff, Eastern, and Pan Am, remains speculative, but anecdotal evidence suggests that thievery and malfeasance played some role in their demise. For example, a Sikorsky S-38 operated by NYRBA (the pioneering airline which Juan Trippe acquired by highly questionable means in 1930) was *stolen* and subsequently crashed by thieves at Rio in 1932. See Jablonski, *Seawings;* Davies, *Pan Am*, 13, 20-21; John J. Nance, *Splash of Colors: The Self-destruction of Braniff International* (New York: William Morrow, 1984), 321-22; Roy Keeler, interview with editor, July 12, 1979, Vero Beach, Florida.

4. Kauffman's observations about the Marines in Haiti during the period of occupation (1915-34) and about race relations in the American South under segregation need little comment. Haitians say today that the American occupation made them realize, for the first time, that they were "niggers."
Interview, National Public Radio, "All Things Considered," July 1994.

#  A Revolution in Cuba

1. Gerardo Machado, Cuba's president from 1925 to 1933, began as something of a reformer and ended as something of a dictator. Machado was supplanted in a 1933 coup by Fulgencio Batista. Batista exercised de facto power in Cuba, either as president or commander of the Army (despite the fact that he had been only a lowly sergeant), until 1959, when he was violently overthrown by Fidel Castro. See William Harris and Judith Levey, eds., *The New Columbia*

*Encyclopedia* (New York: Columbia University Press, 1975), 694; Samuel Flagg Bemis, *A Diplomatic History of the United States,* 5th ed. (New York: Holt, Rinehart, & Winston, 1965), 507, 990.

2. Although Juan Trippe's personal morality, in the conventional sense of marital fidelity and normal social intercourse, was unquestionably of a high order, in matters of business it was something else. Stories of Trippe's sharp business dealings are legendary, and that he would pay bribes there can be no doubt. The cornerstone of his Pan American system rested on a peculiar transaction between Trippe and Cuban dictator Machado during a 1927 trip to Havana. Somehow, Trippe came away from that session with a document that virtually froze out his competitors. The details are lost to history, but Harold Ickes, Roosevelt's Secretary of the Interior, noted in his diary that Trippe was "an unscrupulous person who buys his way. He has made quite an unsavory reputation in South America." Bender and Altschul declared bluntly of Trippe, "His most disturbing characteristic was his deviousness."

Kauffman's observations about this incident of rejected bribery and Pan American's no-bribe policy are borne out by the recollection of Robert W. Blake (Kauffman's friend and retired pilot, personal communication, June 22, 1995. But in all probability, the individual who unsuccessfully sought bribes had lost his position of influence or power within Cuba and was no longer worth bribing—as Kauffman notes belatedly. Trippe would do whatever was necessary to make Pan Am a success, bribery included. See Solberg, *Conquest of the Skies,* 74-90; Bender and Altschul, *Chosen Instrument,* 14-15, 102-3, 347-48.

3. This was apparently *the* Harvey Firestone (1868-1938), founder of Firestone Tire & Rubber. Firestone had extensive holdings in tropical countries around the world because of his interests in rubber plantations. Firestone evidently liked the languid expatriate lifestyle of the tropics. He would have been sixty-five when Kauffman met him, hardly "elderly" by modern standards. See Harris and Levey, *New Columbia Encyclopedia,* 952.

4. The role of U.S. organized crime syndicates in Cuban gambling is well established. Fidel Castro ruthlessly extirpated Mafia gambling operations in Cuba after overthrowing the Batista regime in 1959, thus earning the lasting hatred of mafiosi. That explains why Mafia members were willing participants in CIA assassination plots against Castro during the 1960s. See Gerald Posner, *Case Closed: Lee Harvey Oswald and the Assassination of JFK* (New York: Random House, 1993), 454-55.

5. Kauffman refers here to FDR's "Good Neighbor Policy," which stood in sharp contrast to the "Big Stick" policy of his predecessors, most notably his cousin Theodore. American gunboat diplomacy directed at the Caribbean and Central America justified itself under the so-called Roosevelt corollary to the Monroe Doctrine. In order to forestall Europeans from taking direct military action over bad debts and other forms of governmental malfeasance, Teddy Roosevelt opted to play the role of regional policeman for them.

Following the Spanish-American War of 1898, U.S. military interventions in the region became routine. Increased U.S. economic involvement in the Caribbean and conventional notions of racial superiority justified Presidents Taft, Wilson, Harding, Coolidge, and Hoover in taking military action.

In addition, the security of the Panama Canal (completed in 1914) caused strategic concerns. Cuba was the focus of these matters because it was the largest and most important island in the Caribbean. In 1902, while U.S. forces still occupied the island, the new Cuban government was forced to accept the Platt Amendment, which, among other things, granted the U.S. the right to intervene militarily. In 1903, the U.S. obtained a military base at Guantanamo Bay on the eastern end of Cuba, which it retains to this day. Direct military interventions in Cuba occurred in 1906-9 and again in 1912.

The change came about in 1934, when FDR sent Under Secretary of State Sumner Welles to Cuba to negotiate a new agreement. Widely seen as part of the overall New Deal program, the Good Neighbor Policy abandoned the Platt Amendment and offered something akin to equality to governments of the region. It was not a perfect success, however. President Eisenhower interfered with Guatemala (indirectly through surrogates) in 1954, and John Kennedy did likewise with Cuba in 1961 at the Bay of Pigs. Lyndon Johnson all but declared the Good Neighbor Policy dead in 1965 when he invaded the Dominican Republic.

For the "Colossus of the North," the only valid historical judgment one can be sure of, with respect to relations with its small, troublesome neighbors to the south, is that the past is prologue. See Harris and Levey, *New Columbia Encyclopedia,* 694, 1155-56; Bemis, *Diplomatic History of the U.S.,* 518.

6. From the historian's perspective, this episode involving the escape of President Machado from Cuba substantiates the allegation that Pan Am was a quasi-governmental agency prior to World War II. Critics of Trippe's influence often claimed that he, not the Secretary of State, determined foreign policy in Latin America. That might be a bit overblown, but Kauffman proves beyond any

reasonable doubt that Pan Am was certainly an *instrument* of official foreign policy. See Bender and Altschul, *Chosen Instrument,* 124-25, 258.

7. Others have described the details of this episode somewhat differently. The revolutionaries did indeed fire at the plane as it escaped, inflicting minor damage. The individual in question, Dr. Orestes Ferrara, had been both Secretary of State and chief of the secret police under Machado. Kauffman, who was only twenty-six at the time, was, by all accounts, extremely lucky to get out alive, since Ferrara was, after Machado himself, the man the revolutionaries most wanted to kill. See Daley, *An American Saga,* 90.

## Planes and Pilots in the Thirties

1. Kauffman is only technically correct about Pan Am retiring its S-38 amphibians in about 1931. Because the airline either owned or had a substantial interest in several subsidiary airlines (such as Cubana), which were fully integrated into the Pan Am system, passengers bound for out-of-the-way destinations would have found themselves making part of the trip on S-38s (still bearing the Pan Am logo) until 1940.

Most pioneer Pan Am pilots would probably disagree with Kauffman's low opinion of the Sikorsky S-38 amphibian and its variants. By its very nature, an amphibian is a compromise, so it incorporates some of the best and worst features of landplane and seaplane design. For example, the landing gear of the S-38 was partially retractable, so it caused little aerodynamic drag in flight. Should a land runway be available, the landing gear weight penalty was worth the price for any pilot seeking to avoid a rough, windy seadrome, with its terrifying possibility of a "porpoise" landing or takeoff. On water, the landing gear could be lowered alternately as steering rudders, which mitigated the weight penalty even in that operational regime.

Had the S-38 been constructed without landing gear, it would not have been nearly so profitable to Pan Am on short routes. All seaplanes must frequently be "beached" for maintenance, repair, and flushing (freshwater hose-downs to minimize saltwater corrosion damage to aluminum skins.) Beaching a pure seaplane requires extra personnel, time, and equipment. Crews must float cumbersome detachable wheels (or a drydock platform) to the aircraft before it can be hauled out. The S-38 required minimal ground support because it could simply lower the landing gear and taxi out of the water on its own power. See Jablonski, *Seawings,* 61-80; Davies, *Pan Am,* 12-13, 26. My own experiences as a U.S. Navy seaplane pilot (1959-64) also support this point. I logged 1,400 hours of pilot time in the Martin P5M (SP5B) Marlin, the last fully operational pure seaplane (that is, it had no landing gear, only detachable "beaching" gear).

2. The New York, Rio & Buenos Aires Line (NYRBA) was a pioneering effort that flew passengers and mail to Latin America before Pan Am. Kauffman's casual mention of the lack of an airmail contract as the reason for NYRBA's failure only hints at the truth. Of all Trippe's many sharp business deals during his swashbuckling spurt of expansion between 1927 and 1931, the NYRBA acquisition skirted closest to ethical transgression.

NYRBA was the creation of Ralph A. O'Neill (1896-1980), a World War I ace whose career would make a good Hollywood movie. Born in Mexico to parents who were U.S. citizens, O'Neill grew up fluent in Spanish. He made a small fortune in mining prior to World War I, then volunteered for the Army Air Service after the U.S. entered hostilities in 1917. O'Neill abandoned mining for the romance of aviation in the 1920s, helping to create the Mexican Air Force under the Huerta regime. He even engaged in combat operations against rebels. In the late 1920s, O'Neill became Boeing's agent in charge of warplane sales to Latin American governments. While touring the continent in a Boeing F-2B single-seat fighter, trying to drum up business, O'Neill became obsessed with the idea of creating an airline that would span the continent's jungles and mountains. Trading heavily on his war hero status, O'Neill accumulated financial support for his airline that rivaled Trippe's.

Backed by financial and industrial titans such as James Rand of Remington Rand and Reuben H. Fleet, president of Consolidated Aircraft, O'Neill's NYRBA had real promise, since it held the Argentine government airmail contract. Argentina, which generated sixty percent of all Latin American mail to the U.S., was essential to Trippe's imperial plans. So Trippe purposefully undermined O'Neill in every way he could. For example, in October 1929, when Lou Hoover, the First Lady, arrived at the Anacostia naval base to dedicate NYRBA's Commodore, *Buenos Aires,* O'Neill expected to give a short welcoming speech before she swung a bottle of fizzwater (owing to Prohibition, the abstemious First Lady would have nothing to do with champagne). But much to O'Neill's surprise, who should emerge from the presidential limousine with Mrs. Hoover, surrounded by a phalanx of guards, but Juan Trippe! O'Neill was pushed aside, and although not completely excluded from the ceremonies (as he later claimed, incorrectly), he found himself playing second fiddle to Trippe, who made it appear that Pan Am owned NYRBA's Commodore. Screened away from the First Lady by Secret Service agents, O'Neill could do nothing but fume.

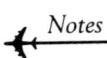 

NYRBA began service in August 1929 and completed its first scheduled New York to Buenos Aires trip in February 1930. The size, grace, and creature comforts of its Commodore flying boats (which carried twenty-two to thirty passengers, depending upon seating configuration) generated enormous publicity for NYRBA, even by the frenzied standards of that aviation-crazy era.

About all O'Neill and NYRBA did not have going for them was the U.S. airmail contract to Latin America. Trippe held it and thus had the critical weapon he needed to destroy NYRBA. With the support of Postmaster General Brown, who favored Pan Am as the "chosen instrument" of Post Office-supported aviation activities in Latin America, Trippe eventually forced NYRBA into a merger that was really a surrender. In August 1930, NYRBA's board bowed to the inevitable and accepted Trippe's offer of Pan Am stock—worth about one-third of their original $8.5 million investment—in return for the airline and all its assets, including the Argentine mail contract and all fourteen Commodores. When Trippe offered him the job of running the absorbed NYRBA as a "division" of Pan Am, the bitter O'Neill said, "Listen, Juan, you're the last man on earth I would work for." So disillusioned was O'Neill that he abandoned aviation and resumed his prewar career in mining. See Leary, *Airline Industry,* 313-15, 335-39; O'Neill, *Dream of Eagles,* 199-202; Davies, *Pan Am,* 20-21; Bender and Altschul, *Chosen Instrument,* 166-76.

3. The Commodore, with its hundred-foot wing span, sixty-eight-foot fuselage, and twin 575 horsepower Pratt & Whitney Hornet engines, established new standards of comfort and efficiency. The NYRBA exterior paint scheme was coral, cream, and black. The Commodore's interior was divided into six separate Pullman-style compartments, each with four facing seats and a different pastel color scheme. Each compartment offered panoramic views and was separated from the others by a central domed aisle in which passengers could stand erect. It was luxuriously carpeted and had waterproof, silk-like upholstered seats and shaded reading lights. In the rear, the Commodore had a lounge and lavatories. Passengers could also send messages via wireless, since a radio operator was aboard as part of the crew.

Consolidated's Commodore flying boat was the lineal predecessor of the famous PBY Catalina flying boat of World War II. The Commodore was designed originally as a U.S. Navy patrol aircraft, under a contract specification that called for it to be able to fly nonstop without refueling from California to Hawaii. The Martin Corporation eventually won the Navy contract, but Ralph O'Neill ordered the civilian model of the Admiral (as Consolidated called the Commodore's military version) for NYRBA in March 1929. For long-haul operations, the elegant Commodore was much superior to the smaller Sikorsky S-38 Pan Am was flying. Trippe desperately wanted the Commodore for Pan Am, but O'Neill had ordered fourteen of the aircraft, enough to keep Consolidated's factory busy for more than a year. NYRBA had eleven Commodores in service at the time Pan Am acquired them in the "shotgun marriage" of 1930.

Although not particularly fast, the Commodore could sustain flight at about 100 mph for over a thousand miles with a full load of twenty-four passengers and cargo. Beginning in December 1930, Pan Am used the Commodore on the Kingston, Jamaica-Barranquilla, Colombia "cutoff" route, which at six hundred overwater miles was the longest scheduled route flown by any airline in the world. The last Commodore, operated by Bahamas Airways (in which Pan Am had a forty-five percent interest), was not retired from service until September 1946. See Davies, *Pan Am,* 20-21; O'Neill, *Dream of Eagles,* 197-200.

4. Kauffman's discussion of the unique nature of piloting for Pan Am pertains almost entirely to the relatively brief era of the great flying boats, which ended with the close of World War II. The inherent difficulties of waterborne operations meant that once land-based facilities were available, Pan Am would quickly abandon seaplanes in favor of landplanes, so this elaborate structure of pilot qualification and training would become obsolete. During World War II, military construction of land-based airfields all over the world eliminated the flying boat's sole advantage—its ability to operate where no landing other than on water was possible.

The highly specialized curriculum Kauffman helped to set up in the early 1930s was actually the opening shot in a battle over pilot unionization that culminated when Pan Am's pilots affiliated with ALPA and eventually won a collective bargaining contract on June 16, 1945.

ALPA, founded in 1931, modeled itself upon professional unions such as the Great Lakes Pilots Association and other maritime unions of masters and mates. In 1933, Decision 83 of the National Labor Board (an agency of the New Deal's National Industrial Recovery Act) granted airline pilots special status. Subsequent New Deal airmail legislation in 1934 and 1935 and the cornerstone Civil Aeronautics Act of 1938 made airline pilots practically wards of the federal government, with their wages, working conditions, and right to unionize guaranteed. Pan Am's pilots benefited from unionization, which resulted in their being paid more than many managers who supervised them. Pilot pay occasioned much grumbling among executives such as Kauffman, whom Trippe (a notorious

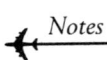 

penny-pincher) savagely underpaid for years. See Hopkins, *Airline Pilots,* 11-13, 19-29; Stuart Nixon, "A Capsule History: ALPA's Fifty Years," *Air Line Pilot: The Magazine of Professional Flight Crews* 50, no. 7 (July 1981): 11; Bender and Altschul, *Chosen Instrument,* 188-89, 463; ALPA, *Proceedings,* 1934 Convention, 845.

5. Pilot training has historically been one of the most contentious issues in a three-sided battle among ALPA, management, and the government. In the early 1930s, ALPA tried to get the government to establish an airline pilot academy similar to the U.S. Merchant Marine Academy at King's Point, New York. That effort failed. Until fairly recently, most airline pilots received their training from the military. Training after hiring has always been the responsibility of each company. Some airlines had reputations for rigorous in-service training, while others were fairly lax. Pan Am fell somewhere in the middle, as one might expect, since it contracted out pilot training. Other airlines, like TWA and United, established their own training schools in the early 1930s. Since all pilots faced recurrent flight checks from government examiners, inadequate training could result in loss of federal licenses and hence dismissal. So training was a significant issue in labor-management relations. See Hopkins, *Flying the Line,* 255; Hopkins, *Air Line Pilots,* 162-64.

6. Airline pilots vehemently opposed merit promotion. In their minds, a pilot was either competent or not, and so merit was meaningless. By ancient practice, dating back to the period between 1919 and 1927 when the Post Office Department's Air Mail Service provided almost the only steady employment for professional pilots, promotion rested upon seniority, not merit. Pilots feared that consideration of intangibles such as merit would result in promotion based upon favoritism rather than ability. At its 1934 convention, ALPA approved a resolution that stated bluntly: "The purpose of pilot seniority is to improve individual efficiency by discouraging favoritism."

Although Pan Am's pilots would not have a formal collective bargaining contract guaranteeing seniority rights until 1945, this passage confirms that they had a de facto seniority system, despite Kauffman's talk about merit promotions. Pan Am's pilots were active in union affairs almost from the very beginning. Roy Keeler (b. 1899), elected regional vice-president for ALPA in 1934, went to work for Pan Am in January 1929, flying the Miami-Havana run in Ford Trimotors. Keeler confirms that pilots insisted, as a matter of self-protection, on a seniority system.

Keeler learned to fly shortly after World War I (he had been an aircraft mechanic in the Signal Corps during the war) and then flew for the Ford company, promoting the "Tin Goose" on barnstorming tours. In the late 1920s, Ford supplied planes for a profitable little sightseeing operation, Skyview Lines, which flew over Niagara Falls during the summer. Keeler occasionally flew these excursions (on loan from Ford), when Skyview's two regular pilots were unavailable. Gregarious and friendly, Keeler liked flying passengers. "Labor Day it was just like pulling a shade down on Skyview," Keeler remembered during a 1979 interview. "Skyview had a deal to fly sightseers in Florida during the winter of 1928, and so Harold Gray and I were assigned to fly a brand new Ford down." (Gray, another legendary Pan Am pilot who worked for Skyview at the time, would later become Pan Am's president and chairman, personally chosen by Juan Trippe upon the occasion of his retirement in 1967.) "We got to Miami, and I heard that Pan Am was looking for pilots," Keeler continued. "So I went over and got a job, just quit Ford on the spot. In seniority I was pilot number six for Ford, and I was also number six for Pan Am. Harold Gray stayed with Skyview until the end of 1929, then he came over to Pan Am, too." So not only did Pan Am honor seniority among pilots, but the powerful, anti-union Ford Motor Company did, too. See Hopkins, *Airline Pilots,* 35-51; Roy Keeler, interview with editor; Bender and Altschul, *Chosen Instrument,* 265-66, 496-514.

7. Despite what Kauffman says, Trippe paid pilots well because he had no choice. Federal legislation required adherence to minimum standards of pay and working conditions as a condition of holding a mail contract. Decision 83 had been written into all airmail laws after 1933, and therein hangs a tale.

FDR's 1934 cancellation of the airmail contracts let by Hoover's Postmaster General Walter F. Brown generated fierce denunciations within the industry. Because the Navy lacked the capability of flying long overseas routes, Pan Am escaped the cancellation. When the Army foolishly tried to fly the domestic routes, the result was a disaster, both aeronautically and politically. Airline spokesmen called the cancellations "socialistic, even communistic." Charles A. Lindbergh all but called FDR a murderer when several Army pilots were killed flying the mail. This split between FDR and Lindbergh endured through the divisive "America First" isolationist movement and beyond.

Alone among all the industry's insiders, David L. Behncke, the gruff United pilot who had founded ALPA in 1931, supported FDR. It took courage, for most of Behncke's rank-and-file domestic airline pilots found themselves furloughed. Behncke shrewdly argued that FDR would have to return the airmail to private contractors—as he did after only three months. Behncke convinced his nervous pilots that if ALPA loyally and openly supported FDR in what historian Arthur

Schlesinger subsequently called "the New Deal's first great fiasco," he would protect them in subsequent legislation.

Events proved Behncke right. Upon sending new airmail legislation to Congress in 1934, FDR declared, "The occupation of air line pilot is hazardous. Therefore the law should provide for a method to fix maximum hours, minimum pay, and a system of retirement annuity benefits." The legislation FDR eventually signed stated, "It shall be a condition upon the awarding and holding of any air mail contract that compensation for pilots shall not be less than the rate paid in 1933 *as* modified *by the decisions of the National Labor Board* (emphasis added)." Unlike domestic airlines, Pan Am received waivers on flying time and duty hours owing to the singular nature of its long-range, overwater operations, but ALPA used these waivers to increase pilot pay—even before a formal collective bargaining contract was signed in 1945. Indeed, the pilots' union did not sign its first labor contract with any airline until the eve of World War II, because it did not need to.

So long as the airlines remained regulated public utilities, with management allowed to pass costs along to the public and the Post Office, unionization flourished. In 1978, when Congress passed the Airline Deregulation Act, thus ending federal economic control, the airlines had the highest percentage of unionized workers of any industry. Deregulation contributed mightily to Pan Am's failure in December 1991, as it did to the demise of Eastern and Braniff. See Hopkins, Airline Pilots, 143-57, 188-89; Hopkins, *Flying the Line,* 279-90; Paul S. Dempsey, *Flying Blind: The Failure of Airline Deregulation* (Washington, DC: Economic Policy Institute, 1990), 1-6.

8. Early airlines emphasized the skill and responsibility of their pilots as a means of reassuring nervous passengers. In the late 1920s, several airlines seemed to hit simultaneously upon the idea of uniforming their pilots and giving them the prestigious title of captain. The operation manager of one early airline said, "No longer do we speak of pilot so-and-so, but rather of captain so-and-so."

Aviation magazine, the fledgling industry's principal organ, in many articles published between 1926 and 1929 praised airline managers for building pilot prestige as an important step in luring passengers. Ironically, airline managers publicized the high pilot salaries government forced them to pay, citing them as proof of caution and probity in the cockpit. See private Hopkins, *Airline Pilots,* 16-17.

9. Pan Am's pilots were perhaps less inclined to unionize than domestic airline pilots because so many of them had Navy backgrounds and thought of

themselves as an elite. But their difference from domestic airline pilots was merely a matter of degree. Two legendary pilots, Edwin C. Musick and Basil L. Rowe, who in the 1930s served as chief pilots at New York and Miami, respectively, were notoriously hostile to ALPA. This merely meant that ALPA supporters among Pan Am pilots adopted a low profile.

The Mexican subsidiary *Compania Mexicana de Aviacion* (CMA), founded in 1924 by two Americans, W. L. Mallory and George Rihl (who managed the company's subsidiary for Trippe), became a Pan Am feeder line in 1930. CMA's pilots were originally all U.S. citizens, but by the early 1930s, rising nationalism forced the hiring of a few Mexican pilots. By 1932, CMA's U.S. pilots, fearing loss of their jobs as more Mexican pilots became available, openly affiliated with ALPA in hopes that the union could protect them. It couldn't. The leader of CMA's pilots, Frank Ormsbee, who had won the Congressional Medal of Honor as a Navy pilot in World War I, was fired for his union activities. ALPA subsequently made Ormsbee its Washington representative in early 1933, using his war-hero status to good advantage and fighting with Pan Am over his reinstatement. It came to nothing; Ormsbee got another flying job with a private company in 1934 and was killed in a crash almost immediately thereafter. But the Ormsbee affair proved that ALPA could play the game of public relations, and it forced Juan Trippe to do some artful dodging to defuse the criticisms of prolabor congressmen and senators. Trippe learned more quickly than most airline executives that tangling with ALPA was potentially dangerous. See Hopkins, *Airline Pilots,* 59-87; Davies, *World's Airlines,* 76-77; Bender & Altschul, *Chosen Instrument,* 129-72; Roy Keeler, interview with editor.

## Across the Pacific

1. Sumner Slichter (1892-1959), Lamont Professor of Economics at Harvard, was an influential and unorthodox scholar in the developing field of industrial relations during the early twentieth century. A Wisconsin native, Slichter earned his doctorate at the University of Chicago in 1918, then taught at both Princeton and Cornell before moving to Harvard in 1930. He is best remembered today for coining the phrase *creeping inflation,* which described the modest rise in prices Keynesians believed necessary for economic growth. Slichter was associated with the Brookings Institution (a liberal think-tank) and served on the staff of the Senate Finance Committee (1946-47), where he played an important role in creating the national unemployment insurance program. Slichter accurately predicted that the economy would convert to peacetime production without large-scale unemployment after World War II.

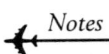 

An exemplar of the burgeoning liberal ethos taking root in academia during the 1930s, Slichter taught a generation of future business leaders that labor unions were not inherently evil. His courses featured guest lectures by labor leaders, who often surprised Harvard's elite students with their erudition, thus moderating stereotypical notions about class and social difference in the labor movement. Slichter's *The Challenge of Industrial Relations: Trade Unions, Management, and the Public Interest* (1947) was a seminal work that influenced decisionmakers far beyond academia.

Clarence N. Sayen (1919-1965), president of the pilots' union, ALPA, from 1951 to 1962, guest lectured frequently in Slichter's seminars. A former Braniff pilot, Sayen was witty and urbane and held advanced academic degrees. No future business leader, after exposure to the likes of "Clancy" Sayen, would have come away unaffected.

The interaction Slichter encouraged between labor and management was very influential. His "reeducation" of American business leaders had much to do with the relative peace that characterized labor-management relations for a generation. See Leary, *Airline Industry,* 420-21; Hopkins, *Flying the Line,* 164-74; *New York Times* (September 29, 1959), 39.

2. Juan Trippe's notorious parsimony kept junior executives in a constant state of frustration. Trippe exploited their loyalty to Pan Am—there is no other way to put it. Grumbling about Trippe's stinginess increased greatly after 1934, thanks to the pilots' successful campaign in Washington to stabilize their salaries at high levels as a condition of holding a mail contract. It irked Pan Am executives that they often earned less than the pilots they supervised. But Trippe kept the lid on executive protest by paying himself an absurdly low salary. Of course, Trippe made his money through stock options, which were not available to his subordinates until the 1950s, when, upon the defection of several talented managers to other airlines, he grudgingly allowed them. See Hopkins, *Airline Pilots,* 161-89; Bender and Altschul, *Chosen Instrument,* 462-64.

3. Trippe's imperious decision-making was legendary. He would conceptualize some vast, expansive scheme, and then airily leave the details to subordinates. Trippe habitually scrawled out orders in his own handwriting (a new route across a new ocean, or a new plane to be ordered) and expected his subordinates to accomplish it while he remained splendidly isolated in New York City. See Daley, *American Saga,* 96-97.

4. Kauffman has identified the major reason trans-Pacific service by Pan Am preceded transatlantic service. The Atlantic crossing was shorter and had

more economic potential, but existing aircraft technology would not permit a *direct* crossing from U.S. soil to Europe. The British were able to block transatlantic service because they controlled landing rights in Canada's northeastern maritime provinces and Bermuda. The DC-4, a four-engined aircraft developed during World War II, was the first plane capable of flying to Europe directly from U.S. airfields with anything approaching a profitable load of mail and passengers. Pan Am explored the possibility of flying its seaplanes to Europe as early as 1932, with an en route fueling stop in Bermuda during winters or Newfoundland during summers. Although not economically feasible, the British denied all transatlantic service until their own international airline, Imperial Airways (a quasi-governmental instrument of national policy) could compete. Pan Am would have been completely dominant on the Atlantic routes because of better aircraft and more frequent service in the mid-1930s.

Because he needed British cooperation, Trippe made a deal with them. The language of this "gentlemen's agreement" required Pan Am to wait until the British were competitive before beginning transatlantic service. Trippe had already acquired an aircraft capable of crossing an ocean (the Martin M-130), so he expanded Pan Am into the Pacific first. It was far more difficult to fly, and far less lucrative than the Atlantic, but the U.S. already owned the stepping-stones: Hawaii, Midway, Wake, Guam, and the Philippines. See Daley, *American Saga,* 205-13, 229; Jablonski, *Seawings,* 113-46.

5. Kauffman's infrequent mentioning of people like John Borger and Bill Taylor presents something of a problem. Both men were well-known among Pan Am insiders and important to the airline's history. But of the two, only Borger achieves mention in either of the two modern histories of Pan Am, Daley's *American Saga* (1980) and Bender and Altschul's *Chosen Instrument* (1982). Neither gains mention in two older histories, Henry Ladd Smith's *Airways* (1942) or Matthew Josephson's *Empire of the Air* (1943).

Borger and Taylor were proteges of André Priester who performed as jack-of-all-trades engineers, working on both airplanes and supporting facilities like landing fields and seadromes. After Kauffman, Borger became Pan Am's chief engineer after Priester's retirement and in the mid-1960s oversaw the technical development of the Boeing 747, which Pan Am was the first to fly in 1970. See Bender and Altschul, *Chosen Instrument,* 515; Daley, *American Saga,* 249, 436; Davies, *Pan Am,* 78-79.

6. Leroy L. Odell, who became Pan Am's chief airport engineer, had been associated with Juan Trippe since 1924. In the mid-1920s, before Pan Am took

shape, Odell (whose rank of captain stemmed from World War I Army service, not flying an airliner) teamed with Trippe and Major Lorillard Spencer (also a World War I veteran) to form a primitive aviation consulting service. Both Odell and Spencer were older than Trippe, but each deferred to the younger man.

In 1935, as it became apparent that Trippe's personal diplomacy with the British would not gain the necessary landing rights for an Atlantic service, Odell became the Pan Am official Trippe directly charged with building the Pacific facilities. It was a monumental logistical task, involving vast amounts of equipment, supplies, warehousing, port facilities, a ship, and finding and hiring the personnel who would sail into the remote Pacific, there to spend an indeterminate time constructing those facilities. In March 1935, the *North Haven* (Odell's leased ship) steamed out of the Golden Gate with 118 men and everything that would be needed in the coming months. The ship returned in July, leaving nearly half the original complement behind, at work on Midway and Wake islands. See Bender and Altschul, *Chosen Instrument,* 62, 234-35.

7. Pan Am's pioneering radio navigation experiments were in the hands of Hugo C. Leuteritz (b. 1903), a Navy-trained engineer whom Trippe hired away from RCA in January 1929. Leuteritz had developed a primitive radio homing device for Pan Am in 1927 while on loan from RCA. Early pilots flew entirely "contact" (or seat-of-the-pants), always keeping the ground in sight, and they navigated with visual reference to landmarks. They flew in clouds or fog only in emergencies. While pilots had enough primitive instrument flying equipment to keep their planes right side up "in the soup," they had no way of navigating because of inadequate ground-based facilities. Not until the mid-1930s would pilots be able to fly "on the beam" of government-built radio ranges and navigate "on the gauges."

The ninety miles between Key West and Havana had no physical landmarks by which pilots could navigate, but neither did it have any mountains they could hit. So Pan Am's pilots could fly the Havana-Key West route "blind" in 1927, if they only had a system to guide them to the immediate vicinity of the seadrome, where they could usually let down safely until they could see the ocean's surface. The flare system of locating the immediate vicinity of an island (either in bad weather or because of radio failure) was begun in the Caribbean. Although flares were installed in the Pacific as a backup, they were unnecessary; radio navigation had improved rapidly. See Bender and Altschul, *Chosen Instrument,* 158-65; Hopkins, *Flying the Line,* 18-23; Keeler interview.

8. The connection between the Navy and Pan Am was always fairly direct, particularly in the public's mind. Pan Am would, until well after World War II, display a marked preference for hiring ex-Navy pilots as well as enlisted men for its ground support staff. In the 1930s, everything about Pan Am said "Navy," from its pilots' uniforms to the seaplanes they flew. But the connection was more than mere image. While the Navy publicly disavowed any formal connection to Pan Am's Pacific facilities (young men eager to work for Pan Am in the Pacific often wrote directly to the Navy Department in Washington), the Navy rendered enormous assistance to Pan Am. The Navy wanted facilities on Wake, Midway, and Guam, but it had refrained from building them in order to allay Japanese fears that they were intended as defensive fortifications. Pan Am provided the perfect cover, so the Navy did everything in its power to assist Pan Am, including lending the airline technical support and personnel. See private Bender and Altschul, *Chosen Instrument,* 232-36.

9. Kauffman was not alone in being unable to figure out Trippe's complex financial maneuvering. His secretiveness and imperiousness with regard to financial arrangements was the reason Pan Am's directors temporarily ousted him from operational control of the airline on March 14, 1939. This would have been at about the time Kauffman noted the placards in Boeing 314 flying boats indicating that they were owned not by the airline but by banks.

Pan Am's board, heretofore chosen by Trippe himself and noted mostly for subservience to him, necessarily added lenders' representatives after 1935. Up to the opening of the Pacific routes, Pan Am had been quite successful financially, largely owing to the fact that in Latin America, Trippe never began flying until he had a U.S. mail contract in hand, and thus guaranteed profits. But the Pacific operation was different. The political climate in Washington changed after the Democrats and FDR arrived in 1933, and Pan Am was under scrutiny as the aviation pet of the previous Republican administration. The upshot was that Trippe had to invest heavily in the Pacific operation before Pan Am could begin drawing government funds. Since the Pacific airmail route was insufficient to generate a profit on mail alone, Pan Am began losing money. The airline lost nearly a hundred thousand dollars per month during the three years following inauguration of Pacific service in 1936.

Despite these losses, Trippe plunged ahead to open the Atlantic routes in 1939. The bankers on his board, worried about their loans, opposed what they saw as Trippe's reckless expansion. So they engineered a boardroom coup that replaced Trippe with his aristocratic Yale classmate and Pan Am cofounder, C. V.

"Sonny" Whitney. Many details of Trippe's ouster and demotion to figurehead president are in dispute, and the company's records are vague on the actual disposition of power. Trippe claimed that he never really relinquished operational control, but he nevertheless had to surrender his prestigious corner office on the fifty-eighth floor of the Chrysler Bulding—a humiliation for him.

It soon became clear that Whitney was incapable of running the airline on a day-to-day basis. His real interest in Pan Am was in making ceremonial speeches as chairman of the board, so long as they didn't conflict with his other interests, mainly womanizing and horseracing. Trippe's exile from power ended on January 9, 1940, when the board formally reinstated him.

These events were sandwiched in time around the outbreak of World War II in Europe, which brought tremendous profits to Pan Am. Trippe's foresight in positioning Pan Am to fly the oceans made his running up of a huge debt seem prescient. In 1939, Pan Am earned nearly six million dollars in profits after taxes, and Whitney clearly had nothing to do with this windfall. Seeprivate Daley, *American Saga,* 231-40, 252-53.

10. Although Pan Am had 121 planes in service in 1935, the largest fleet of commercial aircraft in the world, most of them were smaller amphibians and landplanes scattered throughout its extensive Latin American route system. The airline's premier aircraft of the 1930s were the great four-engine ocean flying boats. These aircraft, the only ones named Clippers, dominated Pan Am's romantic image, but they were never very numerous.

The first four-engine Clipper, the Sikorsky S-40, was merely an enlarged version of the twin-engine S-38. Pan Am had only three S-40s, the Clippers *American, Caribbean,* and *Southern,* all of which were used exclusively in Latin America because of their relatively short range. The improved S-42, which flew the pioneering survey flights in the Pacific, eliminated the "birdcage" external struts, boom-mounted tails, and underslung engines of the S-40 in favor of engines mounted internally in the leading edge of the wing. Pan Am ordered ten S-42s in October, 1932, and began regular passenger service on the Miami-Rio route with them on August 16, 1934. Pan Am would eventually own eleven S-42s, but when the Pacific service began, it had only three on hand.

The Martin 130 was only marginally superior to the S-42 in range and carrying capacity, and inferior to it in speed—130 mph vs. 150 mph. But it was arguably the most famous airplane in the world when it opened regular passenger service across the Pacific on October 21, 1936. Millions of Americans thrilled to the live radio broadcast describing the first trans-Pacific M-130 departure from

San Francisco. As Kauffman notes, however, there were only three M-130s, the Clippers *Hawaiian, Philippine,* and, most famously, *China.* Trippe never ordered any more, and he was frequently warned that should one aircraft be lost, the service could not continue. When the Clipper *Hawaiian* was mysteriously lost without a trace east of Manila on July 28, 1938, Pan Am suspended its trans-Pacific service indefinitely.

Neither the S-42 nor the M-130 was entirely satisfactory as a trans-Pacific aircraft. The S-42 could not carry any passengers or mail at all; it had to carry extra fuel in makeshift tanks installed in what would have been the passenger and cargo spaces (a highly dangerous situation because of fumes), so it was used exclusively for route surveys and support services. The M-130 could carry a maximum of only eight passengers and some mail, not enough to be profitable. If all the M-130's passenger seats were filled, it could not carry enough fuel to cross the longest overwater portion, the San Francisco to Hawaii segment. It could carry a few more on the shorter segments to Midway, Wake, Guam and Manila, but there were seldom more passengers aboard an M-130 than its crew members.

So Pan Am never ordered any more M-130s, preferring instead to put out bids "on speculation" (or "spec") for a true trans-Pacific flying boat, offering a fifty-thousand-dollar prize for the winning design in 1936. Glenn Martin felt betrayed when Juan Trippe asked for additional bids, denounced him with considerable bitterness, and claimed that the losses he incurred in developing the three M-130s nearly ruined him. Martin believed that he should have been allowed to improve the M-130 and recover his development costs. Thereafter Martin would confine his flying boat business exclusively to the Navy.

Igor Sikorsky, likewise irritated by Trippe's cavalier treatment, also declined to submit another money-losing spec flying boat bid without some kind of guarantee of follow-on orders to recover costs. This Trippe would not do. Only Boeing showed any interest in Trippe's 1936 spec competition. Their design would result in the most successful flying boat in history, the Boeing 314. But only twelve such aircraft would be built. See Daley, *American Saga,* 165-75, 194, 223-24; Davies, *Pan Am,* 36-43.

11. Charles N. Monteith, who moved from academic life to the practical application of his knowledge in business, was a leading theoretical aerodynamicist who tended toward the conservative in aircraft construction and design. His association with Boeing began in the early 1930s, when the company elected to diversify from its primarily military business into commercial airliners. Monteith won plaudits for his contributions to the first truly modern all-metal airliner, the

Boeing 247, which first flew on February 8, 1933. The B-247 was a pathbreaking aircraft that incorporated almost every technological advance available in aviation at the time: retractable landing gear, controllable pitch propellers, monocoque construction (stress-bearing skin), and cantilevered (no external struts or braces) wings.

Despite Monteith's achievements, his conservative streak showed when he said of the B-247, "They'll never build 'em any bigger." Monteith thought the twin-engine, ten-passenger, 13,650-lb. airliner had reached the size limits for structural safety. He was quite wrong. Eventually, his B-247 would lose out to similar Douglas aircraft, the DC series, because Donald Douglas's design could be "stretched" or enlarged from the DC-2 into the DC-3. With its inherent design limitations, Monteith's B-247 was not stretchable. See Solberg, *Conquest of the Skies*, 151-53; Taylor, *History of Aviation*, 230-33; Roger E. Bilstein, *Flight in America 1900-1983: From the Wrights to the Astronauts* (Baltimore: Johns Hopkins University Press, 1984), 85-89.

12. The most critical phase of the westbound trans-Pacific crossing was the first, from San Francisco to Honolulu. The prevailing westerly winds slowed down these flights and created a critical "point of no return" roughly midway in the 2,400-mile trip, at which (under certain conditions) the airplane could neither reach Hawaii nor return safely to San Francisco. Predicting the shifting location of this point was one of the great practical engineering challenges of trans-Pacific operations. Each time a Pan Am flight had to return because of this factor, it cost the company money. To his credit, Trippe never second-guessed a pilot's decision to return to base (providing his calculations checked out), saying, "The greatest courage is sometimes the courage to turn back." See private Daley, *American Saga*, 178.

13. One of the most extraordinary aspects of the Pan Am story involves the life of its crews living on these remote atolls, often for many months under primitive conditions. The first personnel dropped off by the North Haven in 1935 included a high proportion of college boys eager to seek adventure with Pan Am in the exotic Pacific. One of them was Bill Mullahey, a star swimmer at Columbia University, who, with only goggles and swim fins (SCUBA had not yet been invented) and no previous experience with explosives, would spend the next year clearing the Wake Island seadrome by blasting coral heads out of the lagoon. See Daley, *American Saga*, 150, 162, 176-80.

14. Edwin C. Musick (1894-1938), Pan Am's chief pilot, was the most famous pilot of his day, second only to Lindbergh. A self-taught aviator, Musick

worked as a barnstormer and mechanic prior to World War I. During the war, he became a Marine officer and flight instructor. From 1919 to 1923, Musick worked as a pilot for Aeromarine Airways, flying fourteen passenger Curtiss flying boats between Miami and the Bahamas. When Aeromarine folded in 1923, Musick (like many another pilot during Prohibition) flew bootleg whiskey between Cuba and Key West.

Musick's legitimate aviation career resumed in 1926, when André Priester hired him as a pilot during the five-month Philadelphia Rapid Transit experimental airline between Philadelphia and Washington, D.C. In 1927, when Trippe hired Priester as Pan Am's operations manager, Musick was an obvious choice as a pilot for the Havana-Key West run. Musick was Priester's kind of pilot: meticulous, conscientious, and sober in his habits. He flew the survey flights in the Pacific because Lindbergh, the route explorer of Latin America, had by 1935 gone into self-imposed English exile following the kidnap-murder of his son. Musick got enormous publicity in the mid-1930s. He was the first of several airline pilots who would become sought-after public heroes during the 1930s, entertaining offers to endorse everything from cigarettes to shaving cream. Musick's terse shyness was reminiscent of Lindbergh's, perfectly fitting stereotypical notions of the strong, silent, unflappable aviator. His fame was partially attributable to a series of eyewitness newspaper accounts of the Pacific route surveys, ghostwritten by Pan Am's indefatigable public relations specialist, William Van Dusen. See Daley, *American Saga,* 165-75; Leary, *Airline Industry,* 380-81; Hopkins, *Airline Pilots,* 10-12, 126-27.

15. The story of Kauffman's and Musick's typhoon encounter between Guam and Manila illustrates either how memory plays tricks on eyewitnesses or how historians get things wrong. Kauffman made the Pacific crossing several times, often with Musick. On this particular crossing, with both Priester and Boeing's chief engineer Monteith (the cigar swallower) aboard, was Musick the pilot? Robert Daley, a careful historian working from documents, believes that Mike La Porte, not Musick, was the M-130 captain. What makes this impossible to know, for sure, is that in *American Saga,* Daley cites Kauffman, in a letter dated July 11, 1978, as his source that La Porte was the pilot. See Daley, *American Saga,* 179, 493n.

16. Unfortunately for the Portuguese, Trippe had no real interest in seedy, decayed little Macao. He always went first class, and he had a nose for social status that always impelled him toward the best of everything—accommodations and clothes, of course, but also destinations for Pan Am. Trippe would have Hong

Kong, the premier destination of Far Eastern travel, as Pan Am's terminus, or he would have nothing. Shrewdly, Trippe figured that Hong Kong's business community, fearful of losing the advantages of trans-Pacific air service, would force London to grant him access to Hong Kong. He was merely using Macao as a ploy. Trippe spent a few dollars building a makeshift seaplane base there, then sat back and waited. Things worked out exactly as he planned. The British came to *him* asking that Pan Am serve Hong Kong, rather than Macao. See Daley, *American Saga,* 181-82.

17. John Leslie (b. 1905) did pioneering work in long-range cruising techniques to save fuel on trans-Pacific crossings. He also supervised critical preparations for the first scheduled mail flight of November 22, 1935 (the first scheduled passenger flight would not come until October 21, 1936). Shortly after takeoff, Ed Musick discovered that he could not get the heavily loaded M-130 to climb out of "ground effect," the cushion of compressed air between the plane's wing and the surface. Until the M-130 lightened its load by burning off fuel, Musick could only fly straight ahead toward the unfinished Oakland Bay Bridge, which was festooned with dangling cables. While millions listened via live radio hookup to the announcer's breathless description, and multitudes more watched from the shore, the M-130 skimmed under the bridge, narrowly missing the cables. Crew members recalled involuntarily ducking as the flying boat passed underneath the bridge. Leslie, who went on to a long and distinguished career, eventually become a vice-president at Pan Am. He always claimed that watching Musick's under-bridge takeoff instantly turned his hair prematurely white. See Daley, *American Saga,* 165-75.

18. A later generation would react to the *Challenger* space shuttle disaster much as Kauffman's generation did the loss of the S-42 *Samoan* Clipper on January 11, 1938. The best evidence as to what happened is that fuel vapors collected in the hub tower, which connected the high wing to the fuselage of the S-42. The hub tower contained the S-42's electrically powered flap motors. While dumping fuel, Musick almost certainly shut down all equipment that could have generated a spark and opened all the airliner's windows to get rid of the highly combustible fuel-air vapors. But he apparently forgot about the enclosed hub tower. When he engaged the flaps, a spark probably ignited the vapors. See Daley, *American Saga,* 194-201.

# A Base in Newfoundland

1. This concurrent operation illustrates the "gentlemen's agreement" Trippe struck with George Woods-Humphrey, managing director of Imperial Airways in 1928. Trippe, who badly needed British landing rights, had no alternative but to honor this agreement long after he would have been able to open a transatlantic service on his own, in the mid-1930s. In February 1937, the U.S. State Department approved the simultaneous service concept in Clause H of an Anglo-American diplomatic agreement on transatlantic service. The Justice Department later raised antitrust questions about the clause, but by then the point was moot; both Imperial and Pan Am had already begun flying the Atlantic.

2. Pan Am had discovered through trial and error that docking barges for servicing flying boats were often superior to fixed piers. For one thing, barges were portable and could be moved when the airline's routes shifted. In these far northern latitudes, piers were impractical; enormous tides raised and lowered by more than twenty feet the surfaces of the protected bays and fjords that flying boats needed to land safely. Keeler interview.

3. The flight described was the first of several survey flights, proving runs for later scheduled service. They carried some mail, mainly for ceremonial purposes, but they were not *scheduled* flights, which would not begin until 1939. The specially modified S-42, the *Pan American Clipper III,* made the 1,900-mile crossing from Botwood to Ireland in twelve hours and thirty minutes, but it could have flown for 3,150 miles—all the way to the Italian boot heel, if necessary. In contrast, the British S-23 Empire flying boat *Caledonia,* which simultaneously left on the westbound crossing, battled adverse winds and took three hours longer to cross. It only barely made Newfoundland. Pan Am would make three crossings that summer; the British, five.

The four-engine S-23 Empire flying boat for which the British were waiting, and upon which they staked their hopes for a successful transatlantic aircraft, proved unsatisfactory. Although faster than American flying boats, the Empire lacked range and was only just able to cross the Atlantic in a stripped-down condition. The British flying boats were flying bombs, sloshing with makeshift fuel tanks, and were flown "stripped to the bone." John Leydon, an Irish aviation official, wanted (for the sake of Irish national pride) to be the first passenger across when the plane left Shannon. When told that the S-23's seats had been removed, Leydon offered to sit on the floor. But the floor had been removed too! There was literally no place for him to sit or stand.

The S-23's uselessness as a commercial vehicle was why regularly scheduled service across the Atlantic would be delayed until 1939, when the improved S-23 G-class flying boat was at last ready. See Davies, *Pan Am,* 36-40; Daley, *American Saga,* 211-13, 217-18; Jablonski, *Seawings,* 168-69.

4. Manufactured by Short Brothers, Ltd. (named for founders Eustace, Horace, and Oswald Short, who began as balloon makers prior to World War I), the Empire was no match for American flying boats, particularly the Boeing 314. When Pan Am and Imperial Airways simultaneously inaugurated service between Bermuda and the U.S. mainland in June 1937 (in accordance with the 1928 "gentlemen's agreement" about reciprocal service), the Empire *Cavalier* had to be transported from Britain to Hamilton, Bermuda, *by ship*—it was incapable of flying there, even with en route fueling stops in the Azores. Despite modifications over the years, the Shorts' flying boats never achieved sufficient range or carrying capacity for the central Atlantic route via Bermuda and the Azores and were only marginally satisfactory performers over the shorter northern route via Newfoundland. Given the iced seadromes along the northern route during most of the year, ability to fly the central Atlantic route was critical in the era of flying boats. See Josephson, *Empire of the Air,* 127; Daley, *American Saga,* 207-13; Taylor, *History of Aviation,* 79; Bender and Altschul, *Chosen Instrument,* 265; Davies, *Pan Am,* 40; Jablonski, *Seawings,* 168-69.

## ✈ Opening Up Alaska

1. Harold M. Bixby (1890-1965) is perhaps best remembered today as one of the original St. Louis backers of Charles A. Lindbergh. In fact, it was Bixby, a St. Louis banker, who coined the name *Spirit of St. Louis* for the famous Ryan monoplane that "Slim" Lindbergh flew to Paris in 1927. Had it not been for Bixby, Lindbergh would never have succeeded. At a particularly low point, when Lindbergh was near despair and on the verge of giving up on the Paris flight because of financial difficulties, Bixby talked him out of it, saying, "You just leave the finances to us, and we'll leave the flying to you."

An Army balloon pilot during World War I, Bixby saw his bank fail after the stock market crash of 1929, and he needed a job. Lindbergh personally escorted him to Juan Trippe's New York office and insisted that Pan Am hire him. Trippe, always in awe of Lindbergh, hired Bixby in December 1932 specifically to go to China to manage China National Aviation Corporation (CNAC), a Pan Am subsidiary. Bixby was successful in China and went on to a long and distinguished

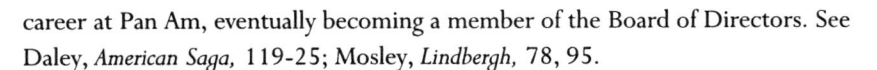

career at Pan Am, eventually becoming a member of the Board of Directors. See Daley, *American Saga,* 119-25; Mosley, *Lindbergh,* 78, 95.

2. Actually, Trippe became involved in Alaskan aviation as early as 1926, when he formed Alaskan Air Transport and persuaded Pan Am's board to finance it. He operated a single war surplus DH-4 airplane there for several months but withdrew upon failing to get an airmail contract. In 1931, Pan Am indirectly sponsored Charles Lindbergh's exploratory "great circle" flights to Asia via Alaska. The fact that Lindbergh took along as crew his winsome bride, Anne Morrow Lindbergh (daughter of Dwight Morrow, former ambassador to Mexico and chairman of the Morrow Board, appointed in 1925 by Calvin Coolidge to study national aviation policy), only added to the publicity surrounding these flights. Using a specially built single-engine Lockheed Sirius floatplane, the Lindberghs traversed the great arc, finally winding up in China. Lindbergh reported to Trippe that scheduled service to Asia via Alaska was feasible with existing aircraft.

In 1932, Trippe acquired two foundering airlines, Alaskan Airways and Pacific International Airways, primarily to obtain experience operating in Alaska before opening the northern great circle route to Japan and China via the Pacific maritime provinces of the Soviet Union. These plans eventually came to nothing, but Trippe, who always took the long view, continued to invest in Pan Am's Alaskan subsidiaries despite the fact that both were money losers. See Daley, *American Saga,* 14-15; Bender and Altschul, *Chosen Instrument,* 71-74, 201-3.

3. Indicative of the transitional times, Trippe hedged his operational bets in Alaska by using both the Sikorsky seaplanes and a landplane, the new Lockheed Electra. Unlike the Boeing 247 (a comparable airplane technologically), the Electra could be "stretched." Eventually it would become one of the most familiar short-haul airliners of the 1930s and went into wide production during World War II as the *Hudson* (Army) and *Ventura* (Navy) light bomber, used mostly for coastal patrol. The Electras were very fast for their day, cruising at 190 mph while carrying from ten to eighteen passengers, depending upon the model. Pan Am ordered a dozen Electras in December 1933. Only two went to Alaska. The remainder went to Pan Am's South American subsidiary, Panair do Brasil. Pan Am operated its internal Alaskan routes during the 1930s with a ramshackle collection of obsolete Consolidated Fleetsters, Fairchild Pilgrims, and a lone, single-engine Ford 8-AT (the only single-engine model of the famous Ford Trimotor ever built), acquired with the purchase of the Alaskan and Pacific International Airways. See Davies, *Pan Am,* 32-33.

4. In fact, Wiley Post (1898-1935) crashed less because of his missing eye than because of his faulty airmanship. Post, an entirely self-taught pilot with virtually no formal education, will be forever associated with the death of his passenger, Will Rogers, one of the most popular entertainers of his day. That fatal crash en route to Point Barrow, Alaska, capped a meteoric career of round-the-world stunt flying that made Post, briefly in the early 1930s, a national celebrity. Success in the high-stakes game of air racing, which became a national mania in the decade after Lindbergh's flight, earned Post tickertape parades and public acclaim.

The crash that killed Post and Rogers was caused by a misdesigned airplane. Post had married an inappropriate wing to its fuselage, making it nose heavy. It would fly so long as the engine was running, but should it fail, it would not glide. When Post lost power while attempting to take off at Whitehorse, Alaska, on August 20, 1935, his Lockheed Orion-Explorer nose-dived fatally. Captain Joe Crosson, a Pan Am pilot, flew the bodies home in a Lockheed Electra, to intense national mourning. See Davies, *Pan Am,* 33; Stanley R. Mohler and Bobby H. Johnson, *Wiley Post, His Winnie Mae, and the World's First Pressure Suit* (Washington: Smithsonian Institution Press, 1971), 1, 112-15.

## ✈ *Luxury Passenger Service*

1. Weighing 82,500 lb., with a wing span of 152 feet, the B-314 was enormous. Boeing adapted the wings and tail from its unsuccessful XB-15 bomber and constructed the fuselage using the latest in hull designs. The B-314 had a clean, modern look with no drag-inducing floats hanging from its wingtips. Instead, it had "sponsons," a kind of waterwing attached to its hull at the waterline to stabilize it while taxiing. The B-314 was designed for the new "compound" Wright engines (with double rows of cylinders), which burned the new 100-octane aviation gasoline; previous aircraft engines had used lower-octane automobile gas.

Pan Am's first B-314 was supposed to be delivered by December 21, 1937. However, a harrowing series of problems during flight testing delayed it. The B-314's poor water handling characteristics nearly caused it to sink on one occasion, when the sponsons failed to keep the wingtips clear of the water. Once, while taxiing in a strong crosswind, the wingtip submerged almost up to the outboard engine. It also had inadequate rudder control. In the latter case, during the first flight, the test pilot could not turn the aircraft except by manipulating the engine throttles. Miraculously, he got it back on the water safely, but extensive reengineering was necessary, eventually resulting in the B-314's distinctive triple tail. The delivery of the first B-314 to Pan Am did not occur until January 27,

1939—over two years late. See Davies, *Pan Am,* 42-43; Daley, *American Saga,* 223-30; Harold Mansfield, *Vision: A Saga of the Sky* (New York: Duell, Sloane, & Pierce, 1956), 128-32.

2. André Priester was adamantly opposed to serving liquor aboard Pan Am airplanes. In 1927 he had fought a hard battle to keep Pan Am pilots from drinking, and he thought it a bad idea to allow passengers to imbibe. But airline passengers in the 1930s were a self-consciously chic lot, who favored cocktails before dinner and wine with it. Trippe knew that Pan Am's clientele often brought their own bottles aboard and pressed the all-male stewards to serve as bartenders. But Trippe deferred to Priester on the drinking issue until he returned to power after the Sonny Whitney interlude ended in early 1940.

Upon regaining control of Pan Am in January 1940, Trippe punished executives who (in his opinion) had shown too much enthusiasm for Sonny Whitney. Priester had accepted promotion to vice-president under Whitney—a fatal error. Overruling Priester on inflight liquor service was the first in a long series of deliberate slaps by Trippe, which would culminate in Priester's complete removal from a position of authority. Trippe allowed Priester to remain with Pan Am, but after 1940 he was disheartened and never understood why Trippe sought to destroy him. See Daley, *American Saga,* 244, 417-19; Leary, *Airline Industry,* 380-81; Keeler interview. Robert Blake recalled Priester "did not have the same control of the operation of the airline that he had before 1940. By then Pan Am had five separate operating divisions and had gone to a decentralized management which gave most of the day-to-day control to each Division Manager. but there was always consultation with Priester on technical matters and he remained in charge of Pan Am's new aircraft development programs at Boeing, Lockheed, and Douglas," personal communication, June 22, 1995.

3. The stewards were all male until after World War II began. Personnel shortages required Pan Am to hire female stewardesses beginning in 1943, and there was great doubt that they could do the work of men, because it was so arduous. Roy Keeler, a pioneer flying boat pilot working the Latin American routes in the 1930s, said, "Those boys worked like dogs"; Keeler interview. Making beds, cooking and serving meals, and running errands for the passengers was strenuous work when done at altitude, where oxygen deprivation left stewards constantly exhausted. On many routes, the stewards also had to assist with the flying boat's docking and ground handling.

Cabin noise in propeller-driven "reciprocating" engines was a formidable problem, and the bigger the engine, the noisier. Not until jet engines began to replace "recips" in the 1960s did air travel really boom with the public, partly because jet engines had less vibration and consequently made less noise inside the cabin. Of course, noise outside, for residents living near airports, was much worse with jets. See Daley, *American Saga,* 244-47; Georgia P. Nielsen, *From Sky Girl to Flight Attendant* (Ithaca: Cornell University Press, 1982), 11, 46.

4. Priester ordered Boeing to build access passageways into the wings of the B-314 because he thought it might be necessary to perform minor mechanical work while airborne or after an emergency open-sea landing. This decision proved expensive and also pointless, owing to the increasing reliability of engines. Priester's tendency to overengineer Pan Am aircraft also played a role in Trippe's growing dissatisfaction with him. "André, we can't be out in front of the entire aviation industry," Trippe said in countermanding Priester on one occasion. See Daley, *American Saga,* 243, 418; Roy Keeler, interview with editor.

5. Because of the modified open-sea landings the B-314 had to make in the Azores, Pan Am pilots were especially wary about what they called the "sea state." Under certain conditions, the sea was simply too rough and the swells too large to permit either takeoff or landing. For example, during the winter of 1940-41, only fourteen of twenty-five scheduled crossings were completed because of violent weather and water conditions at Horta in the Azores. These weather conditions exacerbated the B-314's terrifying tendency to "porpoise" on landings. This problem had bedeviled seaplane operations from the beginning, but the size and complexity of the B-314 made it particularly acute. Initially, Pan Am's pilots were reluctant to admit the problem, fearing that it might reflect upon their competence. But after a series of incidents involving minor structural damage, their complaints forced Boeing to fix the problem. Once the hull was modified, the B-314 became one of the best rough water seaplanes ever built, able to handle the difficult landings in the Azores. See Daley, *American Saga,* 248-50, 305, 497-98.

6. Bill Del Valle was an important figure in the technical and engineering areas for Pan Am in the 1930s and 1940s. He served for many years as Pan Am's technical representative to Boeing, and consequently he lived most of the time in Seattle rather than New York. Apparently, this hurt his chances for advancement within Pan Am's hierarchy. Del Valle, who spoke Spanish, is best remembered today for his role in Pan Am's takeover of the Colombian airline, SCATDA, as World War II approached. Since most of SCATDA's personnel were German (although naturalized Colombian citizens), the military and the State Department wanted them removed. The idea of German-born SCATDA pilots bombing the

Panama Canal was pretty far-fetched, but the U.S. government was taking no chances after World War II began in 1939. So in 1940, Juan Trippe, under pressure from the government, ordered Del Valle south to Colombia, where he engineered the firing of all German SCADTA employees. Del Valle could do this because Trippe had secretly bought control of SCADTA in the early 1930s. For reasons having to do with Colombian national pride, Pan Am's ownership of SCADTA was kept quiet.

John Borger (b. 1914) was one of the original crew who went into the Pacific in 1935 to establish Pan Am's island bases. A twenty-one-year- old MIT-trained engineer, Borger later went on to a long and distinguished career at Pan Am, retiring as chief engineer with the rank of vice-president in 1979. See Daley, *American Saga,* 297-301, 492.

7. The first scheduled B-314 mail service across the Atlantic took place on May 20, 1939. The first flight carrying paying passengers was on June 24, 1939. Trippe, with his usual genius for marketing, had sold rights to fly Pan Am's first transatlantic crossing ten years earlier. Mr. W. J. Eck, a resident of Washington, D.C., had reserved his ticket in 1929. He paid $375 one way (a round-trip ticket cost $675). There were twenty-two passengers on the first flight. See Daley, *American Saga,* 242-43; Davies, *Pan Am,* 42-43.

8. Eastern Airlines' Edward V. "Eddie" Rickenbacker (1890-1973), an Ohioan, quit school after the seventh grade. He became, by turns, a successful race car driver, then a World War I fighter ace—perhaps the most famous American pilot of the war—and a winner of the Congressional Medal of Honor. Leary, *Airline Industry,* 398-415.

## ✦ *The Beginning of World War II*

1. Kauffman's truncated version of the early part of World War II leaves out the fall of France in the spring of 1940—an earthshaking event followed by the phony war (or Sitzkrieg, as it was jokingly called), during which France sat behind its Maginot Line of defensive fortifications, awaiting Germany's attack. The celebrated Battle of Britain, during which the Royal Air Force narrowly defeated the Luftwaffe's bombing campaign (nicknamed the Blitz) during the summer and fall of 1940, made the northern route, which terminated in England (via Newfoundland and Ireland), too dangerous a destination for Pan Am's oceanic flying boats. There was no choice for Pan Am but to concentrate all its aircraft on the more southerly route, which crossed the Atlantic directly via the Azores, to Lisbon, located in neutral Portugal.

Pan Am's transoceanic business boomed with the outbreak of World War II, and Trippe wanted to order more aircraft. But by then, the original six B-314s, plus a supplemental contract for another six, would be all he could get. In response to Hitler's victory over France in 1940, the Roosevelt administration secured passage of huge increases in the defense budget, including the largest single appropriation ever passed up to that point, the Aircraft Procurement Bill of 1940 (the "fifty thousand planes a year" bill). Civilian manufacturers would be busy building fighters and bombers for the Lend Lease program, which supplied Britain and, after Hitler's 1941 invasion, the USSR. Indeed, several of the B-314s would be commandeered by the military after Pearl Harbor.

The twelve B-314s would be the finale for flying boats as commercial aircraft. Pan Am paid $804,925 for each B-314. Trippe sold three to Britain in 1940, at a nifty profit of $600,000—the British had never succeeded in developing a true oceanic flying boat; one was lost in a crash (with fatalities) at Lisbon in February 1943; the rest were scrapped after being sold. The romantic era of the magnificent flying big boats would end almost before it began, outpaced by the rapid development of wartime landplane technology. Today, not a single example of the B-314 survives, although visitors to Miami International Airport can view a magnificent one-sixteenth-scale model suspended from the ceiling over the passenger concourse, complete with turning miniature props. See Davies, *Pan Am*, 42-49; Daley, *American Saga*, 257-58; Bender, *Chosen Instrument*, 350-51; Micheal Sherry, *The Rise of American Air Power* (New Haven: Yale University Press, 1987), 91; Flint Du Pre, *Hap Arnold: Architect of American Air Power* (New York: Macmillan, 1972), 79-80.

2. The military's reliance on Pan Am for help in training personnel for wartime expansion was a tribute to the technical advances commercial aviation had made since the early days. In the late 1920s, the military had actually been more technically advanced than the airlines. But after government cutbacks during the Depression, the private airlines had surged ahead in almost every technical area. The prodigious expansion of training saw the government turn to the only ready source of expertise. In 1938, for example, the entire Army Air Force (AAF) had trained a mere three hundred pilots and had only limited and rudimentary facilities for training navigators. By 1941, AAF pilot training had increased to three thousand per year, but navigator training was almost nonexistent until Pan Am created it. See Sherry, *Rise of American Air Power*, 214-15; Du Pre, *Hap Arnold*, 79-84; Hopkins, *Flying the Line*, 32-35, 56.

3. The Doolittle raid on Tokyo, carried out on April 18, 1942 by B-25 Mitchell landplane bombers launched from the aircraft carrier USS *Hornet* (or *Shangri La*, as FDR called it over the radio—a fictitious location in Tibet from the 1939 movie *Lost Horizons*), was indeed primarily for the purpose of boosting U.S. civilian morale, as Kauffman indicates. It did have military value, however, because it forced the Japanese into an ill-advised attempt to extend their defensive perimeter, most notably at Midway Island, Pan Am's seaplane base in the central Pacific. This hasty effort allowed the U.S. to score a decisive victory at the Battle of Midway, June 3-6, 1942. See Sherry, *Rise of American Airpower*, 123; Du Pre, *Hap Arnold*, 85-88.

4. Rickenbacker and Cyrus Rowlett Smith (1899-1990) were major players during commercial aviation's initial flowering. Although alike in that each came from humble origins and fatherless homes, Smith and Rickenbacker differed in education and temperament. Smith, a Texan, worked his way through the University of Texas and became an accountant. As heads of two of the "Big Four" airlines (the others were TWA and United), Rickenbacker and Smith did not compete directly with each other in a business sense (indeed, under direct government economic regulation, which ended in 1978, airlines barely competed with each other at all), but they often found themselves at odds. Perhaps this antagonism had as much to do with personality as issues. Kauffman's anecdotal account illustrates the barely concealed dislike each man had for the other. See Leary, *Airline Industry*, 398-415, 435-46.

5. Henry H. "Hap" Arnold (1886-1950) was a career Army officer who, at about the same time Juan Trippe founded Pan Am, was toying with the idea of resigning from the service and starting his own airline. He resisted this urge and went on to become commanding general of the AAF during World War II. In effect, Arnold had command of all civilian aviation during the war. The civilian airline fleet shrunk by nearly half during the war, as Arnold commandeered aircraft to serve the needs of the ATC. He also had first claim on new airliners. See Du Pre, *Hap Arnold*; Daley, *American Saga*, 27-28.

## ✈ Pan Am Enters the War

1. Kauffman's rise to an important position coincided with André Priester's decline. In January 1940, when Juan Trippe returned to power, he allowed Priester to retain the empty title of vice-president for engineering but shifted active control to a group of younger executives, among whom was Kauffman. See Daley, *American Saga*, 231-40, 247, 255.

2. The history of Pan Am's African subsidiary began with a conversation between Trippe and Winston Churchill in June 1941, at the height of the Battle of Britain. Trippe had traveled to London both to assess Pan Am's prospects for resuming passenger service to Britain under wartime conditions and to give the annual Wilbur Wright Memorial Lecture before the prestigious Royal Aeronautical Society. Pan Am had discontinued direct passenger service to Britain in 1940, so Trippe had to get there by flying aboard one of his own B-314s to Lisbon and then taking a KLM flight from Portugal. It was a harrowing trip, involving extended rerouting over open ocean under blackout and radio silence conditions. Although usually German fighters did not attack airliners (the British could easily retaliate against Lufthansa flights to Portugal, some of which flew over international waters in the Bay of Biscay), such incidents were always possible in the chaos of wartime. In June 1943, the Germans downed a KLM DC-3, killing film star Leslie Howard, apparently because they believed Churchill was aboard. (In chapter 11, Kauffman reports having heard that the plane was downed in order to kill Leslie Howard.)

After Trippe delivered his speech, Churchill unexpectedly invited him to a private dinner at 10 Downing Street, where he urged him to extend Pan Am's routes across Africa in order to ferry American lend-lease supplies to British forces in Egypt. But Trippe was a businessman, not a warrior, and he saw little profit and much risk in such a venture. So Churchill appealed to Roosevelt.

FDR's relationship with Trippe was always shaky, not only because Trippe was a lifelong Republican who exhibited the animosity his class generally felt toward the New Deal, but also because Pan Am had received such favorable treatment from the preceding Republican administrations. Furthermore, Trippe had proven himself adept at mobilizing congressional opposition to several Roosevelt Administration aviation measures that would have hampered Pan Am. So it was a bitter pill for FDR to have to ask Trippe for help. The president at first delegated the job to General Hap Arnold, who literally tried to conscript Trippe into the Army! But Trippe, a master at obfuscating delay during negotiations, refused to be drafted, thus permanently making an enemy of Arnold, who would later do much damage to Pan Am after the war.

FDR finally had to personally call Trippe to the White House. Under this kind of pressure, Trippe had no choice but to agree to set up an African operation. Trippe structured the deal so that it would be virtually without financial risk to Pan Am. In July 1941, Trippe created two subsidiaries, Pan American Airways—Africa, Ltd. (to carry cargo and passengers), and Pan American Air Ferries (to ferry lend-lease warplanes to Egypt). See Daley, *American Saga,* 310-14, 344-46; Solberg, *Conquest of the Skies,* 267-69.

3. Called the Airport Development Program (ADP), this venture actually began before the African operation. Financed by secret appropriations controlled by FDR, ADP originated in a 1939 top-secret military study that warned of an attack on the U.S. by Germany via the "hump" of Africa, across the narrow waist of the Atlantic, then by stages up the east coast of South America from the "hump" of Brazil. Although it appears far-fetched today, this projected Axis invasion of the Western hemisphere was taken seriously at the time.

The military could not construct these airfields stepping down through the Caribbean to Brazil, because of those nations' national pride and deep historical distrust of the U.S. Pan Am was the perfect cover for what was essentially a military construction project, but Trippe was adamantly opposed to it. FDR eventually bullied him into building the twenty-five landplane airfields (spaced 450 miles apart) and nine seaplane bases, but it had to be kept totally secret. The twelve million dollars Pan Am was paid for constructing the fields barely covered costs. Although the airline would inherit the fields after the war, if word of direct U.S. government involvement in paying for them ever leaked out, it would have done enormous damage to Pan Am in Latin America, where it was already too closely identified with the hated Yankees.

The airfields were never used for their original purpose of resisting an Axis invasion of the Americas, but they eventually proved valuable in supporting the flow of lend-lease war materiel to the battle fronts. See Daley, *American Saga,* 302-9.

4. The Douglas DC-3 ("Douglas Commercial" model 3) was far and away the most successful and versatile airliner ever built. An outgrowth of the fourteen-passenger DC-2 (220 of which were manufactured between 1934 and 1935), the 180-mph, twenty-one-passenger DC-3 entered domestic airline service in 1936. It set new standards for comfort, efficiency, and profitability, quickly displacing all other airliners (notably the Boeing 247) from the marketplace. Over thirteen thousand DC-3s of all types (military and civil) were built before production ceased just after World War II.

With a maximum range of only eight hundred miles, the DC-3 was unsuited to most of Pan Am's overwater routes. Consequently, when Juan Trippe began belatedly ordering this aircraft in 1937, it was entirely for Pan Am's subsidiary airlines in Latin American and China. Eventually, Trippe would buy ninety DC-3s, but at the time the military began forcefully transferring the aircraft to Pan Am, his airline was flying only about a dozen.

The domestic airlines complained bitterly about the injustice of having to turn over their prized and profitable DC-3s to Pan Am, yet they arranged very favorable lease arrangements and came out of the war in better shape financially than did Pan Am. In fact, Pan Am did not exploit its position to make excess profits during World War II. Perhaps if Trippe had been willing to enter the military, he might have positioned Pan Am to profit more significantly from wartime contracts. C. R. Smith of American Airlines accepted a direct commission in the Army Air Corps and became the head of the Air Transport Command (ATC) in 1942, a job Trippe had earlier declined. American's wartime profits nearly doubled Pan Am's, even though it flew fewer route miles. See Daley, *American Saga,* 335-446; Davies, *Pan Am,* 44-47; C. V. Glines and Wendell F. Mosely, *The Legendary DC-3* (New York: Van Nostrand Reinhold, 1979), 197.

5. As World War II approached, the Army authorized the Civilian Pilot Training Program (CPTP). In 1939, the CPTP offered refresher training to civilian flight instructors in order to standardize procedures and make it easier to train airmen who might later be inducted into the service. Congressional appropriations allowed many thousands of young men (and even a few women) to undergo flight training through the CPTP at hundreds of civil airfields across the nation. But the available pool of pilots remained quite small until 1944. When Pan Am needed pilots immediately, the only source was the military's half-trained pilots.

The wartime pilot shortage would be remedied by programs like the CPTP, but in the early days it was a severe problem. Several domestic airlines had to train their own pilots. United Airlines ran its own training school at Tracey Field, California. Because so many pre-Pearl Harbor domestic airline pilots were Army reservists, the domestic airlines suffered more from the pilot shortage than did Pan Am. With its preponderance of ex-naval aviators, Pan Am did not lose nearly as many pilots to military reservist call-ups, for the simple reason that the Naval Air Reserve was so small and there were so few billets for naval aviators who wanted to remain active in the reserves. See Hopkins, *Flying the Line,* 113-15; Sherry, *Rise of American Air Power,* 214-15; Roger Bilstein and Jay Miller, *Aviation in Texas* (Austin: Texas Monthly Press, 1985), 91; Stewart W. Hopkins, phone interview with editor, August 5, 1991. Hopkins, a retired admiral of the U.S. Naval Reserves and former first vice-president of ALPA, went to work for Chicago & Southern Airlines in 1934.

6. Josip Broz Tito (1892-1980), head of the Yugoslav Communist partisans, and Draza Mikhailovitch (or Mihajlovic, 1893?-1946), leader of the "Chetnik" Serbian guerillas, were bitter enemies forced into a temporary alliance during World War II. Evidence exists that Mikhailovitch often cooperated with the Germans because he considered Tito and the Communists a bigger threat. Eventually, strategic factors dictated the choice of Tito as the Allies' favored guerilla leader. Mikhailovitch fought against the Communists after World War II, but he was captured by Tito's forces, tried, and executed for treason and war crimes. He was certainly guilty of war crimes (as anybody familiar with the current situation in what used to be Yugoslavia would understand), but the charge of treason was largely political. See Harris and Levey, *New Columbia Encyclopedia,* 1775, 2755, 3032.

7. Randolph Churchill (1911-1968), British Prime Minister Winston Churchill's only son, although a disappointment to his father in nearly every way, did his duty in World War II. He was seldom sober while doing it, however. See William Manchester, *The Last Lion—Winston Spencer Churchill: Alone, 1932-1940* (Boston: Little, Brown, 1988), 254-55.

8. Anne Marie Monahan Archibald (1897-1953) was the widow of a Marine pilot who died in a 1928 crash. Trippe hired her as a secretary for his Washington office in 1929. Known as Little Orchid Annie because of her fondness for the flower, she was a rarity at Pan Am, a successful female executive. She rose to become an essential Pan Am employee whose inside knowledge of government was indispensable to Trippe. Utterly indifferent to women, Trippe's operation was unapologetically male. Archibald was never promoted beyond the rank of assistant vice-president, despite the fact that she performed vice-presidential duties. See Daley, *American Saga,* 351-52, 510.

## ✈ More on World War II and Its Aftermath

1. Pan Am's contribution to the war effort was truly remarkable, even more so when one considers that Trippe assiduously avoided even the appearance of profiteering. Pan Am's mileage flown in support of the war exceeded the combined mileage flown by all the domestic airlines, and it was done at a piddling profit. Indeed, since so much of Pan Am's war work was done under top-secret conditions, it could not profit even from publicity. See Daley, *American Saga,* 344, 361-62.

2. Ironically, Charles A. Lindbergh contributed mightily to these technical innovations, even though he received little credit for it, and despite Pan Am.

Lindbergh had made himself *persona non grata* with the White House because of his isolationist political activities prior to Pearl Harbor. After the U.S. entered the war, Lindbergh patriotically volunteered his services to the nation, but since he had resigned his Army Reserve commission earlier, he had no practical way of doing this. The Army, conscious of his political liabilities, declined to reinstate Lindbergh's commission. Lindbergh then turned to Juan Trippe, seeking a renewed association with Pan Am. But Trippe, taking revenge against Lindbergh for his neutrality during the 1939 Sonny Whitney takeover, refused him, pleading political pressure from the White House.

Trippe was dissembling. Lindbergh was unpopular with FDR, but when the Ford Motor Company's United Aircraft Technologies Division (which was manufacturing the B-24 Liberator heavy bomber, under contract from Consolidated) hired Lindbergh as a technical adviser in 1942, there was no retaliation. Nor was there ever any pressure from FDR to keep Lindbergh from rejoining Pan Am. In his role as a "technical representative" for United Aircraft, Lindbergh actually flew combat missions in the South Pacific and helped teach military pilots the techniques of fuel management during long-range missions he had pioneered for Pan Am in the early 1930s. See Daley, *American Saga,* 330-32, 397; Mosely, *Lindbergh,* 315-27.

3. CNAC, founded by Trippe's rival Clement M. Keys in 1930 as a joint venture with the Chinese government, was acquired by Pan Am in March 1933. Keys's pioneering transcontinental plane-train route, Transcontinental Air Transport (TAT), did poorly following the 1929 stock market crash and was forced to merge with TWA in 1930. Keys, overextended financially, had no choice but to sell CNAC to Trippe, who, owing to his Latin America subsidiaries, had experience in joint-venture airlines.

The story of CNAC, played out against the vast backdrop of Japan's 1937 invasion of China, World War II, and the civil war between Communists and Nationalists that followed, is one of the great sagas of aviation. Thanks to talented subordinates like William Langhorne "Bondy" Bond (1893-1981) and Harold Bixby (the original Lindbergh financial backer from St. Louis who had become a Pan Am vice-president), CNAC managed to stay in business and even earn a profit under the most difficult conditions imaginable. Throughout its history, CNAC was run as an entirely autonomous operation, and Trippe had virtually nothing to do with it. Indeed, when Trippe involved himself in CNAC's management, his thinking was mostly wrong. For example, Bond (who actually ran CNAC) urged Trippe to reduce Pan Am's percentage of participation after World War II, because he saw the Chinese civil war coming and expected Mao's Communists to defeat Chiang Kai-shek's Nationalists. Trippe disagreed and instead saw a bright future for Pan Am in a postwar China dominated by the Nationalists. Trippe ultimately bowed to Bond's "in country" expertise, but only after he threatened to resign. Bond was, of course, right. See Daley, *American Saga,* 117-25, 281-90; Davies, *History of the World's Airlines,* 147-49, 189-90; Hopkins, "Transcontinental Air Transport," 22-28.

4. The portion of this route that crossed the Himalayas from India into wartime China was known as "the Hump." It was almost as hazardous as flying combat missions. There were no emergency landing fields, and the twin-engine DC-3s and Curtiss C-46 Commandoes used on this route could not sustain the extremely high altitudes necessary for crossing the awesome Himalayan cordillera on a single engine. So failure of one engine meant almost certain death for the air crews. See Davies, *Pan Am,* 60.

5. Flight Safety, International, is a highly respected commercial flight training school with locations scattered around the US.

6. The "boot" Kauffman mentions is a rubberized pneumatic covering over the leading edge of the wings and other control surfaces which, when ice begins to build up, a pilot can break off by inflating. Although a primitive technological fix to the problem of inflight icing, it is still in use today on the kind of commuter planes serving hub airports. The big passenger jets used by major airlines have electrically heated wings to melt ice away from the leading edges. (The lifting surfaces of the wings, upon which ice generally cannot accumulate in flight, must still be de-iced with sprays of liquid glycol prior to takeoff.) Ice is dangerous to aircraft not only because it adds weight but also because it changes the aerodynamic shape of the wings, thus raising the stalling speed. Ice menaces flight safety in many other more subtle ways as well.

See "Last, Heart-Pounding Minutes of Flight 4184," *Chicago Tribune,* Nov. 3, 1994, 6; Nance, *Blind Trust,* 124-32.

7. Claire Lee Chennault (1890-1958) was a roughhewn Texan who enlisted in the Army in 1917 and, despite being physically unqualified, somehow managed to win a commission and pilot's wings. In 1937, Chennault retired from the Army for medical reasons, then promptly accepted Chiang Kai-shek's offer to create and command the American Volunteer Group (AVG) in China. The AVG was a thinly disguised U.S. effort to help China resist the Japanese. The airmen who staffed it were often regular U.S. servicemen who had permission to temporarily "resign"

while fighting and flying for the AVG. After Pearl Harbor, the AVG was absorbed into the U.S. military.

Kauffman somewhat overstates Pan Am's involvement with the AVG, at least until after Pearl Harbor. In fact, Langhorne Bond did his best to keep CNAC out of all direct military involvement. He argued with Chinese officials that CNAC was far more valuable as a noncombatant instrument of transportation than as a makeshift military unit. Ultimately it proved impossible for CNAC to remain neutral, but Bond kept the Flying Tigers (as the AVG was nicknamed) at arms, length for as long as he could.

See Claire L. Chennault, *Way of a Fighter* (New York: G. P. Putnam, 1949); John Keegan, *The Second World War* (New York: Viking, 1989), 547-48; Frank Friedel, *Franklin D. Roosevelt* (Boston: Little, Brown, 1990), 380; Daley, *American Saga,* 281-90.

8. Bond got into aviation because of Lindbergh's 1927 solo flight to Paris. A Chicagoan, Bond was not working in aviation at the time, but he was so impressed with Lindbergh's achievement that he took flying lessons and gradually worked his way into the industry, although not as a pilot. He was working for CNAC in China when Pan Am acquired it in 1933. His first loyalty was always to CNAC (not Pan Am), and he technically resigned from Pan Am when the Sino-Japanese War of 1937 broke out, in order to lessen the direct connection between Pan Am and war-tormented CNAC. After Pearl Harbor, Bond briefly resumed his formal affiliation with Pan Am. When Chiang's Nationalists collapsed in 1949, Bond handled the negotiations with their government-in-exile on Formosa, selling out Pan Am's remaining twenty-percent share for $1.25 million. CNAC had been profitable for Pan Am, largely because of Bond. Once CNAC's existence formally ended, Bond had little interest in remaining with Pan Am. He formally retired from Pan Am in 1950 at the age of fifty-seven, and despite heart trouble (he had already experienced two heart attacks before retiring), he lived until 1981. See Daley, *American Saga,* 119-23, 320-22, 342-44, 393-95.

9. This incident was typical of the harrowing, makeshift, "can do" daily operation of CNAC. Many aircraft, crew, and passengers were lost to hostile Japanese action and to crashes that were largely the result of the threat of Japanese attack. For example, CNAC's pilots flew mostly at night and in cloudy, rainy weather, when Japanese fighters (which were not capable of all-weather combat) were grounded. Because of the primitive nature of China's aerial navigation system, these flights were inherently dangerous. See Daley, *American Saga,* 288-89.

10. Pan Am's divestment of CNAC in 1949 was carried out against the chaotic backdrop of the Nationalists' defeat on the mainland and their escape to Taiwan. CNAC employees who sided with the Communists (including the airline's Chinese director, C. Y. Liu) turned over part of CNAC's fleet of aircraft to them. Because Pan Am owned twenty percent of CNAC's stock, it was able to freeze the airline's U.S. bank deposits. This was the critical maneuver that allowed William Langhorne Bond to negotiate the sale of Pan Am's twenty percent of CNAC. Bond was responsible for the fact that Pan Am's share of CNAC had been reduced from a forty-five-percent participation to twenty-five percent. Trippe opposed reducing Pan Am's share in CNAC and only acceded to it after Bond, who was keenly aware of the Nationalist government's weakness, threatened to resign. See Daley, *American Saga,* 341-43, 393-95.

11. John J. McCloy (1895-1989), a Philadelphia lawyer, diplomat, and scholar, is best remembered today as a member of the Warren Commission, which investigated the assassination of President Kennedy. He held an impressive series of government posts, including the presidency of the World Bank after World War II and then service as high commissioner for Germany (1949-52). See Harris and Levey, *New Columbia Encyclopedia,* 1642.

12. Yet another example of the hostility that pervaded military thinking about Pan Am, mostly a legacy of the run-in Juan Trippe had with Hap Arnold at the time of the creation of the ATC in 1942. See Daley, *American Saga,* 336-37, 345, 377.

13. Kauffman's fanciful speculations about a Tokyo raider, Jimmy Doolittle-type launch of DC-4s from the decks of aircraft carriers were obviously advanced for the purpose of getting a mulish military man's attention. But since this is Kauffman's first mention of the DC-4, some background is in order.

The four-engine DC-4, the first true transoceanic landplane to be mass produced, would end the romantic era of the great flying boats. Because landplanes are so much simpler to handle and maintain than seaplanes, aircraft like the DC-4 (notably Lockheed's Constellation) would quickly supersede seaplanes on all the world's air routes when they became available for civilian use following the war. Pan Am, for example, substituted the DC-4 for the B-314 on its primary San Francisco-Honolulu route in October 1945. The greater speed of the DC-4 was reason enough for this switch. The DC-4 covered the distance in a mere ten hours, compared to the B-314's twenty hours.

The DC-4 began as a joint project sponsored by Pan Am and the "Big Four" domestic airlines (Eastern, American, United, and TWA) in 1936. The first model

DC-4 actually flew June 7, 1938, but never entered regular airline service. In 1940, a redesigned version was ordered by all the airlines originally involved in the project, except TWA, which had switched its business to Lockheed. Featuring a nosewheel instead of the conventional tailwheel, the DC-4 was the first large aircraft with "tricycle" landing gear—a major technological improvement that made landing and ground handling easier. Pan Am ordered only three of the first production batch of sixty-one aircraft, but its planes were to be pressurized, a major advance in passenger cabin comfort. Pressurization seals the cabin so that a constant altitude can be maintained regardless of how high the aircraft flies. While the cruising altitude might be 30,000 feet, in the cabin, pressurization makes it feel like only 5,000 feet to passengers, who need not wear cumbersome oxygen masks either. Technological problems stopped the pressurization of Pan Am's three DC-4s, thus allowing Boeing to produce the first true pressurized aircraft, the B-307, which entered limited service with TWA in July 1940. Only five B-307s were built, and they were quickly commandeered by the military after Pearl Harbor, so the plane's impact on commercial aviation was negligible until after the war, when the improved B-307B model, christened the Stratoliner and reequipped with tricycle landing gear, became available.

The outbreak of World War II halted promising European versions of the DC-4, notably Focke-Wulf's four-engine Condor, which had made several non-stop transatlantic crossings in 1939. So Donald Douglas had the market pretty much to himself, largely owing to superior production techniques his company had honed while mass-producing the redoubtable DC-3. Enormous orders for military versions of the DC-4 lowered the unit price to a bargain basement $160,000 per aircraft. Eventually 1,163 DC-4s were built, of which Pan Am operated at least 90, mostly acquired as quite serviceable war surplus and then refurbished for airline use. Powered by four 1450-hp engines, the DC-4 could carry forty-four passengers at a speed of 215 mph—a quantum leap in both efficiency and profitability for the postwar airlines. See Davies, *Pan Am,* 52-53; Chant, *Aviation,* 181; *Legacy of Leadership* (Kansas City: Trans World Airlines, Flight Operations Department, n.d.), 111-31.

## Labor Relations and Policies

1. John C. Cooper, Jr. was one of the first experts in the new field of international aviation law. Hired by Trippe in 1933, Cooper was, like so many other Pan Am executives (Kauffman included), a "Yalie." Prim, pompous, wearing three-piece suits and viewing the world suspiciously through rimless eyeglasses,

Cooper eventually became vice- president of Pan Am's legal department and spent most of his professional working life at Juan Trippe's elbow. With his gold Phi Beta Kappa key dangling from his vest pocket, Cooper was involved in every important negotiation and legal crisis in Pan Am's history. Cooper's fussy nitpicking often infuriated those with whom Trippe was negotiating. See Daley, *American Saga,* 134, 275; Bender and Altschul, *Chosen Instrument,* 225, 265-79, 326-54.

2. The International Air Transport Association (IATA), founded in 1945 as World War II ended, was the direct offspring of the European Air Traffic Association (EATA), the cartel founded in 1919, just after World War I. A kind of clearinghouse for rules of "fair competition" (involving details as small as standardizing inflight meals), IATA set economic restrictions that were the bane of Juan Trippe's life. At the time, all non-U.S. carriers were state-subsidized monopolies (or "chosen instruments" of their nations' international airline service) that were incapable of competing with the Americans at any level—particularly just after World War II. Pan Am and the other American international carriers in the immediate postwar period—TWA, American Overseas Airlines (a subsidiary of American Airlines), Braniff, Eastern, and Northwest—favored a more free-market approach, particularly when it came to setting transatlantic airfares. But they had to submit to IATA rules, because otherwise the Europeans would deny the U.S. carriers access to their airspace. The fares IATA set were far too high to lure the large numbers of tourists that airline executive like Juan Trippe saw as the industry's future. IATA's fares were designed to keep European national airlines solvent by soaking U.S. citizens, who constituted the lion's share of tranatlantic passengers.

Always contentious, IATA rules were widely disregarded, owing to the outrageous cheating of some member nations. Its authority gradually weakened with the passage of years, growing crossnational ownership, and U.S. political pressure. IATA still exists but is no longer of much significance. See Leary, *Airline Industry,* 243-44.

3. Kauffman is discussing the confusing role of the IATA, whose functions were primarily economic, and the International Civil Aviation Organization (ICAO), which was the government arbiter of technical aspects of aviation. The committees on which he served later became part of the ICAO. Confusion about the two organizations is easy because they were, in fact, linked. The ICAO grew out of a 1944 wartime conference in Chicago on the future of postwar aviation. It hammered out a diplomatic "convention" that would ultimately be ratified by

fifty-two nations in 1946. When the ICAO began operating in 1947, it was as a specialized agency of the United Nations.

The technical committees of the IATA on which Kauffman served in 1945 were themselves outgrowths of the 1944 Chicago ICAO conference. As soon as the ICAO was ratified by member states, it assumed jurisdiction over the temporary IATA technical committees. Kauffman is right about English. Since the Americans and the British were dominant, it was logical that English would be selected as the international language of aviation. Among the examples of IATA/ICAO-sponsored international cooperation, that is probably the one most widely remembered today. See Leary, *Airline Industry,* 246-47.

4. Kauffman's complaint that FDR forced unions down the throat of American business was a common one among people such as himself. But it was also dead wrong. FDR was less responsible for the fact that Pan Am had to start dealing with the unions than the incontrovertible fact that labor was in short supply during World War II, and thus the climate was favorable for unions. In fact, FDR was an old-fashioned, conservative-leaning, Grover Cleveland Democrat on most labor questions. He always felt uncomfortable with union support, most of which he did little to either encourage or earn. Labor's "bill of rights," the Wagner Labor Relations Act of 1935, owed little to FDR. It was organized labor's growing support in Congress and the country that moved FDR toward accommodation with unionism, not the other way around.

So far as aviation labor was concerned, the pilots' union, the Air Line Pilots Association (ALPA), spearheaded the unionization of Pan Am employees. As early as 1934, an astounding ninety percent of Pan Am's far-flung pilots were dues-paying members of ALPA. During World War II, ALPA took the leadership in forming alliances with other airline workers (baggage handlers, flight attendants, and the like), even going so far as to advise, house, and give financial support to an umbrella group of nonpilot airline labor, the Air Line Employees Association (ALEA), which is still in existence. It should be noted that ALPA came into existence in 1931—*before* the New Deal and FDR. See Hopkins, *Airline Pilots,* 162; Leary, *Airline Industry,* 17-19, 176; Friedel, *FDR,* 3, 158, 240-43.

5. Kauffman's description of the problem of "technological unemployment" for navigators and radio operators, and how Pan Am handled it after World War II, illustrates the role of unions and government regulation, and why to some degree both will be a factor in the American economy. It is difficult to imagine Juan Trippe voluntarily paying these technologically displaced workers any kind of severance pay had there not been a union to represent them and government

pressure to treat them fairly. Kauffman implicitly makes this point, but it is also wise to remember that under the pre-1978 system of airline regulation, it was government policy that "the hardships borne by adversely affected employees should be mitigated by provisions for their benefit." See McKelvey, *Cleared for Takeoff*, 126.

6. Despite the fame of a few female celebrity pilots, such as Amelia Earhart and Jacqueline Cochran, aviation was a profoundly male environment for much of its history. Domestic airlines began hiring "sky girls" in 1930, partly for their obvious sex appeal but also to psychologically reassure passengers that flying was safe; it was an unspoken assumption that stewardesses would shame timid male passengers into flying. Juan Trippe, however, was a monogamous straight arrow who would have been totally oblivious to the sex-appeal arguments for using female flight attendants. Pan Am would not have hired women in the war years, had not the dire necessity of the wartime labor shortage necessitated it. As Kauffman points out, the work of Pan Am's male stewards was extremely arduous in the days of the great flying boats. Pan Am never used female cabin attendants on flying boats. Once those conditions changed with the advent of faster land-planes, which did not require cabin attendants to help with ground handling and docking, women were hired in greater numbers. Until the mid-1960s, no airline hired any female pilots at all, and then only because of court challenges and the pressure of federal antidiscrimination statutes. See Leary, *Airline Industry,* 173-78; Hopkins, *Airline Pilots,* 214-16; Nielsen, *From Sky Girl to Flight Attendant;* Daley, *American Saga,* 244-45.

7. J. Franklin Gledhill (1898-1975) was an engineering graduate of Yale who went to work for Pan Am in 1929, the same year as Kauffman. A superb haggler, Gledhill was the man Trippe interposed between himself and aircraft manufacturers. His job was to milk the last advantage for Pan Am out of every aircraft deal. Like most Pan Am executives, Gledhill ran his own show, with Trippe exercising only the loosest control until a final decision had to be made. Probably as close personally to Trippe as any Pan Am executive, Gledhill played a major role in the purchase of every aircraft throughout the jet era. Both an engineer and a pilot, Gledhill became vice-president in 1940 and a member of the board of directors in 1946. See Daley, *American Saga,* 223, 403, 507.

8. Kauffman's anecdotal account of the pervasive racism that characterized aviation in its infancy proves that it was not merely a regional phenomenon. While blacks occasionally held menial positions in the industry, no U.S. airline hired a black pilot until 1965, when a Colorado state court ordered Continental Airlines

to hire Marlon D. Green, a former USAF pilot. Continental appealed the decision to the federal courts but lost. The initial constitution of the pilots' union, adopted in 1931, contained a whites-only membership clause. In 1942, ALPA president David L. Behncke had it deleted. Behncke did so because, in response to pressure from the NAACP, several airlines used ALPA's racial restriction as an alibi for not hiring African-Americans. Behncke wished to embarrass airline management and succeeded in doing so, pointing out that there had been no black pilots prior to ALPA's birth and that management should not be able to blame this state of affairs on a racially repugnant union covenant. Another twenty-three years would pass before an airline hired its first black pilot. See Hopkins, *Airline Pilots,* 71-72, 214-16; Charles E. Francis, *The Tuskegee Airmen: The Story of the Negro in the U. S. Air Force* (Somerville, Mass.: Bruce Humphries Publishers, 1955), 11-17.

9. Kauffman does not make clear that this episode involved a jurisdictional dispute between two cockpit unions, ALPA (the pilots' union) and the Flight Engineers International Association (FEIA). ALPA insisted, for both economic and professional reasons, that all "flight deck" crew should be "pilot qualified" during long, overwater flights. Federal regulations mandated a flight engineer (or third crewman) on all aircraft weighing more than 80,000 lb. but were mute on whether the flight engineer should also be able to fly the aircraft. A tiny number of nonpilot flight engineers could not qualify for a pilot's license, but ALPA was willing to "grandfather" them in. A flight engineer would benefit from having pilot qualifications, because it would make him eligible for promotion to captain—which paid vastly more. The problem was that once a flight engineer became eligible to manipulate the flight controls, he had to switch unions. Faced with the eventual and certain death of their union, the FEIA waged a bitter fight against ALPA over the nature of the third crewman's qualifications. Federal regulators took a neutral stance, so airline management was caught in the middle of this dispute, which the pilots' union finally won after many years of intense strife. See Hopkins, *Flying the Line,* 175-86; Leary, *Airline Industry,* 18, 179-80.

10. ALPA won this dispute with management the way it had won so many times previously, by gaining the support of federal regulators. The federal regulation requiring a third crewman on aircraft weighing more than 80,000 lb. remained in place until it was modified by new federal regulations governing the first generation of short-haul passenger jets (notably the Douglas DC-9 and Boeing 737), which began to appear in the mid-1960s. Technologically, there was no longer any reason for a third crewman on these jets, unlike earlier jets, such as the B-727. ALPA tried to hold the line, arguing that even though the third crewman

had no actual duties, a third pair of eyes in the cockpit made his presence worthwhile. ALPA's official position appeared to be featherbedding, and many pilots were unsympathetic to it. ALPA was bound to lose this fight, and it eventually did, after many years of bitter internal strife and at least one pilot strike, on Wien Air Alaska, which lasted from 1977 to 1979. In 1981, a presidential emergency board found for the two-pilot concept in aircraft designed and certified for two pilots, regardless of weight. See Hopkins, *Flying the Line,* 290-92; Leary, *Airline Industry,* 504; R. E. G. Davies, *Delta: An Airline and Its Aircraft* (Miami: Paladwr Press, 1990), 79.

11. ALPA's contract with Pan Am required it to pay for engineers' flight training. This contract provision added greatly to the bitterness of the jurisdictional dispute between ALPA and the FEIA. See Hopkins, *Flying the Line,* 238-39.

12. What Kauffman does not say is that ALPA was internally divided over the age sixty rule. Older pilots hated it; younger pilots loved it. The union was stuck in a no-win situation. While everybody knew that there was some point at which a pilot should retire because of age, there was never any scientific evidence as to just when that age occurred. Today, the age sixty rule remains in force. All airline pilots must retire on or before their sixtieth birthday. Hopkins, *Flying the Line,* 258.

## ✈ The Beginning of the Jet Age

1. Jet-assisted takeoff (JATO) was one of those technological quick fixes that have dotted the history of aviation. Originally developed by the Navy early in World War II, JATO was a solid-propellant rocket that could be attached to an aircraft for the purpose of giving it a temporary boost on takeoff. The standard JATO "bottle" produced 1,000 lb. of thrust, delivered in a few seconds. Typically, a heavily loaded aircraft would begin its takeoff run; then, at about 45 mph, the pilot would trigger the JATO unit, and the aircraft would quickly accelerate to flying speed. JATO's value was that it not only saved wear and tear on engines but also quickly boosted an aircraft through the transition zone of low-speed flight, where an engine failure was most dangerous. But JATO was expensive and scarily abrupt. Consequently, JATO was more suitable for military than civilian use. See William E. Trimble, *Wings for the Navy* (Annapolis: Naval Institute Press, 1990, 180-81.

2. Kauffman refers to an aircraft known as the Bristol Brabazon. The British aircraft industry's history after World War II was one of early promise, followed by unsatisfactory long-term results. All British commercial aircraft development

had ended after the outbreak of war in 1939. With the coming of peace, British aircraft manufacturers hoped that their military technology could be quickly adapted to civil aviation. But such was not the case, largely owing to the war-weakened state of their industrial facilities, which were worn out after six years of round-the-clock fighter and bomber production.

During the war, the Ministry of Aircraft Production had conducted design studies (not production) of postwar jet-propelled transports capable of transatlantic flight. Since the ministry's chairman was Lord Brabazon, each entry in the design competition was called a "Brabazon" type. Only one Bristol Brabazon (an "elegant white elephant," in the words of British aviation historian Christopher Chant), was built. Although technically innovative, the airliner's huge size defeated every engine design available—piston, jet-prop, and turbojet. The Bristol Brabazon was finally canceled in 1958 after it became clear that it could not compete with Boeing's 707. See Taylor, *History of Aviation,* 373-76; Chant, *Aviation,* 277-81.

3. The De Havilland Comet, the world's first production jet airliner, first flew in 1949 and entered regular scheduled service with British Overseas Airways Corporation (BOAC) in 1952. Developed originally as a Brabazon type, it was intended as a high-speed, transatlantic mail plane that would carry a mere six passengers. Ultimately, modification allowed it to carry forty passengers. Cruising at nearly twice the speed of contemporary piston-powered airliners, the Comet stood on the verge of revolutionizing air travel. Pan Am actually placed an order for three Comets, which would have made it the first British-built airliner ever to fly for a U.S. airline and the first foreign aircraft Pan Am had bought since the early Fokkers. Trippe did not think the Comet was suitable for Pan Am, primarily because of its short range. But he ordered three Comets anyway while privately telling friends that he doubted Pan Am would ever take delivery of them. Nevertheless, the Comet was a sensation, performing spectacularly.

Then disaster struck. In rapid succession, two Comets crashed under mysterious circumstances over the Mediterranean in early 1954. At first, sabotage was suspected, and the remains of the two Comets were retrieved from the seabed for careful examination. But the cause of the crashes was metal fatigue, brought on by repeated pressurization of the Comet's passenger cabin. The corners of the square-cut cabin windows had cracked, followed by explosive depressurization that destroyed the Comet's structural integrity. A simple technological fix—making the windows round—cured the problem, and later-model Comets went on to achieve a satisfactory service record. But the horror of those crashes fatally damaged the Comet's reputation, and it never recovered enough to be commercially successful. The Comet was, in the words of the eminent aviation historian R. E. G. Davies, a "magnificent false start" to the jet age. See Taylor, *History of Aviation,* 386; Davies, *World's Airlines,* 451-55; Daley, *American Saga,* 400-401.

4. Propeller failure is one of the most terrifying experiences in aviation. Not only can props "run away" or overspeed—eventually wrenching themselves from the engine, with catastrophic results—but they can also disintegrate in flight, sometimes slicing through the passenger cabin. Whirling through unprotected air, props are also vulnerable to nicks and chips from pebbles and other foreign objects. These nicks can develop into stress fractures, leading to eventual failure. Metallurgical manufacturing defects, which Kauffman cites, have largely been eliminated in recent years by x-ray examination.

Jet engines are not immune to a species of prop failure: the disintegration of turbine fan blades. Blade failure caused the spectacular Sioux City, Iowa, crash of a United Airlines DC-10 in July 1989. The failed turbine blades knifed through the airliner's hydraulic flight control system, making the plane all but uncontrollable. Miraculously, Captain Al Haines, facing a pilot's nightmare and with only differential power on the two remaining engines available to control the aircraft's direction, managed a "controlled crash," witnessed by millions via an amateur video. Miraculously, 184 of the 296 passengers survived. See "The Mystery," *Newsweek* (Sept. 19, 1994), 27.

5. Pan Am was almost alone among major airlines in skipping entirely the turboprop phase of technological development. Mechanically, jet engines were simpler than piston engines, but they gulped vast, uneconomical quantities of fuel, particularly at low altitudes. By marrying a jet engine to an external prop, aeronautical engineers got the benefits of mechanical simplicity and some of the fuel efficiency of a piston engine. For aircraft operating on short-haul routes or flown mostly at low altitudes, this compromise proved useful. Turboprops still dominate short-haul, commuter routes. See Hopkins, *Flying the Line,* 251-53.

6. Donald Douglas (1892-1981), one of the giants of American aviation history, was a Naval Academy dropout who later graduated from MIT in 1914. He apprenticed as an aeronautical engineer for seven years with Glenn Martin in Baltimore, then headed west in 1921 to set up his own company in Santa Monica, California. Douglas Aircraft became the dominant company in commercial aircraft production during the 1930s and remained so throughout the piston-engine era. Lockheed stood second, with Boeing a distant third.

Douglas reached the pinnacle of piston-engine airliner development with the DC-6 and DC-7 aircraft. Faster and larger than the wartime DC-4, both aircraft were also pressurized, thus allowing them to cruise at high altitude, while the cabin altitude remained lower for the comfort of passengers.

Pan Am ordered forty-five DC-6s in September 1950. The first DC-6 went into service in May 1952, coincidentally at the same time BOAC introduced the Comet jetliner. Unlike the Comet, the DC-6 proved to be a moneymaker. Although slower by nearly 200 mph than the Comet, the DC-6 carried twice as many passengers (eighty-eight) and was easier to fly and maintain. Douglas built 704 DC-6s and 311 DC-7s between 1947 and 1955. Pan Am operated the DC-6 until 1968, well into the jet age.

The final piston-engined Douglas, the DC-7, could fly the Atlantic nonstop in either direction in all weather conditions, and the polar great circle route from California to Europe—the first airliner capable of that feat. Although not as profitable as the DC-6 (it carried four fewer passengers), the DC-7, along with the Lockheed Super Constellation, extended piston technology to the limits. Pan Am flew the DC-7 for barely two years before the new Boeing 707 displaced it from the premier routes in October 1958.

Douglas, complacent and satisfied with the technology and production techniques he had mastered, was understandably reluctant to jump into risky jet transports when Gledhill and Kauffman approached him with Pan Am's proposal in 1954. This reluctance would cost Douglas dearly. Boeing, capitalizing on its experience with military jet bombers, stole a march on Douglas, built the Boeing 707, and displaced Douglas as the industry leader. Thus did fortune reverse for these two companies: in 1932, Douglas had won the TWA-sponsored competition that resulted in the DC-3, which displaced Boeing, maker of the B-247, as the industry leader. See John Newhouse, *The Sporty Game* (New York: Knopf, 1982), 127-40; Solberg, *Conquest of the Skies,* 155-56; Daley, *American Saga,* 396-414; Davies, *Pan Am,* 62-67; Davies, *Airlines of the U.S.,* 568.

7. Wellwood E. Beall was one of the first academically trained aeronautical engineers. As an undergraduate University of Colorado engineering student, Beall was, like so many other young men, smitten with the romance of aviation following Lindbergh's 1927 Paris flight. He resolved to study aeronautical engineering, which he was able to do because a few elite universities (such as MIT) had set up aeronautical engineering programs under grants from the Guggenheim Fund for the Promotion of Aeronautics in 1926. Beall went to work for United Aircraft & Technology Corporation in 1929 and became the primary designer of the fabulous B-314 flying boat. He also played a major role designing other famous Boeing aircraft, including the legendary B-17 Flying Fortress of World War II. See

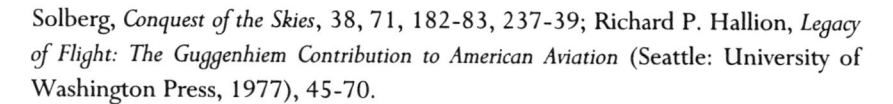

Solberg, *Conquest of the Skies*, 38, 71, 182-83, 237-39; Richard P. Hallion, *Legacy of Flight: The Guggenhiem Contribution to American Aviation* (Seattle: University of Washington Press, 1977), 45-70.

8. William E. (Bill) Boeing (1881-1956), founder of Boeing Aircraft, was the son of a wealthy Michigan lumberman. Upon turning twenty-one, he dropped out of Yale and migrated west to Seattle, where he entered the lumber business for himself. After amassing a substantial fortune, he learned to fly and began dabbling in boat and aircraft construction around 1910. He teamed with Eddie Hubbard, a pioneer airmail operator, to start an airmail service between Seattle and Canada in 1916, using a flying boat Boeing had built. Boeing actually flew some of these early international airmail flights, which allowed him to claim credit for starting the first international U.S. airline.

Boeing's first financial success in aviation came when his factory built fifty planes for the Navy during World War I. In 1927, Boeing and Hubbard again teamed up to create Boeing Air Transport (BAT), which ultimately became United Airlines. In July 1927, BAT won the segment of the Post Office's transcontinental airmail service that connected Chicago with San Francisco. Critics complained loudly that Boeing was cheating, because he controlled a company that was already manufacturing a state-of-the-art mail plane, the Boeing 40, which made use of a new air-cooled radial engine. These ethical and potential antitrust problems led Boeing to sell both the Boeing Aircraft Company and BAT to United Aircraft Corporation in 1928. He served briefly as chairman of the board of the new United Aircraft Corporation but sold his shares late in 1929 and had nothing further to do with either the aircraft company or the airline that bore his name. See Leary, *Airline Industry,* 214-16, 477; Davies, *Airlines of the U.S.,* 40, 60, 195; Solberg, *Conquest of the Skies,* 53-62.

9. Howard Hughes (1905-1976), the eccentric billionaire who controlled TWA in the postwar period, was an authentic aviation pioneer whose accomplishments have been all but forgotten today owing to the bizarre lifestyle that marked his declining years. He had an astonishing career as a moviemaker, pilot, airline owner, and aircraft manufacturer-designer. He held the world landplane speed record for more than a decade (1936-47) and won international fame for his round-the-world flight in 1938. He was also the creator of what was (until the Boeing 747 displaced it) the world's largest airplane, the unsuccessful Hercules wooden flying boat, nicknamed the Spruce Goose. See Leary, *Airline Industry,* 217-34.

10. Kauffman's and Gledhill's reaction to the Boeing 707, the world's first successful jet airliner, was fairly typical. Noise, caused mostly by engine vibration, was always one of the most intractable problems with piston airliners. The speed, power, and quietness of jet engines would mean increased passenger comfort and hence a potential boom in traffic—if there were no unexpected economic consequences. By the early 1950s the DC-6 was the backbone of Pan Am's fleet and a very profitable airplane—the most profitable on a "seat-mile" basis (the cost of flying one seat one mile) ever built. No one knew what the B-707's seat-mile cost would be, and the technological leap was immense. The history of commercial aviation was littered with failed airliners that were merely faster than their competition, rather than more profitable.

The military's massive production of piston airliners during World War II—planes later readily available as war surplus—inhibited new airliner development, because profits earned by cheap war-surplus aircraft were so artificially high. Trippe was uncharacteristically slow in acquiring the new Lockheed Constellation aircraft after World War II primarily because of this factor. The "Connie" was faster and carried more passengers (at a slightly higher seat-mile cost than the DC-6), but it was a joint project of TWA and Howard Hughes. Although Trippe eventually acquired thirty-three Connies, TWA got them first and temporarily displaced Pan Am as the leading carrier on the primary North Atlantic route because of it. Constellation acquisition was also slow because Trippe had always been careful to take developments in aircraft technology sequentially, one step at a time, a legacy of André Priester's aeronautical conservatism. Trippe flirted with acquiring the Republic Rainbow (a high-altitude, pressurized piston aircraft) or the British-built Vickers Viscount turboprop but finally decided instead to gamble with being the first to leap into pure jets. But Trippe hedged his bets, ordering only twenty B-707s and twenty-five Douglas DC-8s—both orders placed on the same day, October 13, 1955.

Trippe was determined to regain the lead in this technological revolution, wary though he was of unexpected economic consequences. Thus the mission of Kauffman and Gledhill to Boeing and Douglas in 1954 to assess the new jet airliners was an absolutely crucial event in Pan Am's history. See Davies, *Pan Am*, 54-55, 62-69; Daley, *American Saga*, 396-414.

11. Pan Am's greatest gamble, financially, came with the dawn of the jet era in 1955. The combined order for forty-five DC-8 and B-707 jets amounted to $269 million, and it was just the beginning. Pan Am's net profit for 1954 had been only $10.4 million. Who would loan such vast sums based upon so meager a profit potential? Trippe brushed aside complaints that he was undertaking a gamble

with his stockholders' money, pointing out that the relative risks he took in ordering four-engined flying boats in the 1930s were far greater.

Most experts agree that Trippe was no grand chessmaster of finance and really wasn't much interested in money per se. His approach to raising capital was fairly conventional up to the dawn of the jet era. In Pan Am's early days, Trippe had raised capital mostly by selling stock and mortgaging equipment. For example, Pan Am owned none of the famous B-314 flying boats it flew. Trippe was successful in purchasing aircraft, then mortgaging them at a much higher amount than he had paid for them. The interest payments amounted to less than the amortization costs of purchasing the aircraft.

The jet era saw a major change. Henceforth, Trippe borrowed primarily from insurance companies and a consortium of banks, usually under terms that required payment only of interest at first. The debt proper would be payable sometime in the future. When Pan Am had to amortize that debt, Trippe would roll it over by offering to the public a debenture that could be redeemed for company stock at a fixed price. So long as Pan Am remained profitable, this system was a surefire way of allowing normal monetary inflation to finance aircraft acquisition. The eventual debt was paid off by stockholders themselves, who had no option but to buy more stock to prevent dilution of their equity in the company. It was a textbook case of creative financing, and it worked so long as Pan Am was on an upward financial trajectory, which it was throughout the 1950s and early 1960s. In the first full five years of jet operation (1958-63), passenger traffic doubled. See Daley, *American Saga,* 457-61, 516; Altschul & Bender, *Chosen Instrument,* 446-50.

12. Henry Friendly began handling Pan Am's legal affairs in 1929 as a young associate at the prestigious New York law firm of Root, Clark. It was unusual for a firm like Root, Clark to employ a Jew, but Friendly's credentials were extraordinary. He was a graduate of both Harvard and Harvard Law, had clerked for Supreme Court Justice Louis D. Brandeis, and, after moving into private practice, he had become a brilliant practitioner in the new field of aviation law. Indeed, Friendly played a major role in shaping much of the aviation legislation of the 1930s. Trippe trusted Friendly with all of Pan Am's major legal matters until 1959, when he was appointed a federal judge by President Eisenhower. See Bender & Altschul, *Chosen Instrument,* 144-45, 171, 321, 411, 490.

13. While this might have been motivated by fear of antitrust action, the company's financial exposure, should jets fail to significantly increase traffic, was a far more important factor. Confronted with this possibility, it must have seemed

wise to spread the risks by permitting other airlines to share in the gamble, albeit with some delay while Boeing filled most of the orders already placed by Pan Am.

14 . The IATA meeting Kauffman describes, held at the Waldorf-Astoria Hotel the same week Trippe ordered the jets, was a bombshell for another reason: Trippe announced his massive order of jets to IATA delegates casually and incidentally, during informal chats at a cocktail party at his Gracie Square apartment overlooking the East River. His guests were stunned. The Jet Age was dawning, with potentially disastrous financial consequences for all of them. If Pan Am were ordering forty-five jets, that meant the airline would (because of productivity increases) replace nearly twice that many piston airliners, which would go on the secondhand aircraft market. Since most airlines were heavily mortgaged, this meant that their own piston airliners would soon be dropping in value, with unforseeable financial consequences.

Guests began to leave hurriedly from Trippe's cocktail party. They had to get word to their own airlines about what the future had in store. See Daley, *American Saga,* 412.

15. Calling Lockheed's turboprop L-188 Electra a "disaster" is a bit strong. The Electra was relatively unsuccessful as a commercial airliner, but the military version of the Electra, the US Navy's P-3 antisubmarine aircraft, performed successfully and is still in use. The Electra's bad reputation stemmed (like the ill-fated De Havilland Comet's) from two early crashes. In September 1959 and March 1960, two Electras suffered inflight airframe failure—a nightmarish event. The cause was traced to harmonic vibration set up by the aircraft's engines, which in turn caused the wing to vibrate sympathetically, like a tuning fork. This vibration literally caused the wing to shake itself to pieces. After being temporarily grounded in 1960, the FAA permitted the Electra to resume service, flown primarily by domestic U.S. airlines, but at speeds well below its cruising speed of 400 mph, where harmonic vibrations did not occur. Later versions of the Electra were modified to correct the problem. See Davies, *Delta,* 71; William Green, *Aircraft Handbook* (Garden City, NY: Doubleday, 1966), 213.

16. The Boeing 707 and the Douglas DC-8, the first two "big jets" (as everybody called them then), were remarkably similar aircraft. The B-707 carried 143 passengers at a cruising speed of 600 mph for three thousand miles, while the DC-8 carried 127 passengers at 590 mph for thirty-five hundred miles. Each aircraft would be "stretched" to carry more passengers and modified to improve performance over the years.

Boeing entered this competition with the advantage of experience in building large jet bombers. But when it came to airliners, Boeing's reputation was inferior to Douglas's. Boeing's postwar B-377 Stratocruiser, for example, was simply a luxurious version of the World War II B-29 Superfortress (the atomic bomber), and it was plagued by constant breakdowns. Pan Am bought twenty-one of the fifty-five Stratocruisers Boeing built and acquired another eight through the purchase of its competitor, American Overseas Airlines, in September 1950. The Douglas and Lockheed aircraft in Pan Am's piston fleet during this period performed better and consequently outnumbered Boeings by a huge margin.

Why, then, did Pan Am abandon its long relationship with Douglas in favor of Boeing? It seemed as if Pan Am would stick with Douglas, because it initially ordered twenty-five DC-8s and only twenty B-707s. But Trippe later surrendered his option on six of the DC-8s while increasing his orders for B-707s. Eventually, Pan Am would buy 130 B-707s. The DC-8 fleet was never enlarged past the original nineteen.

The reason for Pan Am's abandonment of Douglas was Boeing's superior jet manufacturing capability. Boeing produced its jetliner more than a year before Douglas. Pan Am took delivery of its first B-707 in August 1958 and inaugurated service in October of that year. Pan Am's first DC-8 was not delivered until February 1960. See Davies, *Pan Am,* 56-57, 66-73.

## ✈ *Jet Travel Becomes a Reality*

1. Kauffman's explanation of the role direct government spending played in the success of U.S. commercial aviation recapitulates contemporary political debate over industrial policy. Put simply, industrial policy is the notion that government should pick "winners" (industries that in the future will provide high-wage jobs and give American business an edge in international markets) and then subsidize these industries directly, with grants of taxpayers' dollars. This approach succeeded in giving America worldwide domination of commercial airliner production after World War II, but those who poured government funding into military jet technology did not do so with this object in mind. That is, government officials did not support Boeing aircraft *primarily* because they believed that someday Boeing would build jet transports capable of dominating world markets. Rather, they supported Boeing for reasons of military security. Contemporary governmental policymakers would have a much tougher job picking fledgling industries to support, if the primary purpose were to identify future commercial winners.

2. Jet engines (technically known as gas turbines) have a long, complex history. A jet engine simply takes air in the front, mixes it with fuel, ignites the

fuel-air mixture, and then expels the hot gasses rearward, thus propelling forward whatever the jet engine is attached to—a simple matter of Newtonian physics. Patents on gas turbines were taken out in the nineteenth century, and they have been considered for aircraft propulsion since at least 1916. Jet engines are simple, reliable, lightweight, and powerful. But jets suffer from high fuel consumption and require advanced metallurgy. Because jet engines operate under extremely high temperatures and pressures, iron and steel (which are good enough for piston engines) simply melt in them.

Rather than merely expelling hot gases out the rear, jets can also be hitched to either external propulsion devices (props) or internal ones ("ducted" fans, rotating blades that propel the air backward around the jet engine itself). But these internal fan blades on modern "turbofan" or "bypass" engines must still be able to withstand tremendous temperatures and pressures.

It is this problem to which Kauffman refers in his discussion of British-built jet engines. Wright Aeronautical Corporation manufactured this engine, known originally as the Conway, under license from Rolls Royce in the 1950s. Although this engine lost out initially to the better Pratt and Whitney jet engines, it eventually would be used on many airliners, including the elegant Vickers VC-10. See Taylor, *History of Aviation,* 395-96.

3. Engine manufacturers had designs on future commercial sales, so they made sure civilian customers were kept well informed. All jet-engine development was done under military contract and classified as top secret, but Pan Am's engineers had full access to all the particulars of military jet-engine progress nevertheless. See Daley, *American Saga,* 401-11.

4. The first engine on production model B-707s was the Pratt and Whitney JT-3C (the civilian designator of the military J-75 version), which generated 13,500 lb. of thrust. Later versions of the same engine on the B-707 series increased thrust up to 18,000 lb. See Davies, *Pan Am,* 67, 71.

5. Scott Flower was Pan Am's chief pilot, a title that needs explanation. A chief pilot was a member of airline management, not of the unionized pilot force. Although qualified to fly regular revenue trips, chief pilots were supervisors of regular line pilots. There was always some confusion about the status of management pilots, because they could gain that designation only by rising through the ranks of regular "line" pilots, and many of them always thought of themselves as pilots first and management second. Even more confusing, pilots often rotated back and forth between management and "line" status. ALPA, the pilots' union, for many years had a membership category called "executive inactive," specifically

to handle this flexible status. See Hopkins, *Airline Pilots,* 116-17; Hopkins, *Flying the Line,* 193; Daley, *American Saga,* 377-78.

6. Pan Am inaugurated the first jet service to Europe on October 4, 1958, and its B-707s began flying New York-Miami (with National flight crews) on December 10, 1958, to howls of protest from National's domestic competitors and Pan Am's international competitors. Under the regulated system that existed prior to passage of the Airline Deregulation Act of 1978, Pan Am was never allowed to fly domestic routes. But because of Pan Am's dominant status in international aviation, the Civil Aeronautics Board (CAB), charged with economic regulation, gradually permitted domestic airlines to compete internationally. As a hedge, Juan Trippe tried repeatedly to acquire domestic routes, without success. National Airlines, which offered logical gateways to funnel domestic traffic to Pan Am, was a target either for takeover or merger by Juan Trippe as early as 1948. This merger finally happened in 1980, after airline deregulation.

The 1958 interline agreement with National Airlines was seen by domestic airlines as an end run around the CAB's repeated denial of domestic routes to Pan Am. It was essentially an equipment swap allowing National to fly Pan Am's new B-707s over its own domestic routes, primarily from Miami to New York. While allowing National to become the first domestic airline to fly jets (not its own—American won that race), Pan Am was also funneling its Latin American traffic through domestic airspace—in Pan Am's planes flown by National flight crews. These interline arrangements were not unknown, but the Pan Am-National agreement also involved a stock swap. In September 1958, Pan Am exchanged six percent of its stock for twenty percent of National's, with each airline thus becoming the largest single stockholder in the other. The CAB nullified the stock swap in July 1960 but permitted the interline aircraft operation to continue. See Hopkins, *Flying the Line,* 230; Davies, *Pan Am,* 66, 82; Davies, *Airlines of the U.S.,* 513-14.

7. Kauffman is referring to the U.S. superiority in metallurgy. The blades are inside jet engines.

8. The pilots' strike of 1959 was over jet pay scales and the collateral issue of crew qualifications, specifically whether or not navigators and flight engineers should also be licensed pilots. See chapter 14, note 9.

The 1959 strike applied only to the six B-707s on hand. The remainder of Pan Am's piston fleet continued to fly with its unionized pilots but, until an appropriate level of pay could be agreed upon for jets, ALPA crews refused to fly them. Management would eventually have to settle with ALPA because management pilots could not staff the jet fleet as it increased in size. Even with only six B-707s, Pan Am was approaching the limits of safety, owing to the FAA's mandate of an eighty-five-hour maximum monthly limit for pilots. Since only about ten percent of Pan Am's pilot force was nonunion or management, most pilots reached their federally mandated maximum in about two weeks. So long as the union pilots could hold firmly together, they could control their own destiny. Their rapidly rising pay bears witness to their success at achieving solidarity. The first B-707 contract paid about thirty-five thousand dollars per year, nearly double the pay for flying piston aircraft. See Bender and Altschul, *Chosen Instrument,* 463; Hopkins, *Flying the Line,* 249-60; Keeler interview.

9. The technical name of the "black box" is the flight data recorder (FDR). It is an armored, fireproof, waterproof, sealed, almost indestructible recording device (that is actually orange, not black), located in the tail of a commercial airliner. The FDR is a tool for investigating accidents. The first FDRs recorded five elements: time, altitude, speed, direction, and vertical acceleration. Later refinements added such things as engine settings and flight control positions. In July 1958, the FAA required FDRs in all airliners weighing more than 12,500 lb. if operated at more than twenty-five thousand feet. The first black boxes were installed in jets shortly after their introduction in 1958.

Another kind of black box, the cockpit voice recorder (CVR), was added in the mid-1960s. The CVR is a continuous-reel recording device that reveals what pilots say. Together, these devices assist investigators in determining the probable cause of accidents. See Nance, *Blind Trust,* 310; R. W. Johnson, *Shootdown: Flight 007* (New York: Viking, 1986), 190; Stephen Barclay, *The Search for Air Safety* (New York: William Morrow, 1970), 160-63.

10. The gracious era of airline travel came to an end with the introduction of jets. Pioneer airline pilots often lament this change, noting that in the old days, all airline service was single class, but it was first class. Long flights encouraged rest breaks, which pilots often took in the cabin, chatting with passengers, rather like sea captains. Because these flights were so long, airlines like Pan Am often had relief pilots aboard to spell crews while they rested. In the early days of commercial aviation, airline passengers were a select lot, drawn primarily from the wealthy and chic, hardly today's mass market. Pan Am's flying boat captains were encouraged to circulate among the cabin passengers during their rest breaks. They almost universally enjoyed these excursions among their passengers. This practice came to an end because jets compressed both time and distance while increasing the pilots' workload to the point that they no longer had time to

socialize. So even if skyjacking had not reared its ugly head, forcing pilots to lock themselves away in the forbidden zone of the cockpit, where they are merely faceless voices pointing out landmarks no one can see from forty thousand feet, human contact between pilot and passenger would have been lost. See Daley, *American Saga,* 184-90; Hopkins, *Flying the Line,* 261-77; Keeler interview.

11. The Concorde, a joint product of the British and French aerospace industries, was originally designed to fly 130 passengers at supersonic speed (about 1,250 mph). The U.S. government planned to build a three- hundred-passenger competitor, designated the SST, with Boeing as the main contractor. The problems facing both aircraft were formidable. Eventually the Concorde, with ruinous effect upon French and British national budgets, flew in March 1969. After much debate about its cost and effectiveness, Congress canceled the SST project in March 1971.

Although still flown commercially, the Concorde has not been a financial success. Only British and French national airlines fly it today, indicating that Congress was wise to cancel the SST. Juan Trippe placed a conditional order for six Concordes in June 1963, simultaneously ordering fifteen SSTs. Pan Am's conditions would be determined by Kauffman and his engineering team. The Concorde did not survive the close scrutiny they gave it. Only one U.S. airline, Braniff, ever flew the Concorde, on an interline agreement with Air France, from Washington, D.C. to Texas in 1978— subsonically. The Concorde could not meet U.S. noise standards when flown supersonically. See Davies, *Airlines of the US,* 572; Leary, *Airline Industry,* 79.

12. A leading-edge device is simply a retractable flap on the front edge of a wing. Normally attached to the wing's rear, flaps add lift by changing its shape, allowing an aircraft to fly more slowly for takeoff and landing. See Nance, *Blind Trust,* 145.

13. In 1981, as part of a general belt-tightening, Pan Am sold its share of the Falcon Jet Corporation. At the same time, Pan Am also sold its lease on the Pan American Building in New York City for $400 million—the largest amount ever, to that date, for a single real estate sale. See Davies, *Pan Am,* 84.

14. Federal Express, the largest "to-the-door" air freight operator, was founded by Frederick W. Smith (b. 1944) in June 1971. As a Yale undergraduate economics major, Smith wrote a term paper that concluded that a demand existed for high-priority, overnight aerial freight service. (Interestingly enough, Smith also revived the Yale Flying Club, which Juan Trippe had founded in 1917.) After serving as a Marine aviator in Vietnam, Smith, who was independently wealthy,

used money from a family trust to start his small package freight service. He agreed to purchase twenty-three Dassault Falcon business jets from Pan Am, but with stock warrants, not cash. He might have learned this trick from fellow Yale man Trippe, who had used it often during Pan Am's salad days. FedEx began service in 1973, serving twenty-two cities. By 1975 it was showing a profit. The deal Smith struck with Pan Am was crucial to FedEx's extraordinary success. See Daley, *American Saga,* 8; Leary, *Airline Industry,* 172-73, 446-51.

## ✈ *The Jumbo Jet*

1. The Boeing 747, the ultimate airliner, originated in 1965 as a collaborative effort among Pan Am, Pratt and Whitney, and Boeing. The phenomenal success of the first generation of intercontinental jets, the B-707 and the DC-8, in attracting a new mass clientele for airline travel, underlay the B-747 project. Juan Trippe, long an advocate of cheap fares and larger airplanes, saw a limitless future for international tourism. The B-747 was integral to his plans.

In December 1965, Boeing, Pratt and Whitney, and Pan Am signed a preliminary agreement on the B-747. Upon completion of engineering specifications, Pan Am agreed in April 1966 to buy twenty-five of the new aircraft. Everything about the proposed airplane was gargantuan, including the initial price of twenty million dollars per copy. (Later versions would sell for well over $100 million.) In terms of performance, the B-747 was no different from the preceding generation of passenger jets. It cruised at just under 600 mph and had a range of just over five thousand miles. But in terms of passenger capacity, the B-747 dwarfed all previous aircraft. Depending upon the seating configuration, it could carry up to five hundred passengers. Typically, most B-747s came with a mixture of first-class and "tourist-class" seating for about 370 passengers. With a full load, the new behemoth of the airlines would have the lowest seat-mile cost ever.

Boeing built an entirely new factory at Everett, Washington, to construct the B-747. Because the B-747's technology was not new, a prototype emerged from the factory in record time. The B-747 was originally scheduled to begin transatlantic service in November 1969, but engine problems forced a delay until January 21, 1970. Still in production, the B-747 is arguably the most successful airliner ever built, and it was remarkably free from the initial "teething" problems new airliners usually encountered.

The B-747's economic problems were another matter, however. Although aeronautically the B-747 was successful, the enormous financial risks Pan Am undertook in pioneering it proved disastrous. The B-747 appeared just as oil prices began to escalate, triggering a worldwide recession. Since tourism, for which the

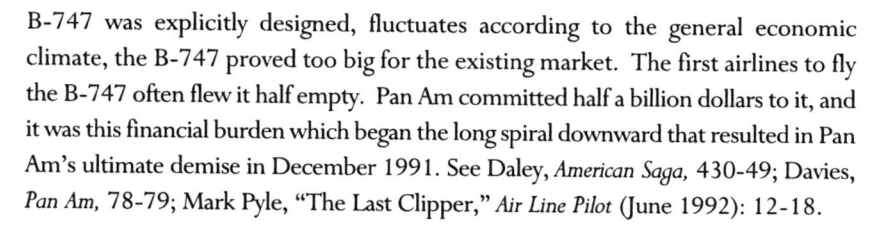

B-747 was explicitly designed, fluctuates according to the general economic climate, the B-747 proved too big for the existing market. The first airlines to fly the B-747 often flew it half empty. Pan Am committed half a billion dollars to it, and it was this financial burden which began the long spiral downward that resulted in Pan Am's ultimate demise in December 1991. See Daley, *American Saga,* 430-49; Davies, *Pan Am,* 78-79; Mark Pyle, "The Last Clipper," *Air Line Pilot* (June 1992): 12-18.

2. "Blind flying" instruments on an aircraft's panel had been pretty well standardized by the early 1930s, in an arrangement called the standard T. But the best way of displaying the actual analog values (numerical equivalents of the flight parameters measured) was always subject to experimentation. Should values measuring such things as altitude or engine temperatures be displayed on round instruments, or vertical bar instruments? Each airline continues to specify different means of communicating the numerical values of flight to their own pilots, as Kauffman's discussion indicates. These variations have caused problems when airlines have exchanged aircraft on interline agreements. Standardization has therefore increased of late, largely because all airlines know that at some point they will sell their planes on the aftermarket to second-line carriers. Under these circumstances, it is best not to confuse pilots with nonstandard instrument flight systems. By the time the B-747 came along, a high degree of standardization in cockpit instrumentation already existed, largely owing to pressure from pilots, exerted through their union, ALPA. See Hopkins, *Flying the Line,* 249-60; Solberg, *Conquest of the Skies,* 125-37; Hallion, *Legacy of Flight,* 101-27.

3. Navigation advances in modern aviation have been nothing short of fantastic. The first generation of airline pilots relied on a technology (optical sextants) only slightly better than Columbus used on his voyage to America. While the inertial navigation systems Kauffman mentions are still available only in commercial airliners, the computer revolution has given rise to a device called a global positioning system (GPS), which allows even "general aviation" (private) pilots to check their position with orbiting navigational satellites. GPS is so widely available that it is often found in private, single-engine aircraft. See Daley, *American Saga,* 146-47; "Portable GPS," *Aviation Consumer* (June 1 and 15, 1992):4.

4. The range and magnitude of change associated with ground handling of an aircraft more than double the size of previous airliners required huge capital investments. To take just one example, the tractors that positioned B-707s on the ground had to be able to pull a 250,000-lb load. The B-747 weighed 710,000 lb. See Davies, *Pan Am,* 67, 79.

5. Landing fees at most airports are based upon an aircraft's weight.

6. The Lockheed C-5 military transport is comparable to the B-747 in size. But not only is it very expensive to operate, it has also become notorious for cost overruns, partly because of the specialized performance requirements Kauffman mentions. See Daley, *American Saga,* 432; Nick Kotz, *Wild Blue Yonder: Money, Politics, and the B-1 Bomber* (New York: Pantheon, 1988), 6, 99-102.

7. In fact,the 747 was too big for the existing market. Many airlines had to mothball their B-747 fleets, hastily ordered to keep up with Pan Am, at tremendous cost. Pan Am eventually bought fifty-one B-747s of all types, but it was hard pressed to pay for the first batch of twenty-five in 1970. Pan Am lost nearly fifty million dollars in 1970, the year the B-747 was introduced, and it owed a staggering one billion dollars on them. Although Pan Am would survive for another twenty years, it was a magnificent cripple during most of that time, and it never really recovered from this debt load. Juan Trippe retired in 1969 after saddling Pan Am with the B-747 debt. See Daley, *American Saga,* 443-49; Davies, *Pan Am,* 78-81; C. V. Glines, "Pan American: The Chosen Instrument," *Air Line Pilot* (June 1992): 12-15, 54.

8. There was another reason for the rapid spread of the B-747 to all the international airlines: Juan Trippe wanted it! While Trippe wanted Pan Am to have the B-747 before other airlines (especially his U.S. competitors, such as TWA), he believed that a lengthy monopoly would damage Pan Am. He believed that foreign national airlines, such as Air France and Alitalia, should have the B-747 soon, and he was willing to give up some of his reserved aircraft delivery dates so they could acquire them faster. But Trippe was hardly being altruistic. If foreign national airlines did not receive the B-747 almost simultaneously with Pan Am, they would in all likelihood raise objections to it on various grounds (including the environmental ones of pollution and overcrowding), which might delay the opening of Pan Am's B-747 service for many months. But if Alitalia and Air France expected to be flying the B-747 soon, they could be counted upon as allies in facilitating government action in their own countries to ease the B-747's path. See Daley, *American Saga,* 433.

## Personalities

1. Kauffman is simply mistaken about FDR ever offering Lindbergh such a job—or *any* job, for that matter. After Lindbergh led the bitter "America First" opposition to FDR's internationalist and antifascist foreign policy in the late 1930s, he was strictly *persona non grata* with Roosevelt. In a 1941 press conference,

the president was asked why he wouldn't allow Lindbergh to return to government service. FDR answered by comparing Lindbergh to Congressman Clement L. Vallandigham, leader of the pro-Confederate "Copperhead" movement in the North during the Civil War. See Freidel, *Roosevelt,* 366-67.

2. As noted previously, Lindbergh did shoot down Japanese planes as a technical rep for United Aircraft.

3. Kauffman has caught the essence of Lindbergh's late-life pessimism. The world-famous pilot even came to doubt the efficacy of aviation itself. There was a time when Lindbergh (and many others) believed that the airplane would be a tool for uniting humanity and bringing peace. But twentieth-century history seemed to ridicule these naive assumptions. Lindbergh actually opposed development of the supersonic transport and the jumbo jet, on environmental grounds. In particular, Lindbergh feared that extensive high-altitude flying might damage the ozone layer. He was years ahead of his time in these concerns. See Joseph J. Corn, *Winged Gospel: America's Romance with Aviation, 1900-1950* (New York: Oxford University Press, 1983), viii, 58-59; Daley, *American Saga,* 430-31.

##  Conclusion

1. Edward P. Warner (1894-1958) was perhaps the leading academic expert on aviation in his day. A 1916 Harvard graduate, Warner later studied aeronautical engineering at MIT. His brilliance was such that MIT offered him a faculty position upon completion of his studies. He taught such future aviation luminaries as Leroy Grumman and James MacDonnell, both of whom went on to found famous aircraft companies. Warner's career rotated between academic appointments and government service. In 1920 he developed the first wind tunnel as a member of the National Advisory Committee for Aeronautics (NACA—forerunner of today's NASA), and in later life he won a reputation as America's leading authority on the technical aspects of international aviation. He was a member and chairman of the CAB (1939-41 and 1943-45) and from 1945 to 1957 headed the International Civil Aviation Organization (ICAO). See Leary, *Aviation Industry,* 493-95.

2. While Kauffman might have thought Pan Am's union leaders were difficult, Pan Am actually had a reputation for labor peace, relatively speaking. Certainly it never had the kind of labor strife Eastern endured. See Roy Keeler, interview with editor; Bernstein, *Grounded,* 23-53.

# *INDEX*